CRADLE TO KINDERGARTEN

CRADLE TO KINDERGARTEN

A NEW PLAN TO COMBAT INEQUALITY

Ajay Chaudry, Taryn Morrissey, Christina Weiland, and Hirokazu Yoshikawa

The Russell Sage Foundation NEW YORK

The Russell Sage Foundation, one of the oldest of America's general purpose foundations, was established in 1907 by Mrs. Margaret Olivia Sage for "the improvement of social and living conditions in the United States." The foundation seeks to fulfill this mandate by fostering the development and dissemination of knowledge about the country's political, social, and economic problems. While the foundation endeavors to assure the accuracy and objectivity of each book it publishes, the conclusions and interpretations in Russell Sage Foundation publications are those of the authors and not of the foundation, its trustees, or its staff. Publication by Russell Sage, therefore, does not imply foundation endorsement.

LIBRARY OF CONGRESS
CATALOGING-IN-PUBLICATION DATA

Names: Chaudry, Ajay, author.
Title: Cradle to kindergarten : a new plan to combat inequality / Ajay Chaudry, Taryn Morrissey,
    Christina Weiland, Hirokazu Yoshikawa.
Description: New York : Russell Sage Foundation, [2017] | Includes bibliographical references
    and index.
Identifiers: LCCN 2016040134| ISBN 9780871545572 (pbk. : alk. paper) | ISBN 9781610448666
    (ebk)
Subjects: LCSH: Child care—United States. | Early childhood education—United States. |
    Equality—United States. | Child welfare—United States. | Family policy—United States.
Classification: LCC HQ778.63 .C4543 2017 | DDC 362.70973—dc23

LC record available at https://lccn.loc.gov/2016040

The paper used in this publication meets the minimum requirements of American National Standard for Information Sciences—Permanence of Paper for Printed Library Materials. ANSI Z39.48-1992.

Text design by Matthew T. Avery.

RUSSELL SAGE FOUNDATION
112 East 64th Street, New York, New York 10065
10 9 8 7 6 5 4 3 2 1

To Alasdair, Cailyn, Lucia, Xander,
and all children

CONTENTS

LIST OF ILLUSTRATIONS

Figures

Tables

ABOUT THE AUTHORS

AJAY CHAUDRY is a writer on social policy issues and a senior fellow at the Robert F. Wagner Graduate School of Public Service at New York University. He also served as a Deputy Assistant Secretary for Human Services Policy at the U.S. Department of Health and Human Services in the Obama Administration.

TARYN MORRISSEY is assistant professor of public policy at the School of Public Affairs at American University.

CHRISTINA WEILAND is assistant professor of educational studies at the University of Michigan.

HIROKAZU YOSHIKAWA is Courtney Sale Ross University Professor of Globalization and Education at the Steinhardt School of Culture, Education, and Human Development at New York University.

ACKNOWLEDGMENTS

The authors are grateful to Michael Laracy of the Annie E. Casey Foundation (grant 215.0334) and the School of Public Affairs at American University for generous support toward the development of this book. Ajay Chaudry would like to thank Peter Edelman and the Georgetown University Law Center, Sherry Glied and New York University's Wagner School of Public Service, and the Russell Sage Foundation for providing writing homes over the course of this project. Hirokazu Yoshikawa would like to thank New York University and the NYU Abu Dhabi Research Institute for partially supporting his time working on this book.

The authors wish to thank the experts who reviewed earlier versions of the manuscript, including Mary Jo Bane, Greg Duncan, Olivia Golden, Bob Granger, Michael Laracy, Joan Lombardi, Hannah Matthews, Christopher Ruhm, Isabel Sawhill, Ruby Takanishi, Jane Waldfogel, Shelley Waters Boots, and Martha Zaslow. Their comments and insights led to important improvements to the book. We want to further thank the two anonymous readers who read the whole manuscript closely and provided many helpful suggestions for revisions. We are very grateful to Sandra Tang, Christopher Wimer, and Sharon Wolf for data analytic support, and to Doug Clements for his generous help with the reprint of his and Julie Sarama's work that appears in chapter 4. Finally, special thanks are due to Bonnie Mackintosh for her invaluable assistance with research and editing.

INTRODUCTION

Benji

About twenty minutes south of the gleaming edifices of downtown Seattle, in a neighborhood surrounded by industrial warehouses, two-year-old Benji is growing up in the house his parents, Bill and Brooke Caldwell,* bought a few years earlier with visions of starting a family.† Their small, low-rise, ranch-style house is typical of the housing stock in this affordable, working-class residential enclave. Bill and Brooke's home sits less than a quarter-mile from the middle school where they first met, and a half-mile in the other direction of where they first started dating their senior year of high school.

Bill and Brooke are arranging Benji's education and care while planning for their second child, who will be born in six months. Both have had steady employment since reaching adulthood. Both completed approximately one year's worth of college courses while also working full-time before losing their financial aid; once they married at age nineteen, their combined earnings disqualified both of them. Bill has been working full-time the past three years at a charity organization, earning $650 per week ($33,000 annually). Brooke works full-time for the local school district as a tutor for English Language Learners, making a $39,000 salary. Brooke was home with Benji for only a month after he was born before she needed to return to work— she had only recently started the job at the school district and could not afford to give up the income.

Brooke's mother cares for Benji at no cost. Bill and Brooke would like to pay her something, especially since she has fewer resources than they do, but she refuses to take any money. They cannot imagine trusting anyone else with his care while he is so young. Brooke says,

"Family is really important to us, him being around his grandma and being able to have a relationship, and our peace of mind knowing he's okay. . . . We are so blessed to have family here or one of us would not be able to work."

Although they are grateful that they can rely on Benji's grand-mother, Brooke and Bill wish they could have enrolled their son in a center-based preschool program by the time he turned two because they feel he is ready. Bill says a center-based program would bring Benji together with other children and offer school-like daily activi-ties that would prepare him to learn:

> I've been at some of those Head Start programs, and you know, they're really cool. I mean, the kids, they learn how to wash their hands, and they're brushing their teeth, and they're eating snack— and you know, just to learn how to act with other kids . . . you know, just things he's ready to do, and he's going to need to learn before he gets into school.

Brooke herself, in fact, attended Head Start, an opportunity to which her mother attributes her love for education. However, Bill points out, they are not income-eligible for Head Start or any other publicly funded early care and education programs, and yet they are also un-able to afford a private preschool: "A lot of the programs around here—you know, it's only for real low-income kids. . . . Most of the time we fall into the category where we don't qualify for any of the services, but we don't really make enough money where we can have extra money to pay for something either." Brooke and Bill have even asked the local Head Start program director whether Benji could at-tend Head Start when he turns three if one of them stops working. They were told that they still would not qualify.

When Brooke and Bill are interviewed again one year later, Benji, who has just turned three, excitedly announces that he has a baby brother, Pedro. Both parents are working full-time at the same jobs; now both Benji and six-month-old Pedro are cared for by their grand-mother. Though things seem stable now, Bill and Brooke report that the last year has been a struggle. Very soon after the interview last year, Brooke had pregnancy complications in her fourteenth week, had to have emergency surgery, and almost lost the child. Put on bed rest for the remainder of the pregnancy, she was out of work for six months. The couple struggled financially, borrowing money from both of their families to make their mortgage payments and avoid overdraft fees. Brooke used up her vacation and sick leave before being put on unpaid leave because she had not been given the necessary paperwork to complete when she was first employed to be eligible for short-term disability insurance. Luckily, both of their families lived nearby and chipped in, cooking meals and buying diapers while Brooke was bedridden.

Because of the financial pressures, Brooke returned to work within two weeks after Pedro's birth, and her mother began looking after the baby as well as Benji at the Caldwells' home. They are grateful for the large network of family and friends who have supported them, and especially for Brooke's mother and her devotion to caring for their children. Still, even with two parents working full-time at better than median-wage jobs, Brooke and Bill are disappointed that they cannot afford better early learning opportunities for their young son. More than ever, they wish they could start Benji in a group learning environment. Brooke puts it this way:

> Bill and I know all the programs near here—there are several within a few blocks. Our restriction is because of our income, which makes it harder. . . . We both wish we could have started Benji in a more structured early education program at least a few days per week when he was two, because we know he wants to be challenged more and that in that type of setting he would be stimulated in different ways, would learn routines, and how to be around and accept care and direction from other adults.

Bill adds: "If there was a drastic change, like we were to have a lot more income or there was more funding, then we could put Benji in a good full-time child care center. . . . Because children really need to have the chance to learn . . . to get an early education."

Adrienne

Diane Harvey[‡] was thirty-three years old when she gave birth to Adrienne, the third child and first girl for her and her husband Daryl. We meet them when Adrienne is two years old. Mother and daughter share a buoyant, almost puckish, spirit. The family of five—Adrienne's brothers are Daryl Jr. and Gary, ages five and seven—lives in a modest apartment in Upper Manhattan.

Diane returned to work within the first two months of her first two children's lives. Little did she suspect that she would be forced into an even earlier return to work after Adrienne's birth. Laid off from her job when she was eight months pregnant, Diane at one blow had lost access to six weeks of paid maternity leave and the additional sixty days of benefits that New York's Temporary Disability Insurance Program provides. Instead, she returned to work just seven days after Adrienne's birth to support her family as the primary earner.

> Con Ed [the electric company] stuck me with a large electricity bill that summer that we still had not paid off, and even though we were paying it down, they said they were going to cut our electricity. I'd been home four days with Adrienne when I am on the phone arguing with the electric company. [That was] when I get a call from G. at the temp agency and asked if I wanted to take a temp job that was paying $16 an hour. I got off the call with [the electric company] and told her to go fax my résumé. I went to work the next day.
>
> I did not want to go back to work right away—she was only a week old. . . . I had to get back to work, and I had no time to arrange child care. So Adrienne went to my mother's, who lives an hour from here in Brooklyn. Her father drove; he picked her up and dropped her off every day on his way to and from his job.

Diane was fortunate that her mother was available to provide free care on short notice. But because of the distance, this was not an arrangement they could sustain long-term, nor could her mother sustain it. When the advertising agency where she took the temporary position offered her ongoing employment, Diane—who took charge of making all the arrangements for the children—began the difficult search for infant care:

> When she was two months, we started sending her to a child care in a woman's home with someone called Ms. Shannon. She lived further uptown [twelve blocks north] from here. She went there from when she was two months until she was six months, and we just paid out of pocket about $75 [per week]. That was a lot less for a two-month-old than anyone else I could find; others were charging $125 or $140, but she was just starting and said, "I know where

I live and what the people in my area make and I can't feel right charging that much." I thought it was great, so I just said thank you.

It turned out that the affordability of this child care setting, with twelve children, was in fact too good to be true:

> It was the lady and her daughter. It was not bad care or anything, but it was not structured. I got the impression the kids watched a lot of television, and [there] were lots of people going through the house. It was also hard because I had to bring all the food. She provided some food for the older kids, but Adrienne was a baby, and formula is expensive.

Diane had applied to the city for child care subsidies from the time her youngest son was one year old. She had called or knocked on the doors of every major infant care provider for a mile in every direction from her home, in search of a subsidy-providing setting. A full five years after she first applied, her persistence paid off:

> I had wised up and knew I would never get off the ACD wait-list. [The Agency for Child Development is the former name for the public agency that handles child care subsidies, and many families still use the acronym ACD for the program, though New York City's Administration for Children's Services absorbed responsibility for the child care subsidies program in the 1990s.] Instead, I went directly to as many of the ACD [contracted] programs in the community I thought looked okay, and put the children on wait-lists, hoping if they got a spot, the program would help push through the subsidy application. . . . Sure enough, Daryl Jr. got a spot with Love Thy Neighbor's after-school program.

When she called to check in with Love Thy Neighbor, she learned that they had an opening not only for Daryl Jr. but also for Gary in their center, and there was an additional opening for Adrienne with a family child care provider in their network. With the subsidies, Diane's weekly copayment was $75 for all three children, covering Daryl Jr. and Gary's after-school and full-time care in the summer, and Adrienne's full-time care with Ms. Spelling. "I liked Ms. Spelling the most of all my children's care providers," Diane says. "She was really organized and had her house arranged with lots of books and toys. She had been providing family child care for almost twenty years. Addy loved her and thought she was her grandmother."

Adrienne would remain with Ms. Spelling for eleven months until Love Thy Neighbor informed Diane that she was no longer eligible for her child care subsidy because her income had increased:

> I got kicked off ACD. That January I had negotiated an increase in my hours and my pay. I had been at $16 an hour for six hours [per day], and I got it up to seven hours for $19 an hour. Now they said I was over-income. We paid Ms. Spelling the full amount for like one week, but we could not afford that. I had to scramble all over again.

Having fought for the raise and extra hours, Diane then faced an increase in child care costs that eclipsed her income increase. Moreover, all of the available alternatives have been poorer in quality. Adrienne, at eighteen months old, is about to start her fourth child care arrangement, this time with a young woman Diane met from church who will also watch the two boys after school.

When Diane is interviewed a little more than one year later, she relates her disappointment that a pre-K slot she had hoped would come through for Adrienne did not:

> We planned to enroll her in school in September, but it looks like Addy won't be able to go. I wanted her in pre-K because she is so bright and could get ready for school, and the pre-K program is free. . . . But today was enrollment day, and they said that I am not in "the zone." You know me, I visited them three months ago, I was the first one at the school this morning, [and] I had already called them five times before that to ask about enrolling her, and no one said anything about a zone. And besides, I am only two blocks from there. What can the zone be?

By the time Adrienne is three, Diane has made nearly twenty-five different primary and secondary care arrangements for their three children. This latest challenge, trying to get Adrienne into pre-K, has left her devastated: "They have such few places that they want to serve those who live closest to the school, and they know there would be no places available. They told me to try another school, but I knew

[that] pre-K program was for fours [four-year-olds]. . . . The lady was just trying to find the soft way of putting the dagger in my heart."

The life of the young child in the United States has changed dramatically over the course of the last two generations. In 1965, three-quarters of children under age six had a stay-at-home mother, and fewer than one-quarter of mothers worked.[1] Most of today's grandparents spent their early years at home with their mothers. In contrast, the majority of their grandchildren are in nonparental care settings by age one. By 2015, the proportion of mothers with young children who were employed had grown to 64 percent, including a majority of mothers who had returned to work before their child's first birthday.[2] Over the last fifty years, the proportion of children living in homes in which their parents work has grown dramatically, and successive cohorts of American families have placed their children in early care and education at younger and younger ages. Nonparental care and education is now the normative experience for young children in the United States and in much of the world. §

In our research over the last twenty years, we have heard stories like those about Adrienne and Benji from hundreds of families all over the country, and we have visited the wide range of early care and education settings where children spend their days.[3] The challenges that the Caldwells and the Harveys face are not unique or relegated to the large urban centers of the country. In fact, in some ways Adrienne's and Benji's family circumstances are not as challenging as those of many of the other families we have met in our research. And New York City and Seattle provide considerably more early care and education resources than many other parts of the country.

Early care and education in the United States is in crisis. Family budgets and routines have been stretched beyond their breaking point. Too many children are getting overlooked during their earliest years when early attention and adequate investments would put them on a more solid path educationally and give them a fair shot in life. In a nation with ample resources to provide good opportunities to all its citizens, we are burdened with a system that creates unequal sets of experiences among our youngest children and growing disparities in cognitive and behavioral skills that worsen rather than remedy inequality across generations. Despite the strong and growing preference of families to place their children in high-quality early care and education, the enrollment of children under five in these settings and public investments lag far behind those of other developed countries and show large disparities by family resources. The crisis affects everyone, but the impact on the middle class and disadvantaged families is much more severe.[4]

Few things matter as much to the prospects of a person, a family, a community, or the nation than the learning, health, and development of young children. There have been revolutionary advances in knowledge in recent years across the diverse disciplines of biology, neuroscience, developmental psychology, economics, and other fields that make it clear that the period from birth until age three is the most promising and possibly consequential stage of human development. The research evidence from developmental science demonstrates the enormously sensitive and expansive learning and development that occur during this period and shows, in fact, that the well-documented gaps in achievement and development begin prior to preschool. The neuroscience literature, which has vastly expanded over the last twenty years, has shown the importance of the earliest period of life for the brain's developing architecture. There is now strong evidence of the importance of early learning opportunities for basic skills development, school readiness, and lifelong learning trajectories.

Indeed, these connections have become widely understood among parents, as shown by their decisions to provide greater early learning opportunities for their children, particularly among those who can afford to do so. Public support for greater public investments in early care and education has increased as well. In recent national polls, ensuring that all kids get a strong start in life was ranked as one of the most important national priorities, tied for first with improving public education and ahead of creating jobs in one poll and second only to creating jobs in a second poll.[5]

High-quality early care and education is in short supply, and when available, it is very expensive relative to most families' means. Across the United States, communities large and small, affluent and poor, lack the infrastructure for the care and education of young children. Over the past few decades, the market has slowly responded, and more affluent families have shifted to investing substantially more in the early learning of their children. Families of lesser means have not been able to keep up. As a result, a great many children simply do not have the opportunity to further develop their skills to move ahead, and socioeconomic disparities in early education, school readiness, and longer-term outcomes in educational attainment and employment have widened markedly. The children of families with means have seen vast increases in parental time and financial investments during the first five years of life, including much higher levels of enrollment in center-based education, than children from low- and middle-income families. As such, early childhood has increasingly become a developmental period when a great many children lose the opportunity to develop a foundation for learning and inequality is reinforced. As presently structured, our system of early childhood care and education replicates social stratification rather than reducing it.

The learning gaps that are rooted early in life are precursors to gaps in longer-term human capital outcomes, including educational attainment and labor market success. The lost opportunities in early childhood limit development later in life because, as the economist James Heckman has termed it, "skills beget skills."[6] The underinvestment in early child development is especially foolhardy given that, to compete in today's information- and knowledge-based global economy, citizens must attain a high level of skills and education. The United States lags behind most other developed nations in public investments in children under age five. The Organization of Economic Cooperation and Development (OECD) ranks the United States near the bottom among developed nations in the level of public expenditures to support early care and education, and thirtieth out of thirty-two countries in enrollment of three- and four-year-olds in early childhood education.[7] The United States trails other nations with advanced economies in levels of college completion, labor force participation, and economic mobility—areas in which it was once a world leader.

As public investments in early care and education have lagged, women have disproportionately borne the burdens of caregiving. Most mothers work and are increasingly family breadwinners, especially in many low- and middle-income families. The lack of an infrastructure for early care and learning opportunities has negative consequences for the productivity and earnings of parents, particularly mothers. Many women have little choice but to return to jobs quickly after giving birth. When they do so, many families then struggle to find and afford reliable and high-quality child care, and this continues to be a critical challenge until the child enters kindergarten.

The central thesis of this book is that early care and education in the United States must be restructured to support children's learning and behavioral development from birth to school entry, in the context of families' work, economic, and caregiving realities. There is a huge gulf between the system we have today and one that will allow children to realize their full potential and provide the nation with the educated population it needs to achieve a more prosperous and secure future. We propose an integrated set of national and state policies that can support families in nurturing their children's learning and development to promote not only the children's long-term success but also our nation's.

Large and Growing Gaps in School Readiness and Later Outcomes

From birth, there are wide disparities in access to opportunities for growth and learning. Higher-income parents are more likely to have paid parental leave benefits at work and are more able to take unpaid leave to spend time with their newborn children. Nearly one-quarter of children today are being raised by two college-educated, full-time working parents, and it is these children who most often experience two or more years of formal center-based care and education before reaching kindergarten.[8] By contrast, children growing up in low- and middle-income households typically receive at most one year of preschool learning in center-based settings. In effect, current inequities in early learning opportunities put children from affluent families on a vastly different track compared to children from low- and middle-income families.[9]

For many years, we have known there are large disparities in measures of children's cognitive skills, social and emotional development, and behavior across a range of family and individual characteristics, including family income, race-ethnicity, maternal education, and home language.[10] Figure 1.1 shows the trends in achievement gaps for math and reading test scores based on a comprehensive analysis of

Figure 1.1 *Trends in Achievement Gaps by Family Income by Birth Cohort, 1945–2006*

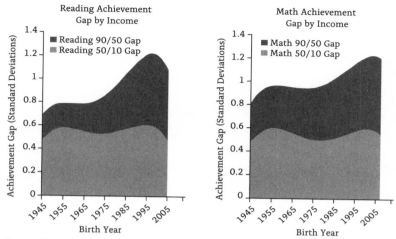

Source: Sean F. Reardon, based on data in Reardon (2011) and Reardon and Portilla (2016); used with permission of the author.

dozens of studies covering the years from prekindergarten to twelfth grade by Sean Reardon and Ximena Portilla.[11] In math and reading, children from families in the top 20 percent of the income distribution (above $120,000) are more than one year—more than one full standard deviation in statistical terms—ahead of their peers from families in the lowest 20 percent of the income distribution (below $25,000). Children from families with the highest incomes also substantially outscore children from moderate-income families (with incomes at the median level, $62,000).[12]

These income disparities have been widening over time. The gaps in test scores between the ninetieth and tenth percentiles of family income (the midpoints of the top and bottom quintiles) grew substantially in the last quarter of the twentieth century—by about 40 percent overall between birth cohorts since the late 1970s. The gap between the top and the middle actually widened even more in these years, enlarging the gap between children from families with incomes at the ninetieth and fiftieth percentiles to be as large as the gaps between those with family incomes at the fiftieth and tenth percentiles.[13] This growing gap has not happened because children from lower- and middle-income families are doing worse—actually, their scores have been increasing modestly over this period—but because children from families with the greatest means have been pulling away in their early skills. Sean Reardon and Ximena Portilla suggest that the significant increased investments made by higher-income families, including enrolling their children in early learning and preschool settings at younger and younger ages, are contributing to the significant gains among this group. This suggests that with the right kind of investments in high-quality care and education opportunities, many more middle- and low-income children could also improve their skills and school readiness.

By the time children start kindergarten, disparities in school readiness across the full continuum of family incomes are already huge. Figure 1.2 shows that the disparity in reading and math school readiness between children from families at the tenth and ninetieth income percentiles amounts to roughly an entire year of early learning (between 1.0 and 1.2 standard deviations). This disparity is similar to the overall achievement gap measured across the school years in figure 1.1. Figure 1.2 also shows that children from families with higher incomes are substantially ahead on measures of social and emotional development, including teacher-reported self-control and approaches to learning.[14]

These disparities begin well before kindergarten, appearing as early as infancy. Disparities by income in terms of cognitive skills, health, and behavior have been found as early as nine months of age. Two-year-olds from lower-income families are already six months behind in language development and word acquisition compared to children from higher-income families.[15] In other words, most of the achievement gap in reading and math skills measured at later points in childhood is present before children first set foot in kindergarten.[16]

Why do these large differences in skill levels and early disparities matter? A great many children in the United States have low skill levels when they start kindergarten and are not nearly as ready as they should be. Data from the Early Childhood Longitudinal Study (ECLS) indicate that nearly half of all children who entered kindergarten in 2010 had low proficiency levels in a range of literacy and math skills: 49 percent had low literacy skills, and 48 percent had low math skills. Furthermore, two-thirds of children whose family income was in the lowest 20 percent had low literacy and math skills (68 percent and 66 percent, respectively).[17] Research shows that read-

Figure 1.2 *School Readiness Gaps at Kindergarten Entry in 2010 Between Children at the Ninetieth and Tenth Family Income Percentiles*

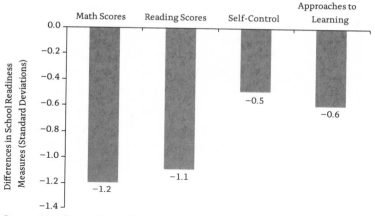

Source: Reardon and Portilla (2016); Early Childhood Longitudinal Study–Kindergarten Class of 2010–2011 (ECLS-K: 2010–2011).

ing, math, and behavior skills in kindergarten and the early primary grades predict later educational and adult outcomes.[18] Longitudinal studies and other research over the last several decades have documented the significantly worse adult outcomes for health, education, income, and criminal activities for those living in disadvantaged circumstances during childhood and into adulthood compared to their better-off peers.[19]

In addition, there is evidence that access to high-quality early childhood services can improve children's outcomes and reduce disparities. The strongest evidence comes from the very few program evaluations that have included both poor and nonpoor families and tested the effects of high-quality early care and education on each group. The Infant Health and Development Program (IHDP) served lower-income, low-birth-weight newborns across eight urban study sites in the 1990s, made frequent home visitations in the first year, and offered full-day, high-quality early care and education beginning when infants were one year old and continuing until they turned three. IHDP essentially eliminated the income-based gap in early cognitive skills at age three and reduced such gaps at ages five and eight by between one-third and three-quarters, thus increasing the predicted lifetime earnings of participants by an estimated 13 percent.[20]

Other evidence to support the particularly strong effects of quality early care and education on children from disadvantaged families comes from national studies of preschool effects and evaluations of universal prekindergarten programs in Boston and Tulsa.[21]

The Head Start program serves many more children than the more intensive IHDP, and there is more variation in quality among its program providers. Nevertheless, Head Start has been shown to increase participants' likelihood of attending college by six percentage points, decrease their likelihood of being teen parents by two percentage points, and decrease their likelihood of being in poor health in their early twenties by seven percentage points.[22] Although these effects are smaller in scale than the long-term outcomes from small-scale demonstration programs such as the Perry Preschool Project or the Abecedarian Project, they still represent sizable improvements. This is especially true given that per-child, per-year spending on Head Start is less than half what it is with the other two interventions, and that these results are based on receiving Head Start program services for one year (the typical amount of time that many children are enrolled in Head Start); children in Abecedarian and the IHDP received five years and three years, respectively, of more intensive and continuous program services.

In sum, the body of evidence suggests that low skill levels and socioeconomic disparities early in life contribute to starkly different long-term adult outcomes, and that early childhood interventions, particularly those characterized by high instructional quality, can improve educational outcomes that reduce disparities. These findings motivate our call for a coordinated plan to fix the early care and education crisis in the United States.

How a New Vision for Early Care and Education Could Reduce Inequalities

School readiness gaps are not intractable problems. Expanding access to high-quality early care and education could significantly increase the level of skills and access for children in low- and middle-income families, ameliorating the sharp inequalities they face and ensuring that many more of them are ready for school. To be sure, investments in high-quality early childhood care and education for all children would not completely eliminate the gaps, since it is likely that many other aspects of inequality contribute to the disparities, including later resources and learning opportunities. But a carefully designed program of subsidies and instructional improvements could significantly improve children's skills, reduce the size of the gaps in school readiness, and shrink subsequent gaps in educational and economic outcomes.

In this book, we point out several deficiencies in the existing hodgepodge of early learning programs: services are underdeveloped, leaving large gaps in coverage; on average, programs are of mediocre quality; and the components of the early care and education system are often fragmented and working at cross-purposes. As a result, the system is not coherent. Another important deficiency is that those who might benefit the most from high-quality early care and education opportunities are the least likely to attend. All of these deficiencies contribute to maintaining and increasing inequality in early learning and later success rather than reducing it.

Many early childhood policy efforts tinker at the edges, focusing on single incremental steps that could prove feasible for one program area (for example, state pre-K) or on one problem with existing services (such as low-quality care or lack of equity in access). We present a comprehensive policy proposal spanning the first five years of life that will fulfill the promise to provide opportunities in the early years for success for all, while helping to close the large and growing gaps in access to high-quality early childhood experiences.

We believe that a framework to support the development and education of young children requires a comprehensive approach grounded in an understanding of how current gaps in early child care access and quality contribute to the growing deficits in school readiness and educational outcomes over time. This book offers a proposal that addresses those gaps with the most evidenced-based policies to support children's early learning and long-term success.

Principles to Help Guide Early Childhood Investments

Our plan addresses what we see as the key challenges across the range of early childhood services. In addition, it is based on research evidence and guided by a set of core principles.

First, the proposals we offer *tackle disparities in both access and quality*. We describe how large and growing gaps in access and quality by family income at each developmental stage have contributed to the widening of school readiness disparities. Both access and quality problems present challenges for supporting children's ability to reach their full potential. The widening gap in children's access to early care and education opportunities has contributed to achievement gaps by providing children from higher-income families with the means to race further ahead. Broadening access to high-quality early learning can level the playing field so that more American children can have an opportunity to succeed and development and school readiness gaps can be narrowed.

Second, in designing our early childhood proposal, we have aimed to *support both children's early learning and parents' employment*. These two goals can be complementary when high-quality, affordable care and education are designed to reflect the needs of working families. We expect that improved early care and education resources in the very earliest years not only supports children's development but can also lead to increased and more stable parental employment.

Third, we seek to *support parents' own choices for nurturing their children's early development*. The family is most influential in shaping children's development. The policy framework that we advance aims to expand families' access to a broader set of early learning opportunities by improving their availability, quality, and affordability. Our policy framework does not offer a "one-size-fits-all" solution.

Fourth, this vision *accords a central role to equality of opportunity in learning and education* in shaping policy for early care and development. Developing their capacities through educational endeavor is a principal means by which individuals achieve social mobility and success. In enhancing the development and learning opportunities that begin from birth, our policy framework is consistent with the value this country has historically placed on providing a level playing field: in the establishment of universal public primary and secondary education, antidiscrimination policies in employment and housing, affordable health care, and voting rights.[23]

Fifth, *supporting children's developmental needs in the early years is a shared private and public responsibility*. Even as the costs of paying for children's care prior to school entry have often been considered a private family responsibility, children's elementary and secondary education in the United States has long been viewed as an area of public responsibility in that it supports the development of future workers and the citizenry. Many states and localities are coming around to this view of early education in the preschool years as well. We believe that the public and private responsibility for children's early care and education need not be viewed dichotomously. It seems reasonable to expect parents to contribute to the cost of nonparental early care and education to the extent that their resources permit because doing so is their core responsibility and they are best positioned to make decisions regarding the most appropriate investments. Yet stable and high-quality early learning environments are often beyond the financial reach of many families. As vital as early education is to skill development in the years before formal schooling and to a child's ability to make the most of the public schooling that follows, public resources are needed to supplement the resources that parents can reasonably commit for this purpose.

We consider and discuss these core principles in more detail as they arise in the context of the specific policy proposals across this book's chapters. Our aim in developing and discussing the policy framework here is not to prioritize any one principle over the others, but to consider how together they can inform a comprehensive plan for early care and education.

The Organization of the Book

This book presents a vision for an early care and education policy to meet the challenges of the coming decades. Our proposal centers on integrated supports to allow families to nurture their children's development. Chapters 2 through 5 are devoted to each of the components of our policy proposal. Chapter 2 proposes a new *paid parental leave system* to provide parents with time and support after birth. In chapter 3, we propose two related policy mechanisms to support families' capacity to pay for high-quality child care: a *child-care assurance or guarantee* for low- and moderate-income working families with young children, and an expansion of the existing *child care tax credit* to help support the child care costs of families across a broader age spectrum. In chapter 4, we argue for *universal, high-quality early educa-*

tion that starts by age three. Chapter 5 describes our proposal for a *reconceptualized Head Start* that begins at or before birth and targets the highest-need children and families with early and continuous intervention and developmental services until school entry.

In chapter 6, the final chapter of the book, we summarize the key elements of our strategic vision and present how the four components of our policy proposal are integrated and coordinated. We discuss the proposal's merits, estimate how many families and children will be served, develop cost projections, and describe long-term benefits. We briefly describe how the components could be sequenced and phased in over time within a ten-year window. Finally, we discuss the challenges and opportunities for making this vision a domestic priority for our children, ourselves, and our posterity.

PAID PARENTAL LEAVE   2

The first weeks of life are vital for the formation of strong, lifelong bonds between children and the most important caregivers in their lives: their parents. Newborns need consistent, sensitive, and responsive caregiving in their earliest days if they are to forge strong, loving relationships. This early period of care is often cut short for many families in the United States, however, because parents need to return to work to continue to earn income.

The majority of children in the United States are born into families of working parents. Nearly two-thirds of women work while pregnant, and approximately two-thirds return to work within the year after giving birth, with many returning quickly after birth. Twenty-eight percent of mothers are back to work within two months of childbirth, and 41 percent within three months.[1] Those who have the fewest resources and can least afford to not work are the most likely to return to work very soon after giving birth. Both Benji's and Adrienne's mothers are examples of the millions of working mothers across our nation who give birth each year and return to work quickly—Adrienne just seven days later—because they have no access to paid leave. Without the option of job-protected paid leave, these parents face the heart-wrenching choice between leaving their newborns in someone else's hands to go back to work or confronting financial losses from unpaid leave or job loss. These decisions can have cascading, long-term consequences for maternal health, child well-being, and family economic security.

The Effects of Paid Parental Leave

PAID PARENTAL LEAVE AND CHILDREN

The newborn and early infancy period is a critical time of life for parents and children. A period of leave from work enables them to establish important caregiving and feeding patterns during this very early period, including breast-feeding, which is associated with improved child health and mother-child bonding.[2] A large body of research on the effects of maternal employment on children's outcomes suggests that any negative effects are confined to intensive levels of employment during the first nine or twelve months of life, primarily in non-Hispanic white, middle- and high-income families; mothers' employment during later developmental periods has largely been found to have neutral or even some positive effects.[3]

Research findings show that the rapid return to work characteristic of American parents predicts poorer child outcomes.[4] Multiple studies provide evidence for causal associations between mothers' return to work within twelve weeks of their children's birth and lower rates of breast-feeding as well as fewer immunizations and increased child behavior problems.[5] In addition, a growing body of research demonstrates negative effects on child outcomes from income volatility and parental job loss, which are more common and severe in younger families.[6] Policies that help families smooth income and maintain secure employment over the critical newborn period—like job-protected paid parental leave—can promote health and development and improve economic security.

The majority of the research on the effects of paid family leave on child well-being has been conducted in countries that have robust family leave policies, such as in Europe and Canada. In general, this research finds evidence for positive impacts of paid leave on child health. A recent study of parental leave in 141 countries found that the provision of at least ten paid weeks of maternity leave is associated with a 9 to 10 percent reduction in neonatal mortality, infant mortality, and under-five mortality rates.[7] Another recent study found that paid maternity leaves of twelve weeks or longer are associated with increases in the likelihood of well-child doctor visits and receipt of recommended vaccines.[8] Research examining the introduction of parental leave in sixteen European countries from the 1970s to the 1990s found that the provision of more generous paid leave is associated with substantial reductions in death rates among infants and young children and in low birth weights.[9]

In recent years, three states—California, New Jersey, and Rhode Island—have implemented publicly funded paid leave systems by building upon the infrastructure of their Temporary Disability Insurance (TDI) systems and largely funding these programs through small increases in employee payroll taxes.[10] Since 2004, California has provided up to six weeks of leave at partial pay for both mothers and fathers to care for a new child or seriously ill or injured family member. The emerging evidence from the few evaluations of these new state programs is positive. Since the California program was enacted, parents have been more likely to take leaves, and to take longer leaves.[11] An evaluation of this program found that women in California who used the paid leave benefit breast-fed twice as long as those who did not.[12] A recent study from the Centers for Disease Control and Prevention (CDC) found that compared to seven states with no paid parental leave policies, California showed a significant decrease in hospital admissions for pediatric abusive head trauma, a leading cause of death from maltreatment, among children younger than two following the 2004 implementation of paid leave.[13]

PAID PARENTAL LEAVE AND PARENTS

Maternity leave is often viewed as a time for mothers to recover from childbirth. Indeed, in states with TDI systems, mothers during the period after childbirth—or prior to it as well if pregnancy complications are present—are considered eligible for disability insurance. Research suggests that maternity leave is important for mothers' health and psychological well-being. Mothers who take less than eight weeks of paid leave have poorer overall health and increased depressive symptoms, according to some findings, and women who take longer leaves following a child's birth report lower levels of daily family stress than women who transition back to work sooner.[14]

The birth of a child, particularly if there is no source of wage replacement for the time away from work, can lead to a significant decline in family income and trigger the descent of some families into poverty.[15] Many women must take unpaid leave from work, or leave their jobs altogether, and consequently face wage reductions due to time out of the labor force. Also, taking an extended leave or dropping out of the workforce to spend time with a newborn has been found to affect mothers' longer-term labor and economic outcomes.[16]

A great many parents can experience financial stress surrounding the birth of a child, but those with low incomes and those who are single parents without a household partner face deeper financial challenges, especially without paid leave. In 2013, four in ten babies were born to unmarried women, and in about half of these cases (58 percent), the parents were in a cohabitating relationship.[17] Unmarried mothers, even those in cohabitating relationships, are more disadvantaged than their married counterparts, and children born to unmarried mothers are more likely to live in poverty and to have only one parent present for most of their childhood, both of which have negative implications for children's outcomes.[18] Further, considering that mothers now earn the majority of household income in more than 40 percent of families, the lack of paid parental leave has negative consequences for a broad swath of American families.[19]

Although mothers experience pregnancy and childbirth, both parents need time with a newborn to form lifelong parent-child relationships and establish more secure caregiving routines. Fathers' time with newborns is also important for long-term child and family well-being. One study of fathers in four countries (Australia, Denmark, the United Kingdom, and the United States) found that fathers who take leaves of two weeks or more are more involved with their children and with child care–related activities, and that their children score higher on cognitive tests later in childhood.[20]

Research in the United States shows that fathers are more involved in their children's lives when they start early.[21] Fathers on average have increased their involvement in caregiving in the last fifty years from two and a half hours per week in 1965 to seven hours per week in 2011. Yet this is still only half of the time spent on child care by mothers, who put in fourteen hours per week in 2011—a four-hour increase over the ten hours they spent on child care in 1965, despite more of them being in the workforce. A 2015 Pew Research survey found that more than half of mothers (60 percent) and fathers (52 percent) report that it is very or somewhat difficult to balance work and family responsibilities, and full-time working fathers today are more likely than full-time working mothers to report that they do not spend enough time with their children (50 percent compared to 39 percent).[22]

Fathers in the United States and other countries are less likely to take parental leave than mothers, and when they do, they often take short periods of leave that minimize reductions in family income.[23] Studies have found that paid leave can be structured to encourage fathers' leave-taking through gender-neutral paid leave available to both parents, set-asides for father-only leave, and more adequate levels of wage replacement, all of which appear to increase fathers' leave-taking and duration. Compared to evaluations of fathers' use of unpaid leave following implementation of the FMLA, which did not affect their leave-taking, the share of men taking family leave after the implementation of California's paid system increased from 17 percent to 29 percent.[24] The province of Quebec saw an increase in both the use and durations of paid leave by fathers in the years after implementing a set-aside policy of several weeks that only fathers could use.[25]

Research in countries with generous maternity-only leave policies, absent analogous policies for fathers, has found that female-only benefits may inadvertently harm women's income and progression in the workforce by serving as a disincentive for employers to hire or promote women, especially those of child-bearing age.[26] One recent study found that, since the implementation of FMLA, women are 5 percent more likely to remain employed, but 8 percent less likely to be promoted.[27]

Paid leave has the advantage of supporting families' standard of living at a critical stage of family formation and expansion when expenses also increase, as well as encouraging fathers (or a second parent in same-sex couples) to take leave. Fathers are less likely to take leave when it is unpaid, not only because the mother of their child is the one who needs time to recover from childbirth, but also because they face economic pressures to support their family's standard of living.

PAID PARENTAL LEAVE AND EMPLOYERS

The issue of parental leave has grown more salient to employers with the increase in the number of women in the labor force. Compared to other historical periods, women are now more likely to work while pregnant and to work longer into their pregnancy.[28] Because the United States lacks a publicly financed parental leave system, employers bear the costs of any voluntary leave time they provide to employees. Studies on the effects of parental leave on employers are limited, but some research suggests that a publicly supported paid leave system could alleviate some of the financial burden now faced by employers and could also have some positive effects on employee retention. In general, mothers are more likely to return to the labor force (and their prebirth jobs) when their leave is long enough.[29] Google found that its expansion of work-family benefits reduced the attrition rate of new mothers among its employees by 50 percent.[30] Publicly funded leave would alleviate some costs to employers who provide paid parental leave, but more importantly, it would expand the benefits of offering leave to the vast majority of employers that currently do not offer paid parental leave, especially smaller firms. Public paid leave could increase employee retention and reduce the costs of employee turnover, which has been estimated at 21 percent of an employee's annual salary.[31]

Regardless of whether paid leave is employer-provided or publicly supported, employers must temporarily cover the workload of the employee on leave. In a 2014 study in the United Kingdom, which provides up to thirty-nine weeks of paid leave, 58 percent of managers and 48 percent of employees report that leave is "somewhat disruptive" to their businesses. Seventy-two percent of managers report that parental leave affects the efficiency and productivity of their employees. Small businesses in particular express concerns about recruiting and training temporary staff.[32]

Research has shown that firms can mitigate the costs of the short-term loss of an employee, whether on paid or unpaid leave. In a study that followed the implementation of California's paid leave program, 29 percent of large businesses (100 employees or more) report negative impacts on productivity, and the other 71 percent report either no noticeable effect or a positive effect. Just 13 percent of all employers report cost increases due to the new public paid leave law; for those employers, the additional expenses were incurred predominantly in the additional hiring and training needed to cover the work of employees on leave.[33]

PAID PARENTAL LEAVE AND THE ECONOMY

The establishment of a paid parental leave system may affect the overall economy in several ways. There is strong evidence that paid parental leave increases maternal labor force participation and women's economic security, increasing lifetime earnings and retirement savings, particularly among single-mother households.[34] The United States fell from having the sixth-highest female labor force participation rate in 1990 to seventeenth in 2010 among twenty-two OECD countries, as it failed to keep up with other nations in its work-family policies.[35] The establishment of a new paid leave law would probably induce more women to work before and during their pregnancies to be eligible. Christopher Ruhm has estimated that a law establishing three months of fully paid leave in the United States would increase female labor supply by 10 percent or more in the year prior to childbirth.[36]

Research suggests that the children of mothers who take leave may experience long-term benefits. One study in Norway found that the children of women who received paid maternity leave have wages that are 5 percent higher than those of their counterparts at age thirty, though other studies have shown no effects.[37] The fact that more research, however, has consistently found positive short- and long-term impacts of paid parental leave on children's health and development and mothers' well-being implies that paid parental leave could reduce public and private expenditures on child and maternal health, including for treating infectious diseases and maternal depression.[38]

In sum, the research suggests that access to paid leave following the birth or adoption of a child, for an adequate period of time and made available to both mothers and fathers, would improve the short- and long-term outcomes of young children as well as the economic security and stability of their parents. Publicly funded parental leave in particular would expand these benefits to more workers and serve as an investment in the future health of the population and economy. Finally, paid parental leave should be implemented in a way that minimizes costs to employers or avoids incentives to not hire women or men of childbearing age.

Inadequate Access to Parental Leave in the United States

The United States is the only developed nation without a parental leave system that provides income and job protections for parents that enable them to spend essential time with their newborn children.[39] The Family and Medical Leave Act of 1993 is the only federal protection available to workers in the United States. FMLA provides for up to twelve weeks of job-protected unpaid leave, but this protection is limited to full-time employees who have been with their employers for twelve or more months and who work at firms with at least fifty employees. Fewer than half of private-sector workers are covered by the law.[40] Self-employed, low-wage, recently hired, or part-time workers are largely ineligible for the unpaid leave provided by FMLA.[41] A handful of states have Temporary Disability Insurance (TDI) systems that provide partial wage replacement for workers who are temporarily disabled or injured and that consider the period following childbirth an eligible disability.

In recent years, a few states have established paid leave programs that build on their TDI systems to create paid family leave for all parents. California began providing partial wage replacement funded entirely by a new employee payroll tax on January 1, 2004, and New Jersey and Rhode Island followed in subsequent years.[42] In March 2016, New York State passed a paid family leave law that provides up to twelve weeks of paid leave beginning in 2018. Washington State is the one state without a TDI program that has passed a paid parental leave law, but funding and implementation have been delayed for several years. Research demonstrates the popularity and success of the current state leave systems in operation and the positive effects on mothers' and fathers' leave-taking. These systems have also been found to increase the duration of breast-feeding, decrease infant hospitalizations, and improve firms' employee retention.[43]

Table 2.1 provides a summary of the benefits and coverage of the

Family and Medical Leave Act and the state paid leave and TDI programs.

With the lack of public leave policies across much of the country, the majority of American families have no access to parental leave. Although some employers create individual solutions for their employees, these are still rare and very unevenly distributed among American workers.[44] Only 13 percent of positions in the private sector have access to paid family leave.[45] Employers of high-skilled workers in competitive labor market sectors, such as technology firms, are the most likely to provide parental leave, recognizing the importance of this benefit for recruitment and retention.[46] Workers across most industries and income ranges, however, are not offered employer coverage.[47] Low-income working parents, who need paid leave the most, are the least likely to have it. As shown in figure 2.1, 21 percent of workers in the top quarter of earners have paid leave benefits compared to 5 percent of workers with wages in the bottom 25 percent and 13 percent of those in the middle two quarters of the earnings distribution.[48]

The issue of public paid parental leave has received greater policy attention in recent years. Recent public opinion polls show widespread support for paid parental leave among the voting-age population, including majorities in favor of a paid leave system funded through payroll contributions.[49] In 2016, New York State and the City of San Francisco passed laws to implement more generous paid leave systems in 2018 and 2017, respectively. New York's public paid leave benefit will provide up to twelve weeks of leave, and San Francisco will establish a system for 100 percent wage replacement through a combination of California's paid leave program and an employer mandate to provide the additional wage replacement. Proposals to create paid family leave systems have been introduced and actively debated in the legislatures of at least fourteen other states.[50] The Obama administration has been supportive of expanding state efforts, making funds available in the Department of Labor's budget to provide competitive grants to states.

At the federal level, several paid leave proposals have been introduced in Congress. For example, the Family and Medical Leave Insurance (FAMILY) Act would provide two-thirds wage replacement financed by a 0.2 percent payroll tax on employees and employers.[51] To

Table 2.1 *Summary of the Family and Medical Leave Act and State-Paid Family Leave Laws*

Law	Benefits	Who It Covers
Federal Family and Medical Leave Act (FMLA) (1993)	Up to twelve weeks of unpaid leave for specific family- or health-related reasons, including: • Employee's own serious health condition • Mothers for maternity-related reasons • Parents (mothers and fathers) to care for a newborn • Parents for a new adoption or foster care placement • Care of employee's child, spouse, or parent for a serious health condition Employees must be restored to the same or equivalent job upon return to work, and health benefits (if provided) must continue.	Employees working at firms with fifty or more employees who have been working at the firm for twelve months or more. Employers may voluntarily provide full or partial wage replacement. Smaller employers may voluntarily provide paid or unpaid leave.
State Temporary Disability Insurance (TDI) programs	Provides partial wage replacement for short-term injury or illness unconnected to work.	Rhode Island, California, New Jersey, New York, Hawaii, Puerto Rico, and the District of Columbia have TDI systems. Most salaried workers are covered. Employers in other states may voluntarily participate. Typically, only mothers who give birth—not fathers and adoptive parents—are eligible.

Program	Description	Coverage
California Paid Family Leave (PFL) insurance program (2004)	Provides up to six weeks of leave with partial wage replacement to each parent, in addition to TDI benefits, in order to care for and bond with a new child or care for another family member (not available for the worker's own health needs). Wage replacement is approximately 55 percent of earnings (up to a maximum of $1,075 per week of benefits) for each worker. The program is funded through employee payroll taxes. Job protection is not included, but FMLA's job protection applies to covered workers.	Most private-sector and some public-sector employers and self-employed workers.
New Jersey Family Leave Insurance program (2009)	Provides up to six weeks of leave with partial wage replacement to each parent, in addition to TDI benefits, to care for and bond with a new child or care for another family member (not available for the worker's own health needs). Wage replacement is approximately two-thirds of the employee's weekly pay (up to a maximum of $595 per week). The program is funded through employee payroll taxes. Job protection is not included, but FMLA's job protection applies to covered workers.	Most private- and public-sector employers.
Rhode Island Temporary Caregiver Insurance (TCI) program (2014)	Provides up to four weeks of leave with partial wage replacement to each parent, with a weekly benefit rate of 4.62 percent of their wages paid in the highest earnings quarter of their base period (approximately 60 percent, up to a maximum of $752). The program is funded through employee payroll taxes and provides for job protection during leave.	Most private-sector and some public-sector employers.

Source: Authors' compilation.

Figure 2.1 *Availability of Paid Parental Leave in the Private Sector, 2014*

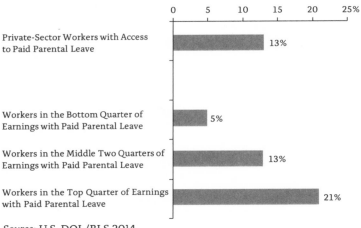

Source: U.S. DOL/BLS 2014.

date, Congress has not taken any action on these proposals.[52] In January 2016, the Pentagon announced an expansion of paid maternity leave from six to twelve weeks and paid paternity leave from ten to fourteen days for women and men in the military.[53] In the 2016 presidential race, candidates from both major parties, including Secretary Hillary Clinton, Donald Trump, Senators Marco Rubio and Bernie Sanders, and Governor Martin O'Malley, all voiced support for family leave for new parents, though their specific proposals varied.[54]

In sum, employer-provided paid leave and the state TDI or paid leave laws cover only a small proportion of new parents. For those eligible, the FMLA is helpful but not sufficient, providing only unpaid leave. As a result, many new parents face the difficult choice of returning to work quickly or losing their income and possibly their jobs, and young newborns and their parents lose out on this important time for setting a healthy developmental pathway.

A Universal, Publicly Supported, Paid Parental Leave System

We propose a system to provide job-protected leave with publicly funded partial wage replacement for workers during pregnancy or when caring for a new child. Similar to other proposals currently being discussed, such as the Family and Medical Insurance Leave (FAM-ILY) Act of 2015, our proposal would be administered through the existing Social Security system.[55] Parents would be eligible to receive up to sixteen weeks of paid leave benefits equal to a percentage of their average weekly salary upon the birth or adoption of a child, with minimum and maximum benefit levels. Like Social Security, the fraction of average earnings that workers receive in benefits would be progressively set based on income, with "bend points" such that the first portion of earnings would receive a greater percentage of wage replacement. We propose 80 percent wage replacement for the first $25,000 of average annual earnings. Above this threshold, subsequent earnings would receive a lower wage replacement level: 60 percent wage replacement for average annual earnings above $25,000 to a $75,000 maximum. These bend points reflect the progressiveness of the policy and are similar to recent revisions that have been adopted in California and proposed in Massachusetts.[56] With these wage replacement levels, we would establish a $160 minimum weekly benefit and a $962 maximum weekly benefit.

Our proposal promotes efficiency by using the existing national infrastructure of Social Security, though it would necessitate additional data and administrative resources for the Social Security Administration (SSA) and the Department of Labor, including ways to link and coordinate benefits for both parents related to the child. The proposed wage replacement levels would offer support to low-wage workers using leave and encourage middle- and higher-income working parents to participate, but would be capped to control costs and target benefits efficiently.[57]

Like FMLA and state-sponsored paid leave plans, eligibility and benefits would be tied to workers, but the total amount of leave time would be allocated per child, requiring coordination between the Department of Labor, the SSA, and the Internal Revenue Service (IRS). Benefits would apply to workers who have stay-at-home spouses or partners. Parents with full or partial custodial rights and responsibilities would be eligible for leave even if they did not reside with their children.[58] The weeks of paid leave would be designated as maternity leave, paternity leave, or gender-neutral leave: eight weeks reserved for mothers; four weeks reserved for fathers or mother's partner; and four weeks that would be parent- and gender-neutral.

This approach would allow families flexibility and promote father involvement through a type of mechanism that has been successful in Quebec.[59] It would bring the maximum period of leave with partial wage replacement to sixteen weeks per birth or adoption (twelve weeks if only the mother takes leave; eight weeks if only the father takes leave).[60] For example, in a two-parent family, if one parent whose average annual income is $25,000 takes twelve weeks of paid leave, the weekly benefit level would be $385, and if the second parent, earning $37,500 annually, takes four weeks of paid leave, the benefit would be $529 per week.[61]

The current FMLA protections would extend the length of the paid leave time for which new parents are eligible to include both the initial weeks of paid leave plus the existing FMLA protections for up to twelve weeks of unpaid, job-protected leave. Employers could voluntarily offer payment during this period or add additional leave time. Both parents could take additional unpaid leave and could choose to do so concurrently, sequentially, or staggered during pregnancy or the child's first year of life, as allowed in the California system and in the United Kingdom. Thus, in a family with two working parents, if the mother and father stagger their paid leave for ten and six weeks, respectively, and each parent takes twelve weeks of unpaid leave concurrently or sequentially, their infant might not need to begin regular nonparental care until six to nine months of age. Although many families might be unable to afford twelve to twenty-four weeks of lost parental income, it would be doable for other families, particularly if their employers choose to provide benefits beyond the period of public paid leave.

Just as the SSA uses individuals' overall work histories to determine eligibility for retirement and disability benefits, our proposed system would use workers' full work histories until the time when leave is sought, not just their current employment status. Further, as with the existing state TDI and paid leave systems, all workers with sufficient wage and earnings histories would be eligible, regardless of the size of their employer or whether they are self-employed. For example, a work history of at least 200 hours in the past twelve months could be used as an eligibility threshold.[62] These benefits would apply to workers with employer-sponsored paid leave as well. Employees could choose the more generous benefits or combine benefits for extended paid leave, while employers could choose to extend or replace the public paid leave benefit level or leave period.

The Social Security system is a cornerstone of American social policy and has evolved over its eighty-year history to meet the changing economic and demographic needs of our country. Adding the economic needs of newborns and their parents to our social policy infrastructure would update the program to meet the needs of today's families.[63] Moreover, the SSA, with its records on workers' employment and earnings, capacity for determining workers' medical or disability eligibility for benefits, and infrastructure to provide payment to a broad group of beneficiaries, would be an appropriate and effective agency for administering this new benefit.[64]

Importantly, we focus our proposed paid parental leave system for care during a new child's first year of life. In contrast with FMLA eligibility, the paid family leave systems in place in California, New Jersey, and Rhode Island, and the leave laws passed in Washington and New York, it is not designed to include leave for family member illnesses or other events outside of the birth or adoption of a child. In California's paid leave program, 87 percent of all leave claims are for bonding with a new child.[65] However, just 21 percent of all leave events that qualify under FMLA are for pregnancy or a new child.[66] Although it is clear that working parents require leave for other events, our program includes duration, wage replacement, and other design features that focus specifically on the period following childbirth—a particularly vulnerable period for both children's development and family economic security that warrants greater public investment to help families both maintain a basic standard of living and provide essential care for their children. The FMLA would remain in place to provide for job-protected unpaid family leave during these other times of need, and states or employers could provide other paid leave benefits. The federal government could consider expanding on a paid parental leave system for other leave reasons in the future.

The benefits of paid parental leave programs should be progressive so that they do not exacerbate socioeconomic inequality. Higher-income and more-educated workers are more likely to be covered by and to use the FMLA.[67] A study of Norway's expansions of paid leave in the late 1980s and early 1990s found that these programs favored middle- and upper-income families, and that these families received proportionately greater after-tax benefits than low-income families.[68] To avoid this outcome, we include a higher wage replacement level of 80 percent for the first $25,000 in earnings for all workers (a level nearly equivalent to the federal poverty level for a family of four). This higher percentage ensures a basic benefit level for all workers and wage replacement levels sufficient to encourage participation by parents with lower earnings. Benefits would increase by 60 percent for the income between $25,000 and $75,000, the maximum level. These thresholds and the maximum income level for wage replacement would be adjusted annually for inflation.

COSTS AND FINANCING

We estimate that our paid leave proposal would cost $18 billion to $20 billion per year within several years after full implementation. Details regarding participants' benefit levels and the overall costs of the proposal can be found in table A2.1 in the appendix; we discuss the cost of the plan's components in chapter 6.

This new social insurance benefit could be financed in one or several ways so that it does not add to long-term budget deficits. First, there could be an increase in the retirement age at which the cohort of children whose parents take leave following their birth could be eligible for Social Security that is financially equivalent to the number of weeks taken by their parents.[69] Here we assume that adults will choose to delay their retirement by as much as three or four months in exchange for having had the assurance of adequate family income and their parents at home with them in the weeks following their birth, given the importance of this time for their own development and economic potential. Parents themselves might accept this trade-off of compensated time around the time of having a new child for a modest delay in their retirement as worthwhile. Heather Boushey has proposed that parents could be allowed to trade weeks of future retirement benefits for leaves to care for new children.[70] Compared to the months following birth—a critical period of development that sets a child's long-term life trajectory—the first months of retirement are a less economically vulnerable period.

As a second option, parental leave could be financed with small increases in employee taxes, employer taxes, withholding, or some combination thereof. For example, the proposed FAMILY Act would increase the payroll tax by 0.2 percent for employers and employees (which averages about $1.50 per week per worker).[71] California's and New Jersey's paid leave systems are financed solely through employee payroll taxes. California's payroll tax rate for paid leave has varied from 0.6 percent in 2007 to 1.2 percent in 2011, and the program's trust fund has grown over time, dispelling earlier fears about the program's potential bankruptcy.[72] If the paid leave system is financed through employee payroll taxes, employees would have less take-home pay and the system could be more regressive than if financed through the progressive income tax structure. If supported by employer taxes, firms' labor costs would modestly increase (or effectively decrease worker wages). Increasing the cap on employee and employer with-holdings under Social Security provides another plausible means of financing the system.[73] We argue that paying additional taxes averaging approximately $1.50 to $2 per worker per week, paid by employees, employers, or a combination, is a good trade-off for ensuring financial security following the birth of a baby, reducing employee turnover, and promoting greater economic equity for families.

Alternatives and Limitations

One alternative to our proposal is to mandate that employers provide paid leave. We believe that a federal social insurance system for paid leave is more equitable and efficient than relying on employers, whether through voluntary means or mandates. A public system can provide universal coverage without creating undue hardship for em-ployers, reaching part- and full-time employees at large and small employers, as well as the self-employed and contract workers, who are not covered by FMLA. Further, a public system can be designed so that it offers equal access and progressive benefits to lower-wage workers.

In addition, today's workforce is dynamic: young workers in par-ticular change jobs, employers, and residences more frequently than in years past. Between 1979 and 2013, workers between the ages of eighteen and forty-eight held nearly twelve jobs on average, changing jobs every two years.[74] Given these patterns, there is little sense in making employers at a particular point in time exclusively responsible for providing benefits to largely new and often mobile employees.[75] Further, some firms, by the nature of their work, may be more likely to employ workers of childbearing age, disproportionately shouldering the burden.

Finally, by spreading the costs of leave across either all employers or all workers, our proposal reduces the disproportionate burden currently shouldered by the employers that voluntarily offer leave to just 13 percent of the U.S. workforce and by the large fraction of infants whose parents cannot afford to take unpaid leave. Employers would still be able to offer additional paid leaves as well as unpaid leave above the base public benefit, but we argue that employers should not shoulder the sole or primary burden of financing paid leave for individual employees, for several reasons. Small employers and the self-employed in particular (currently exempt from FMLA) and other types of firms in certain industries work within tight profit margins. Adding another mandate for these employers could reduce jobs and increase unemployment. Rather, just as retirement is supported by a broadly financed Social Security system, the time following childbirth is a common experience among Americans and should be publicly and broadly supported by all those who experience the benefits and drawbacks, which ultimately is all of us.

A federal system would be more efficient than relying on individual states. Although some states have taken the reins in creating their own paid leave systems in the absence of federal action, their options are limited. Only a handful of states have the TDI systems that have been used as the infrastructure for paid parental leave programs. Without a TDI system, Washington State has struggled with implementation and financing even after passing legislation to establish paid leave. Moreover, while some plans have proposed using the unemployment insurance infrastructure, we believe that the stricter employment-based eligibility criteria and experience or seniority rating would not be appropriate for parental leave purposes; in addition, unemployment insurance systems lack the ability to determine medical eligibility for benefits.[76]

Although our proposal would provide uniform benefits and relatively limited flexibility across the states, we argue that these measures are justified to ensure that all children in the United States get a healthy start when they are born. Further, nothing in our plan precludes states from providing additional benefits beyond the federal system, as states and localities have done with laws establishing higher minimum wage laws and state-earned income tax credits.

Other approaches to expanding the availability of paid leave have been proposed.[77] Scholars at the American Enterprise Institute have proposed making the Child and Dependent Care Tax Credit (CDCTC) available to families following the birth of a child on a refundable basis to low-income families with no tax liability (41 percent of tax returns filed) via advance payment (for example, through negative paycheck withholdings).[78] We are supportive of making the tax credit refundable and available via advance payments. However, as we explain in chapter 3, the tax credit amount must be increased substantially to help families meet their child care and other financial obligations. If used for paid leave only, a tax credit would be highly regressive and limited in the support it offered.

The Independent Women's Forum put forth a proposal for personal care accounts (PCAs) in which workers could save up to six weeks of income (capped at $5,000) per year to become available during times of leave following the birth or adoption of a child. If no leave is taken, or savings remain in the account, it would be treated as an IRA for retirement.[79] Given the low rate of retirement savings among Americans, particularly low-income and young individuals of childbearing age who often use all of their earnings to make ends meet, it is questionable whether these accounts would be used by those who need them most.[80]

These alternative parental leave proposals that do not use a federal social insurance system would each be insufficient to the need and could exacerbate already high levels of inequality by providing greater benefit to those with more resources.

Despite the many benefits of our proposal, it has its own limitations and trade-offs. First, as noted earlier, we limit our proposal to leaves taken in the year following the birth or adoption of a child. Working parents do require leave for other family illnesses and emergencies. In addition, workers who do not have children may resent being required to pay for this benefit via payroll taxes or other mechanisms. Although broadening eligibility to include other reasons for family leave could help alleviate this concern, we focus on a particular length of leave consistent with the needs of a family caring for a newborn. We argue that just as social programs, particularly Medicare and Social Security, rely on the earnings of all workers and future generations, publicly supported paid parental leave would be a wise investment for both those who stand to benefit directly from time off with their children and those who stand to benefit indirectly from the future contributions of the next generation. We have not done a similar analysis for what the appropriate approach or program design would be for other leave reasons, and those should also be considered.

Second, despite targeting both fathers and mothers, mothers may disproportionately take advantage of paid leave, or take much longer leaves than fathers (for example, if mothers take twelve weeks compared to fathers' four weeks); in this event, we might have some of the negative labor market and gender gap consequences found in European countries with generous maternity-only policies and long leaves taken by mothers. However, the specific designation of weeks for each parent and the levels of partial wage replacement offered are designed to limit these potential negative effects and allow families to structure their leave periods to meet their own circumstances. Further, paid parental leave is just one policy that could affect the gender wage gap; it could also be addressed with other policies like affordable, high-quality early care and education, flexible work schedules, and shorter workweeks.[81]

Third, the businesses that currently offer no leave or shorter periods of leave could incur greater costs in temporarily replacing employees or covering their work responsibilities while on leave. This issue is already faced by employers whose employees are covered by the twelve weeks of unpaid leave protections provided by the FMLA, but not currently by smaller businesses (fewer than fifty employees) or those with very high employee turnover. Businesses in California were found to be highly adaptable in using a variety of creative solutions to cover employees' workloads after the implementation of that state's parental leave law, such as voluntary extra shift lists, voluntary overtime, and putting non-urgent work on hold. In firms where employee turnover is high, like retail or food service, the influx of new hires was adequate to cover those on leave.[82] In addition, our proposal would allow workers to take leave in alternate blocks during the child's first year (as opposed to all at once); this possibility could alleviate some of this problem and was appealing to about half of employers in one study in the United Kingdom.[83] However, very small businesses—for example, a doctor's office with five or fewer employees—could find it more challenging if one employee is absent for three or more months, and employers of all sizes that currently do not offer leaves or offer shorter leaves might incur greater expenses covering temporary employee absences. Overall, however, we anticipate that employers would experience reductions in employee turnover, with lower costs involved in hiring and training new workers. In addition, costs could be reduced for employers who either currently offer paid leave or might do so in the future absent public provision.

Summary and Conclusion

The establishment of a publicly supported paid parental leave system would have numerous benefits for children, their parents, and the economy. A system that provides paid, job-protected leave, accessible to workers across states, employers, and the income spectrum, would offer new opportunities for developmentally appropriate parent-child time during a brief but critical period in children's lives. The benefits of this time for both parent and child are multiplicative. Families would benefit through improved child and parent well-being, greater gender equity at home and in the workplace, and enhanced economic security. Employers would benefit through reduced worker turnover and lessened responsibility for offering leave. Finally, paid leave would help build our economy and promote families' economic security by increasing parent labor force participation and lifetime earnings.

Our proposal offers these benefits by providing a minimum of economically secure parent-child time for all families—a floor that is currently set at zero. Moreover, our proposal for a federally administered and financed, universal paid leave system would address the socioeconomic inequalities that begin at birth, disproportionately benefit the low- and moderate-income families who typically lack access to any leave, even unpaid leave, and it would replace the existing system, which relies on employer benevolence.

AFFORDABLE, HIGH-QUALITY CARE AND EDUCATION

3

The period in children's lives before they enter public education has historically received little public investment, despite the developmental importance of these early years. During the very period when brain development is most sensitive to environmental influence, the cost of out-of-home care is at its highest, and largely borne by families without public support. In addition, the quality of the care available during this period is at its lowest, especially for disadvantaged families. As a result, a great many working parents struggle to find and afford high-quality, nonparental early care and education, particularly for infants and toddlers. For many children, the lack of affordable, accessible, and good-quality early care and education represents a lost opportunity to have the enriching early childhood experiences and interactions that can build a solid foundation for school readiness and later success.

Some features of parents and families and of today's job markets contribute to the challenges faced by families with young children. There is enormous complexity, fluidity, and instability in many low- and moderate-income families at just the time when greater economic resources and stability are most needed to support children's development. Most parents of young children are themselves young adults —nearly half are under age thirty—and many are in relatively low-wage employment owing to their age and lack of work experience. Moreover, in the modern labor market, wages for entry-level jobs have been declining, and there have been dramatic changes in the nature of work; more parents today navigate a world of nonstandard or unpredictable work hours with just-in-time scheduling.[1]

Many younger working parents are also continuing their education, working while enrolled in postsecondary and community college programs in an effort to get ahead in today's labor market. Together, the realities of low- and middle-income parents' increasingly precarious work situations and compelling child development research argue for policies that ensure access for American families to affordable, stable, and high-quality early child care and education.

In this chapter, we describe the current economic and policy contexts facing early care and education in the United States. We discuss the reality that most children live in families in which their parents are employed, as well as the importance of high-quality early learning experiences. We propose a new subsidy system for Assuring Care and Education for Young Children (ACE subsidies, or "the Assurance" for short) that would guarantee progressively structured subsidies to low- and moderate-income working families with young children so that all families can access and afford licensed, high-quality early learning and care options. When fully implemented, ACE subsidies would replace the current Child Care and Development Block Grant (CCDBG) program. ACE subsidies would serve families with children between birth and age five years, with care for school-age children (those in kindergarten through age thirteen, who are currently served in CCDBG) shifted to out-of-school and summer programs sponsored by public schools and other service systems. In addition, we propose reforming the existing Child and Dependent Care Tax Credit (CDCTC) to support a wide range of care options and to cover children of various ages across a broader span of family incomes. With more generous subsidies and tax credits providing greater support to low-, middle-, and higher-income families, existing dependent care assistance programs (DCAPs) could be phased out. Besides promoting children's development and family financial security, our system would also streamline the existing patchwork of fragmented early care and education programs in the United States.

The Need for Affordable, High-Quality Early Care and Learning Opportunities

During the infant and toddler years, daily interactions with parents, caregivers, and the environment strongly influence the early cognitive and socioemotional development in children that forms the foundation for later skill acquisition.[2] The fact that a child's brain and development are most plastic and flexible from birth to age three underscores the need to ensure that all children have access to high-quality environments during this period.[3] Research shows that children in low-income families are more likely to grow up with less enriching early learning environments and to experience exposure to toxic stress.[4] It has also been shown that such experiences contribute to early inequality in measured cognitive and behavioral outcomes.[5] Improving the developmental contexts for children early in life can lay the foundation for improved learning and success in school and life.[6]

The normative experience for young children is to spend much of their early years in nonparental care. Where and with whom children spend their first years have changed dramatically in recent years with the sharp increase in maternal employment and the growing use of early care and education at younger ages by families with working and nonworking mothers alike. Data from the Survey of Income and Program Participation (SIPP) indicate that in 2011, 12.5 million children under age five (61 percent) were regularly in nonparental care each week, which was triple the fewer than 4 million young children in any type of nonparental care in 1965.[7] Of these children, 10.9 million were in families with working mothers, and they averaged thirty-six hours per week in nonparental care arrangements.[8] Moreover, many children are cared for in more than one arrangement: in 2011, 27 percent of children under age five with employed mothers were regularly in more than one nonparental early care and education arrangement.[9] Multiple, concurrent nonparental arrangements are more common among families who work extended or nonstandard hours.[10]

Child care is an essential basic need for most working families, but it constitutes a substantial family expense. In the 2011 SIPP data, families with children under five who paid for child care spent an average of $179 per week, or 10.5 percent of family income, on this service.[11] Families with income below 200 percent of the federal poverty level (FPL) (or less than $49,000 in 2016 dollars) who paid for child care spent 22 percent of their family income, while those above 200 percent of FPL spent 7 percent. Notably, these are families' actual out-of-pocket *expenses* for the care they used. As things exist now, working families with low and moderate incomes are spending a large part of their earnings on what is often low- or mediocre-quality care (discussed later in this chapter) because higher-quality care would cost even more.[12] This family expense is incurred precisely when parents are younger and in the lowest-earning years of their careers.

HIGH-QUALITY, STABLE EARLY CARE AND EDUCATION: EXPENSIVE AND HARD TO FIND

Center-based and other licensed child care settings provide higher-quality care on average and less variation in quality than unregulated or informal care. But center care is more costly, particularly for infants and toddlers. The cost of child care is high because the majority of these costs are for labor, and because group sizes and adult-to-child ratios must be low enough for younger children to support quality care environments. For center-based care, families spent an average of $258 per week for all children age zero to five enrolled full-time and $322 per week for infant care, according to 2012 NHES data.[13] There is also considerable across-state variation: other data show that the cost of center-based care ranged from approximately $5,000 per year in Mississippi to more than $17,000 in Massachusetts.[14] Anne Mitchell, who cofounded the Alliance for Early Childhood Finance, has modeled the costs of the components of high-quality care to create estimates of child care costs in several states.[15] She found that, in median-cost states, the cost of delivering high-quality center-based care averages nearly $15,000 per year for a child under three and $10,000 for preschool-age children. Given these high costs, it is not surprising that regulated child care—center-based care and licensed family child care—represents less than one-third of infant and toddler child care arrangements, and that most children are in unregulated, informal care.[16] There is a high level of unmet need for licensed child care, particularly in low-income communities.[17]

Although families have consistently used a range of nonparental care—including relative and nonrelative care in home settings—the use of center-based care by families with working mothers has been increasing, particularly among families who can afford the higher

Figure 3.1 *Early Care and Education Arrangements for Children Under Age Five with Employed Mothers, by Type of Primary Arrangement, 1965–2011*

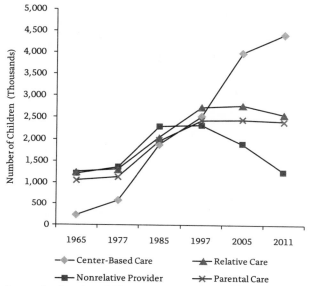

Source: Authors' compilation and analysis of data from Lueck, Orr, and McConnell 1982; U.S. Census Bureau 1987, 2002; and SIPP, 2004 and 2008.

cost of center care. Between 1965 and 2011, there was a remarkable twentyfold increase in the number of young children with working mothers in center-based early care and education, from 228,000 to 4.4 million (figure 3.1). The use of center-based early care and education has continued to grow rapidly since the mid-1990s, even as the pace of growth in the number of young children with working mothers and the use of nonparental care has slowed. Large shares of children have been shifted to center-based care from other types of care. Since 1997, center-based care and education has been the only type of care for which the numbers and percentages of children enrolled have continued to increase among all families.

Over the last two decades, parents have been significantly increasing their use of center care over noncenter arrangements for their children at every age from birth to five. Figure 3.2 shows that the use of center care increased for every age between birth and five while the use of noncenter care decreased between 1995 and 2012. Although home-based care has continued to be the primary nonparental care

Figure 3.2 *Children Under Age Five in Nonparental Care and Education Arrangements, by Type of Primary Arrangement, 1995 and 2012*

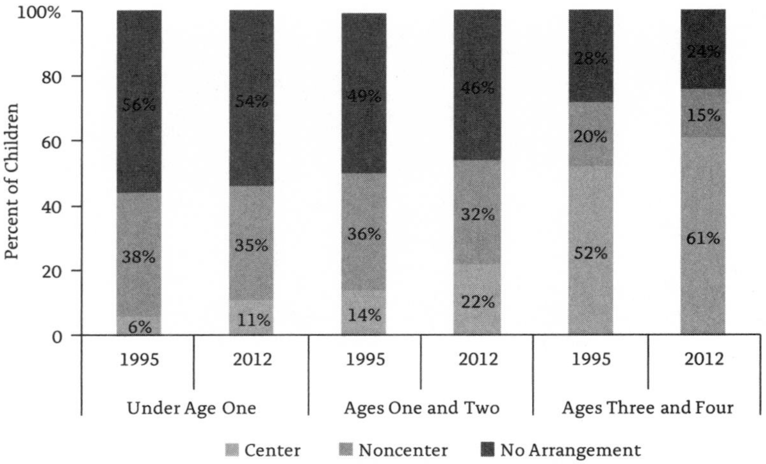

Source: Data from 1995 NHES (from Burgess et al. 2014); authors' analysis of 2012 NHES data.

setting for children before age three, much of the recent growth in center care and the shift away from noncenter care has been occurring for infants and toddlers.[18]

The types of child care that families use reflect a combination of what they prefer, what is available to them, and what they can afford. In 2011, among children under age three with employed mothers in regular child care, more than one-quarter attended an organized child care center; nearly one-third were primarily cared for by relatives; and 17 percent were cared for by nonrelatives (for example, family child care providers, nannies, neighbors, or other informal care providers).[19] Finally, one-quarter were cared for by a parent, including fathers, mothers while they worked, or a split arrangement between parents with differing work hours.[20]

For all children under age three, home-based care arrangements, particularly with relatives, remain the most common setting. However, income gaps in the use of center-based care and education have widened, especially for younger children. The use of center-based care has been increasing, particularly for toddlers ages one and two from middle- and higher-income families, more than one in four of whom are in center-based care (figure 3.3).

Figure 3.3 *Children Under Age Three in Center-Based Early Care and Education, by Family Income and Child Age, 2011*

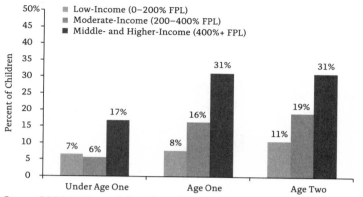

Source: 2008 SIPP panel data for primary arrangements in 2011.

VARIATION IN THE QUALITY OF CARE BY FAMILY INCOME

Several national studies have found that most nonparental care is of low to moderate quality, particularly for infants and toddlers, and that children in low-income families are the most likely to experience low-quality care.[21] Figures 3.4 and 3.5 display scores from the Early Childhood Longitudinal Study–Birth Cohort on observational quality measures for two-year-olds, by care type and family income quintile, respectively. The quality differences by income are displayed in two ways—the overall average scores (figure 3.4), and a measure of the gap in the quality experienced between children in the top income quintile and each of the other quintiles (figure 3.5). Quality is higher with each incremental increase in income—children from the highest-resourced families experienced the highest quality, and children at the bottom experienced the lowest quality, with the children from other income quintiles in the middle. The gaps in quality are especially pronounced in home-based care, and some are quite substantial for home-based relative care—greater than a full standard deviation for children in the lowest-income quintiles, whose families are most often using this type of care.[22]

In addition to low-quality care, many children experience frequent changes in care. Data from the National Institute for Child Health and Development Study of Early Child Care and Youth Development

Figure 3.4 *Average Quality for Types of Care of Two-Year-Old Children, by Family Income Quintile, 2003*

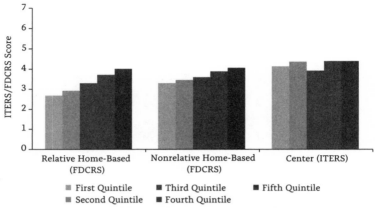

Source: ECLS-B child care observation sample, 2001 birth cohort.
Notes: N=approximately 1,400. ITERS = Infant-Toddler Environment Rating Scale; FDCRS = Family Day Care Rating Scale.

Figure 3.5 *Gaps in Experienced Quality of Types of Care Between Children Under Age Two in Each Income Quintile Relative to Children in the Top*
Income Quintile, 2003

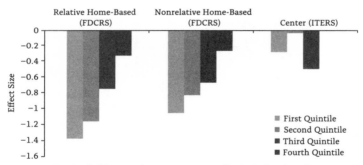

Source: ECLS-B child care observation sample, 2001 birth cohort.
Notes: N=approximately 1,400. ITERS = Infant-Toddler Environment Rating Scale; FDCRS = Family Day Care Rating Scale.

(NICHD SECCYD) show that children experienced an average of seven different arrangements before their third birthday.[23] Unstable care or frequent transitions may disrupt routines, limit the formation of secure child-caregiver relationships, and lead to poor behavior and adjustment.[24]

Early Care and Education in the United States: Falling Short of Families' Needs

There is a severe shortage of affordable, high-quality early care and education in this country, and most families need financial assistance to access higher-quality care opportunities that can both benefit children's development during a critical period and support increased and more stable parental employment. What has been the U.S. policy response to the child care crisis faced by American families?

The existing patchwork of public-sector early learning services is underdeveloped, leaves large gaps in coverage, and does not attend enough or effectively to quality. In the United States, public expenditures on early childhood care and education programs amount to less than 0.3 percent of gross domestic product (GDP), compared to the 3.8 percent that is spent on K-12 education, 0.9 percent on higher education, and 3.2 percent on children's health programs.[25] Public expenditures on K–12 education and children's health in the United States exceed those of most or all other countries with developed economies, while the funds spent on young children's early care, development, and education trail those of most such countries.[26]

The Child Care and Development Block Grant is the main child care subsidy program in the United States, providing funding for child care subsidies for children from a few weeks old to age thirteen.[27] The federal government provides annual block grants to states, which are required to provide matching funds. In 2013, total public spending on child care assistance was $11.3 billion.[28] Although the federal government provides the lion's share of the funding and sets broad regulatory oversight, states have established a wide range of program characteristics, including eligibility criteria, reimbursement levels for the types of care supported, family copayment levels, administrative procedures (such as requirements for applications and recertification), and licensing requirements.[29]

In 2014, 1.45 million children received public child care subsidies through federal and state funding.[30] This is a 20 percent decline from the peak of 1.81 million children served in 2001, due to a steady erosion in public funding for child care in real terms since 2001.[31] According to analysis by the Department of Health and Human Services, 14.2 million children from birth to age thirteen were eligible for child care subsidies in 2012 under federal eligibility guidelines, but only 15 percent of these children received child care subsidies in the average month during that year.[32] The 14.2 million children eligible in 2012 included 3.0 million under age three, and only 600,000 of these received subsidies.[33] Children from families with the very lowest incomes and those receiving TANF benefits were most likely to receive subsidies.[34] Subsidy-receiving families were much more likely to use center-based care than nonrecipients. Seventy percent of children under age three in subsidized care were in centers.[35] Approximately 77 percent of subsidy recipients made copayments to cover a share of the cost of child care, which averaged 7 percent of income.[36]

A second source of financial assistance for families' child care expenses is the federal Child and Dependent Care Tax Credit, which allows families who paid for nonparental care for a dependent under age thirteen (or for a dependent incapable of physical or mental self-care) to reduce their tax liability for a percentage of their child care expenses up to $3,000 of total costs for one dependent, and up to $6,000 for two or more.[37] Families with incomes below $15,000 qualify for a credit for 35 percent of their child care expenses; this percentage declines as income increases, reaching 20 percent for all families with incomes over $43,000. However, the benefits of this credit are unavailable to many low-income families because they do not have significant tax liability and the credit is not refundable.[38] Indeed, families with children in the top two income quintiles (those with family incomes over $68,200 in 2014) receive the majority of the benefits from the CDCTC (nearly 60 percent), while those with incomes below $50,000 represent approximately half of families with children but receive less than 30 percent of the total benefits from the credit.[39] In 2013, 6.3 million households claimed the credit and received nearly $3.5 billion in benefits, with an average credit of $548.[40]

Finally, a third type of financial support for child care costs is an employer-administered dependent care assistance program, a type of flexible spending account (FSA) whereby employers can allow employees to exclude from their taxable income contributions toward qualified child and dependent care expenses. The federal limit of the exclusion, $5,000 annually for a family, has not been increased since the mid-1980s. Families must often choose to use either the DCAP or

CDCTC, which can generate significant confusion for parents about the relative advantage of one over the other. Like the CDCTC, the DCAP structure provides very little benefit to low-income employees with little or no income tax liability. In addition, only about one-third of employers provide DCAPs, and those who work for small employers or employers with a relatively larger share of lower-wage employees are less likely to have access to them.[41] In addition, DCAPs are even more regressive than the CDCTC, since the value of the benefit increases with a family's marginal tax rate, and families with incomes over $100,000 receive 80 percent of the benefit.[42] Approximately 1.2 million families (or tax-paying units) participated in DCAPs in 2012, at an estimated annual program cost of $1.5 billion.[43]

The need for child care assistance far exceeds that available through the CCDBG, the CDCTC, or DCAPs. The eligibility thresholds that states set for CCDBG subsidies are too low to support a great many families who struggle to find and pay for child care.[44] The pressure on state administrators to stretch their limited block grant funds to serve more children and families contributes to extremely low subsidy reimbursement levels that neither cover the costs of high-quality care nor keep pace with increasing child care costs. As a result, most high-quality care is out of reach even for low-income families receiving subsidies.[45] Likewise, the limited reach of DCAPs and the very limited benefit levels and lack of refundability of the CDCTC compared to actual child care payments constrain the ability of these programs to help support low-income families' child care expenses. Given the importance of stable, high-quality care during the early years for children's long-term development, both the subsidy and the tax systems need to be significantly updated and expanded to support all children's access to affordable, high-quality care opportunities, regardless of their families' income.[46]

Child Care Policy Moving Forward

The time has come for a bold initiative to help support families' ability to access and use high-quality early care and education opportunities. We propose two complementary policy reforms to expand access to affordable, high-quality child care that meets children's developmental needs and parents' employment demands:

1 *The Assuring Care and Education for Young Children system:* ACE sub-
    sidies will help low- and moderate-income families with meet-
    ing the costs of the licensed, high-quality, developmentally ap-
    propriate early care and education opportunities that they may
    choose for their young children before kindergarten entry.
2 *A reformed tax credit:* We propose a tax credit that will support a
    broader array of paid care arrangements for a wider range of
    families, including families with school-age children and those
    with incomes above the level eligible for ACE assistance. The
    benefit would be made refundable for the costs of child care in-
    curred by all families with children up to age thirteen, and the
    amount of the tax credit would be significantly increased for
    families with children under five. The tax system would be fur-
    ther streamlined by eliminating the DCAP.

ASSURING THE CARE AND EDUCATION OF YOUNG CHILDREN IN WORKING FAMILIES

We propose that the federal government, together with the states,
significantly increase financial assistance for children's early care and
education through Assuring Care and Education of Young Children
(ACE), the new subsidy system we propose that would guarantee children under the age of five in working families of low and moderate
income access to high-quality care and early learning opportunities
(see table 3.1). ACE subsidies when fully implemented would replace
the subsidy system funded through the CCDBG as well as the trans-
fers that states make to child care through their TANF and SSBG
funding.[47]

The Assurance broadens access for young children with working
parents. Families in which both parents living in the child's household are employed and whose incomes are below 250 percent of the
federal poverty level ($60,750 for a family of four in 2016) would be
eligible for direct subsidies toward the cost of licensed nonparental
early care and education of the parents' choice.[48] The federal government would establish a common maximum income level up to which
all families with young children would be eligible for subsidies at 250
percent of the FPL across all states. Individual states would have the
option of setting a higher family income eligibility ceiling, up to 400
percent of the FPL, while still receiving the same federal match rate,

Table 3.1 *Proposed Subsidies and Tax Credits for Early Care and Education*

Policy Strategy	Eligibility Criteria	Policy Components
Assuring Care and Education for Young Children (ACE) subsidies to support the financial costs of high-quality early care and education for low- and moderate-income families with children under age five	• All parents employed twenty or more hours per week • Family income below 250 percent of FPL ($60,750 for family of four in 2016[a]) or higher maximum income level at state option (up to 400 percent of FPL) • Child under the eligible age for universal enrollment in state or local public education (preschool at ages three or four years or kindergarten at age five) in the child's jurisdiction • Child below age for kindergarten enrollment who requires additional (secondary) early care and education (even if he or she is also enrolled in preschool) to correspond with parents' employment hours (for example, including evenings, nights, weekends, summer hours)	• Subsidy for direct financial assistance toward the cost of licensed nonparental early care and education programs of parents' choice, with subsidy amount determined by family income and the cost of care (by child age, care type, hours in care, and number of children in family who are in care) • Family copayments based on sliding income scale representing a percentage of family income, such that families spend between 3 and 10 percent of total annual income on child care for one child, with families paying a progressively higher percentage the higher their income • Minimum $10 family copayment per child per week (for families under 100 percent of FPL) • Fully replaces the CCDBG and CCDF programs; current level of block grant funding used for school-age child care (ages six to thirteen) could be combined with other summer and after-school programs for elementary school-age children

(continued)

Table 3.1 *(continued)*

Policy Strategy	Eligibility Criteria	Policy Components
Expanded Child and Dependent Care Tax Credit (CDCTC) to provide financial assistance for child care costs incurred by families at all income levels with children under age thirteen, refundable for those without tax liability and with expanded support for families with children under age five	• Any income level • Credit can be used for care expenses related to work or looking for work for children under age thirteen (or older with a disability)	• Tax credit can be taken for a proportion of paid costs for all types of paid care (licensed and unlicensed), though not for ACE subsidy copayments • Refundable tax credit for families without tax liability using paid child care for all eligible care expenses (for children zero to thirteen years) • Increases the amount of eligible child care expenses and credit percentage for families with child care costs for children under age five • Annual cap of $6,000 in child care expenses for one dependent under age five (increased from $3,000), and $9,000 for more than one dependent under age five (increased from $6,000), with these levels indexed to inflation • Applicable maximum percentage of expenses eligible for credit increased to 50 percent of expenses for families with children under age five over an increased range of family income (up to $60,000 with phase-down: less 1 percent for every $1,500 increase in income) as income increases to the minimum credit level of 20 percent of expenses for all incomes above $105,000; these income levels indexed for inflation • Eligible child care expenses and credit percentage remains the same for families with child care expenses for children six and older

Source: Authors' compilation.

[a] U.S. DHHS 2016a.

to reflect the large differences in the cost of early care and education across the country. Individual states would determine minimum work hour requirements for initial eligibility (up to a maximum level of twenty hours per week, on average, in a given month), since many low-wage workers have variable work schedules. Job search periods of up to three months would be allowed for continuing subsidies in the event of job loss. The amount of financial assistance would be based on family income, the type and cost of care, and hours of care used.

The Assurance establishes provider reimbursement levels adequate to support the provision of high-quality care. Unlike the existing CCDBG-funded programs in most states, we expect provider reimbursement levels under this proposal to be set at levels adequate for ensuring access to a wide range of licensed, high-quality early care and education in all states and localities. The provider payment or reimbursement rates across most of the states are set far too low and very often restrict access to only the very lowest-cost providers, and many states go many years without updating their maximum reimbursement levels. Under the Assurance, subsidy amounts would be based on what providers charge for care up to a maximum amount. The federal government would establish a process for creating appropriate and consistent floors and ceilings for state maximum reimbursement levels for licensed types of care, by child age and for full-time and part-time care. These floors and ceilings would reflect regional variations in the cost of care and would be indexed to inflation.[49]

Table 3.2 illustrates potential reimbursement rates, by age of child and type and amount of care, based on modeled costs of high-quality child care from the Alliance for Early Childhood Finance.

Families, States, and the Federal Government to Share in the Costs of Assuring High-Quality Early Care and Education

We propose that the costs of providing low- and moderate-income families with access to high-quality care be the shared responsibility of parents and the federal and state governments. As with the current CCDBG funding structure, both the federal and state governments would contribute funds. To ensure that ACE subsidies are established

Table 3.2 *Illustrative ACE Federal Subsidy Caps by Child Age*

Child Age	Subsidy Monthly (and Annual) Cap for Center Care (Full-Time Care)	Subsidy Monthly (and Annual) Cap for Licensed Home-Based Care (Full-Time Care)	Subsidy Monthly Cap for Center Care (Part-time Care: ~20 Hours per Week)	Subsidy Monthly Cap for Licensed Home-Based Care (Part-time Care: ~20 Hours per Week)
Zero to twelve months	$1,200 ($14,400)	$800 ($9,600)	$600	$400
Twelve to twenty-four months	1,100 (13,200)	733 (8,800)	550	367
Twenty-four to thirty-six months	1,000 (12,000)	667 (8,000)	500	333
Children ages three and four (prior to kindergarten entry)[a]	900 (10,800)	600 (7,200)	450	300

Source: Authors' compilation.

Note: The total cost of care paid to the provider would include the public subsidy plus parent copays. Federal public subsidy caps would be indexed to inflation.

[a] Some three-year-olds and most four-year-olds would be enrolled in universal preschool in their state and might need part-time, wraparound care. Those who do not have access to universal preschool could use the ACE subsidies for full-time preschool.

with consistent minimum standards around eligibility, reimbursement levels, and quality standards, and that the program is implemented efficiently, the federal government would contribute a greater share of the funding to be maintained over time.[50] The federal government would contribute 80 percent of the costs of the subsidies in the Assurance program, as well as 100 percent of the costs for establishing the quality standards, quality assurance systems, and quality improvement supports where needed.

The Assurance system would require that families have "skin in the game" and make out-of-pocket copayments for the early care and education programs they choose, based on a sliding income scale ranging from 3 to 10 percent of family income and increasing progressively with family income. A minimum copay amount would be set at $10 per week (or $520 per year) for families with very low incomes (at or below 100 percent of the FPL), and a family's share of the costs would not exceed 10 percent of income at the state's eligibility ceiling—250 percent of the FPL or a higher level up to 400 percent FPL at the option of the state.

Figure 3.6 shows how the subsidy benefit and the parents' share of the costs for center-based care would vary by family income. Consider a family of three with two working parents who want to enroll their two-year-old daughter in a center serving toddlers. The monthly charge at the center is $1,000 per month, or $12,000 annually (the maximum reimbursement level eligible for subsidy in their state). The family's income is $29,000 per year. Under the Assurance, the family would be eligible for a subsidy for approximately $10,950 of the annual cost of care, while the parents would be expected to contribute approximately $20 per week (or between 3 and 4 percent of their family income).[51] A second example we can consider is a family of four trying to enroll their two-year-old in the same center. This family earns $60,000, closer to 250 percent of the FPL and the maximum income eligible in their state. Their total weekly cost for child care at the center would be $62, or $3,200 per year (between 5 and 6 percent of family income), and the ACE benefit would amount to $8,800. In a higher-cost state that has opted to have higher income eligibility thresholds (up to 400 percent of FPL) and modestly higher maximum reimbursement levels, a family of three making $75,000, or 325 percent of FPL, would pay $7,000 annually for the cost of center care (between 9 and 10 percent of family income), with the subsidy amount representing the difference between the full cost of the care and the subsidy.

States would administer the program, certifying family eligibility with documentation of parents' employment and income through simple means such as electronically filed forms or, if possible, direct matching with state employment or tax records. To ensure stability in children's development and care, and consistent with current law, certification and recertification periods would be no less than twelve months (with states having the option to provide for longer certification periods).[52] In addition, recertifications could be aligned with those of other benefit programs, such as public health insurance assistance programs (Medicaid and health marketplace subsidies),

Figure 3.6 *ACE Benefit Level for Center-Based Care for One Two-Year-Old in a Family of Three with One Child Under Age Five in Care, by Family Income*

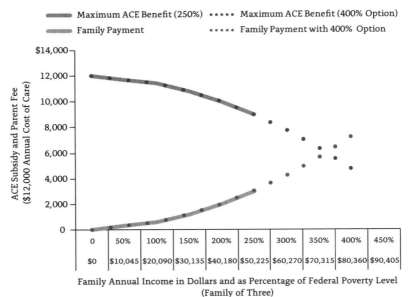

Source: Authors' compilation.

SNAP, and WIC, so that income and other common eligibility information could be shared and updated automatically. Copayments would be adjusted for changes in income at recertification or at the time when significant changes in family income occurred.

The federal contribution to program funding would help to support high-quality standards and a rigorous quality assurance system for early care and education programs receiving public funds in each state. The federal government would set an appropriate floor for the standards that providers would have to meet for licensure, and it would specify the types of providers required to be licensed. States would ultimately set standards at or above the federal regulatory floor, issue the licenses, and enforce the standards. Providers receiving subsidies would be expected to operate within these state and federal guidelines. States would be provided with additional funds and technical assistance from the federal government to design and implement child care setting and provider standards, such as those related to pre- and in-service training and adult-child ratios, over the first five years of the Assurance program.

The quality standards and enforcement system would not apply to nonlicensed care provided by family, friends, neighbors, or other nonlicensed care providers, and these types of care would not be eligible for reimbursement with ACE subsidies. Families' expenses for nonlicensed care would be eligible for the enhanced child and dependent care tax credits (discussed later). Over time, states could provide supports that would serve as incentives to bring more home-based care providers under a regulatory framework. For example, they could support the establishment of networks of home-based providers overseen by high-quality centers or other intermediaries in their area for those interested in becoming licensed; these networks would facilitate administrative tasks and provide opportunities for professional development and sharing of resources (such as children's books and toys). They could also make training available to providers working toward meeting licensing requirements. These strategies could offer providers a pathway to becoming licensed, Assurance-eligible providers.

A portion of Assurance funds would be targeted for underserved communities. The Assurance system would incorporate both demand- and supply-based approaches to addressing the problems of access and quality in early care and education. The availability of ACE subsidies would increase the demand for high-quality child care through its subsidy vouchers, allowing parents to find and afford a range of licensed, private, market-based care settings, thereby effectively increasing demand. Although this initiative would incentivize greater acceptance of subsidy vouchers by existing providers and the entry of new care providers, it is very likely that additional measures would be needed to overcome both affordability and availability constraints. Therefore, the Assurance system would also increase the supply of high-quality child care by expecting states to fund contracted slots in the most underserved low-income or rural communities, or during nonstandard hours. In these circumstances, where geography and hours make the use of a subsidy challenging, states would be encouraged to use the Assurance to establish contracted care facilities and to create networks of home-based providers who could be licensed and made eligible for subsidies. States could also offer higher reimbursement levels for the care that children in these families might need that would otherwise be more difficult to find. The federal government could set a floor or range for the percentage of funds to be used for contracted slots (for example, a minimum of 20 percent or a maximum of 60 percent), but states would be expected to develop a strategic plan based on the distribution of supply relative to demand geographically to determine the right mix of vouchers and contracted slots.

ENSURING QUALITY

Early care and education settings supported with ACE subsidies would be consistently measured and monitored to ensure the quality of the services provided, including measures of both structural quality (the regulated features like staff-child ratios) and process quality (observations of the quality of children's interactions with caregivers); these components of quality are discussed further in chapter 4. Such monitoring under the Assurance could build off the work that many states have been doing for more than a decade in developing quality rating and improvement systems (QRISs). These systems vary considerably across states in terms of quality measures, provider participation, and other requirements. Research to date finds weak links between QRIS measures and improvements in child developmental outcomes, and so more work should be done to further develop and incorporate measures that can be more strongly associated with outcomes.[53] It should be a state's decision whether to employ a QRIS, and it might help for more states to come together to develop a more consistent definition and measurement of quality across states and settings. Such an effort could help parents identify and choose higher-quality care, as well as provide states and programs with feedback on the care features that best support children's positive development. As such, if states do use QRISs, the ratings should be transparent to parents and readily accessible via state-based, easy-to-use websites.

Building on states' existing transparency and public information efforts, all states that establish an ACE subsidies program should be eligible to receive additional resources and technical assistance to establish a public information system in the first two or three years after the Assurance program is enacted. The public information system would provide regulatory reports to the public, along with consumers' ratings and comments on providers. Once fully established, states would be provided with funds and technical assistance to design and implement standards and monitoring procedures.

It is essential to offer professional development opportunities to early care and education providers. A commitment to training, skills, and consistency within the early care and education workforce is needed for sustained improvements in program quality and child outcomes. To provide one example, regular, in-classroom observation and support by an expert coach has been proven effective for teachers of preschool-age children (as discussed in more detail in chapter 4). Though not yet widely tested with infant and toddler teachers and providers, two recent efforts to provide such in-service training have shown positive impacts on both the structural and process features of quality, suggesting that coaching may be an effective component of professional development for this sector of the early childhood workforce as well.[54] Accordingly, we view identification of evidence-based professional development as an area ripe for further study, including via implementation studies, program development, and rigorous program evaluation.

In addition to identifying ways to develop and improve the quality of infant-toddler teachers in center-based programs, there will be a significant need to seed and study new models for assessing and improving the quality of home-based early care and education settings, including the feasibility of integrating more home-based providers under a regulatory framework. There is little research on how to effectively improve the quality of home-based care and establish networks through which providers could receive oversight, support, and professional development but that would require dedicated attention in the first ten years of these reform efforts.

The Assurance would lead to higher-quality services over time by funding evidence-based quality enhancements and innovation. States that implement the Assurance program would be eligible to receive additional federal funds to model, pilot, and test evidence-informed coaching and mentoring systems, continually improve quality measurement instruments, and validate proposed quality monitoring systems across communities. We propose that, for at least the first five years, 1 percent of federal program dollars be set aside to support research and experimentation. Developing brief, scalable, and predictive measures of quality for various types of care—especially home-based care—would help quality improvement efforts in most states. Quality improvement approaches should encompass both center-based and home-based settings and explicitly include approaches for encouraging home-based providers to become licensed.[55]

EXPANDED CHILD AND DEPENDENT CARE TAX CREDITS

The Assurance system would support children from many low- and moderate-income families, providing access to high-quality, licensed early care and education settings, most of which are currently out of their reach. However, early care and education costs are a significant expense for many families at middle- and higher-income levels as well, and these families would not be eligible for the ACE subsidies. Other families who might have difficulty using ACE subsidies include those who choose the care of a neighbor, relative, or other regular caregiver for their infant or toddler, and those with children attending preschool or elementary school who require wraparound after-school and summer care to match their own work hours. Expanding the existing Child and Dependent Care Tax Credit could better serve these families.[56]

We propose several changes for the CDCTC. First, the tax credit would be made refundable and indexed to inflation for families with care expenses for children thirteen and younger, including families not receiving the Assurance subsidies and using nonparental care. Families with no tax liability who currently do not benefit from the tax credit would thus be able to use it to afford better-quality care through refundability.

Second, we would increase the annual cap for early care and education expenses for children under age five from $3,000 to $6,000 for one dependent, and from $6,000 to $9,000 for more than one dependent, and we would index these maximum levels to inflation. Third, we would increase the maximum percentage of families' child care expenses for children under age five that could be applied to calculate the tax credit to 50 percent of expenses up to the cap for families with incomes up to $60,000, with a phasedown of one percentage point for each additional $1,500 in family income and a minimum rate of 20 percent for families with incomes of $105,000 or more. These

Figure 3.7 *Assurance and Child and Dependent Care Tax Credit Benefits for a Two-Year-Old in a Family of Four, by Family Income Level (and Cost of Care)*

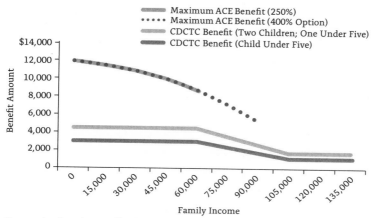

Legend:
- Maximum ACE Benefit (250%)
- Maximum ACE Benefit (400% Option)
- CDCTC Benefit (Two Children; One Under Five)
- CDCTC Benefit (Child Under Five)

Source: Authors' compilation.

changes would expand and simplify the tax system for care expenses, while making it more progressive.[57] Figure 3.7 illustrates benefit levels by family income for the proposed CDCTC, together with the maximum Assurance benefit for a family of four. The maximum effective tax credit that most families with a young child could receive would increase from $600 to $3,000 for one child, and from $1,200 to $4,500 for two or more. Given many families' need for financial support as they incur care costs, parents should be able to incorporate the value of the credit through reduced withholdings in their paycheck, if they choose. Finally, we would eliminate dependent care assistance programs (also referred to as dependent care flexible spending accounts).

Advantages and Challenges of the Proposed ACE Subsidies and CDCTC Reforms

High-quality early childhood care and education is vitally important to children, families, and our nation. Our approach would provide a reliable guarantee of assistance coupled with a broad-based federal tax credit to ensure that all families receive the assistance that they need to access high-quality early care and education for their children. This approach would replace an existing block grant structure in which states must ration very limited funds, restricting eligibility, access, and the level of assistance and care choices that can be supported with the subsidy.

Instituting a guarantee of support for families' early care and child development needs would offer the dual advantages of ensuring access for every child to safe, healthy, and secure early learning environments that foster their development while enabling their parents to work. Because of its influence on children's development and its necessity for parents to work, high-quality, reliable early care and education provides benefits not only for children's development but for their longer-term capacity as future productive members of society.[58] At the same time, supports for parents' employment lead to increased maternal employment and hours in the near term and to parents' more continuous employment.[59]

Our proposal for providing reliable financial assistance would support the importance of work by increasing the number of working parents and improve employment stability and security for current and newly working parents. There is an economic and social interest in policies that support parental employment and remove the barrier to gainful employment of prohibitively expensive good-quality early care and education.

Even as overall employment levels in the United States have recovered since the Great Recession, economists and policy professionals remain concerned about the continuing steady decline in adult, prime-age labor force participation.[60] Women's labor force participation rose rapidly over the last third of the twentieth century, but then stalled after 2000 and actually retreated.[61] Good empirical research has shown the effects of price on nonparental care and education by lowering costs through subsidized provision. Wide-ranging estimates of the positive effects of making early care and education more affordable in the United States suggest that a 20 percent reduction in the cost of care would increase the percentage of mothers' employment by 1 to 5 percent.[62] The Urban Institute has estimated that a set of more modest expansions in the current child care subsidy program would lead to an increase in the number of working parents of between 400,000 and 1.9 million.[63]

Just as important, providing a reliable guarantee of assistance commensurate with supporting access to high-quality care and education would ensure that children are not made worse off when their parents work. Families facing similar financial and employment constraints would be treated equitably and have similar choices, rather than being subject to the almost random rationing of subsidies that now prevails, varying from state to state. Our proposal would convey to parents that if they work and contribute what they can, within their means, toward the cost of care, their children will have access to high-quality early learning opportunities.

THE ASSURANCE AND THE TAX CREDIT: PRESERVING FAMILIES' CHOICE OF CARE

ACE subsidies would provide resources to support the use of high-quality care that is subject to quality assurance standards, meaning that only licensed care—primarily center-based care and family child care in most states—would be eligible for subsidy assistance. Compared to the current provisions in states' CCDF programs, this could be seen in some respects as restricting parents' choices and shifting financial assistance away from informal arrangements. However, the ACE subsidies and the CDCTC are designed explicitly to jointly support families because of the wide range in parents' preferences and circumstances in making care choices for their children at different points in time. The ACE subsidies would put more expensive licensed early care and education opportunities within the reach of low- and moderate-income families and assure them that the arrangement is subject to review and monitoring for licensing purposes by their state. The reformed tax credit would provide a greater level of assistance to the very significant share of eligible families who would continue to use and prefer arrangements with relatives and friends, particularly for infants and toddlers.[64]

Despite the overall benefits from our approach, it will encounter some challenges. Considering that the proposed financial assistance for early care and education for young children would require significant new investments, would the level of financial assistance be worth the cost? Some may say that families have managed to find and make care arrangements that they consider "good enough" and that parents' preference for their young children's care is a private matter. It is certainly true that many parents do find some care for their children when they go to work, and some may have a relative who is available and willing to provide child care. However, as discussed earlier in this chapter and in chapter 2, these informal arrangements are often low-quality, unstable, and inadequate in supporting children's development. Given the important benefits for children of high-quality and stable early learning opportunities, it is important to support good child development options for all families. In addition, reliable financial assistance would increase parents' employment options and hours worked, as well as families' economic security.

In addition, our approach to improving early care and education assistance to working families is built around the most prudent spending choices: funds are targeted to a population—children under age five—for whom care is the most expensive and the benefits of greater access to reliable, high-quality care would be most advantageous. In addition, we would limit the availability of subsidies to licensed forms of early care and education, so that subsidies would be targeted to the care opportunities that families could not otherwise afford. This would incentivize some families to choose higher-quality and more stable care settings.

Finally, though both federal and state costs would increase, we have proposed that a much greater share of the additional costs of these policy changes be borne by the federal government. The federal government would bear all of the tax expenditure costs of an increased CDCTC, a larger share (80 percent) of the costs of the ACE subsidies, and 100 percent of the initial cost of building quality assurance, monitoring, and information systems in the states.

In the concluding chapter, we discuss the overall costs of the plan and the main policy components (see tables A3.1 and A3.2 for the details on the costs for the Assurance and tax credit proposals). We envision that the costs of implementing the Assurance will increase over time as the policy is rolled out to serve more families; after ten years, total public investments in the program could be $21 billion in annual expenditures, which would require $13 billion in new investments above the $8 billion in current expenditure levels across the federal funding streams supporting child care assistance (see table A3.1). This would include full implementation costs for both the direct subsidies and the quality support and monitoring, administration, and information systems. Almost all of the increase in public investments would be federal; states' overall costs would be likely to eventually remain close to the estimated $3.8 billion that they contribute in the aggregate to the federal-state funding streams.[65] This outcome could encourage all or most states to move to the guarantee structure. Parents would be responsible for copayments totaling less than $4 billion.

Our estimate assumes full nationwide implementation of the new ACE subsidies to provide support for the early care and education of 2.3 million children between birth and age five in low- and moderate-income families in which both parents are working. Many ACE-eligible children would also enroll in public preschool as a primary arrangement when it is available to them starting at ages three or four, and they could continue to use the subsidies or tax credits for their secondary care needs. If public preschool for three- and four-year-olds is limited in some states, the Assurance would ensure that all low- and moderate-income families with three- and four-year-olds could be served through market-based preschool in their communities.

The benefits to states and the nation would be substantial, including the increased economic productivity and income tax revenue from more- and better-employed parents and care providers, starting in the relatively near term and increasing with time.[66] In the longer term, benefits could also come from the improvement in children's skills and school readiness. Added to this could be savings over time in spending on other health, education, and social service costs.

Another potential challenge to this proposal could be disagreements about who should be provided a guarantee and up to what income level. Some observers might note that a lower eligibility threshold (say, up to 200 percent of the FPL) for the ACE subsidies would conserve government resources while targeting subsidies to those with the greatest need. Others are likely to note that even with an income cutoff of 250 percent of the FPL, the market costs of high-quality child care still present a significant affordability barrier, and that moderate-income families who earn just above this cutoff would have access to only the more modest tax-based benefits. Still others might suggest that there should be no single national floor or ceiling for eligibility because the costs of early care and education, particularly the labor costs of well-prepared teachers and providers, vary greatly across the country.

We argue that a balanced combination of subsidies with more generous tax credits could lessen the "cliff" effects across the range of states' early care and education markets. In addition, we specify that federal matching funds should be available at the same higher rate for states that wish to establish eligibility up to 400 percent of the FPL, and that higher maximum reimbursement levels above the federal floor should be allowed because we recognize the large differences in costs across regions. With these measures, and by having both the Assurance and the CDCTC, we believe that most families who want to use high-quality care and education for their young children will be able to do so while contributing a fair share—which nevertheless would be less than 10 percent of their family income toward out-of-pocket costs.

As government subsidies through the Assurance become more widely available and maximum reimbursement levels are instituted, we may expect early care and education prices to rise, in part, we would expect, to support higher-quality care. Current average care costs are relatively low, and below what experts deem as adequate to support high quality. In general, higher reimbursement rates will allow providers to hire more qualified providers by offering adequate wages or benefits such as health insurance and paid sick or vacation leave, pay for quality enhancements like professional coaching, and improve facilities and equipment.

We recognize that some providers might inflate prices to seek the maximum reimbursement level, including parental copayments, without making discernable improvements in quality. One safeguard against this response might be a national maximum reimbursement level that is more commensurate with what is known about how much it costs to provide higher-quality early care opportunities, capped to set a maximum level of subsidy support. Another potential safeguard would be to limit providers who serve both children whose families are supported by subsidies and children whose families are paying the full program cost out-of-pocket in how much they could raise prices across the board. States could choose to encourage centers to establish a floor of full-pay families to foster more integration of families by income and establish a "true" market rate for the care they offer, though in some communities it might be difficult to attract a sufficient number of families who could fully pay for the cost of care.

Families' choices and decision-making can also serve as a check, since required family copayments give parents an incentive to seek the best value in early care and education for their children. In addition, with the development of quality assurance measures, the quality of care would become better known and could drive consumer choices as well as the reimbursement policies that offer differential payment rates based on observed quality.

Summary and Conclusion

The proposed combination of Assuring Care and Education for Young Children subsidies and expanded tax credits has several benefits. First, it offers flexibility for families seeking assistance that meets their needs. Many families might end up relying on the tax credits for some periods for their child, and using the Assurance when they want to transition their child to a center. Families might also need ACE subsidies for the care of a younger child and the tax credit for a school-age child. Second, our proposal makes financial assistance for early learning more widely available at the ages when it is most needed—birth to five. Third, our approach provides the necessary resources to encourage higher-quality care. Fourth, it addresses the problems of the lack of affordability and supply of high-quality care through its use of both demand-side vouchers and contracted slots. Fifth, the ACE subsidies ensure flexibility in how states design and implement programs and in the federal resources required to increase the supply of stable and higher-quality early care and education settings. Most importantly, the Assurance brings together the joint goals of supporting both children's development and parental employment through a system of shared public and private responsibility, thus ensuring that parents working for their family's well-being can access and rely on high-quality early learning opportunities that support their children's development.

UNIVERSAL PRESCHOOL   4

Preschool* education in the United States today has reached a cross-roads. Evidence has mounted over several decades that high-quality early education enhances children's cognitive and socioemotional capacities and readiness to learn. American families and the public at large clearly recognize the importance of early learning and value it, as witnessed by the increase in private preschool enrollment by families with the resources to pay and the high support for preschool in public opinion polls and ballot box initiatives. The majority of young children now attend some preschool before they start kindergarten.

Center-based preschool can build on the Assurance proposed in the last chapter. The structure proposed—a combination of subsidies and tax credits for care and education—acknowledges the range of options that parents prefer and may use for their children, particularly in the first three years of their lives. By age three, however, most children are ready for a group learning experience, and the majority of parents prefer high-quality, affordable, center-based preschool. Research also indicates that children can benefit from quality preschool education starting at age three. In this chapter, we present our plan for a universal preschool program for children ages three to five.

Currently, preschool access and quality are very uneven, and public investment in preschool access and quality remains minimal. At a time when 48 percent of families with young children are low-income, with annual incomes below $50,000, the cost of preschool is higher than the cost of college in many states.[1] Children in families with incomes in the bottom three quintiles of the income distribution are mostly attending one year of public preschool where it is available, while the majority of families in the top quintile of family income are most often receiving two or more years of private early education for their children.[2] Three states—Oklahoma, West Virginia, and Georgia—provide universal access to preschool for four-year-olds, the District of Columbia offers universal access to preschool for three- and four-year-olds, and eight states do not yet offer any public preschool education.[3] The United States as a whole ranks near the bottom among high-income nations in the level of public expenditures to support early care, development, and education and in the share of three- and four-year-olds enrolled in early childhood education.[4] Studies of preschool quality indicate that investment in the type of quality that matters most for child development—quality of teaching and interactions—is also minimal.[5] At present levels, high-quality preschool is simply out of reach for many U.S. families. Thus, rather than serving as a source of opportunity and an engine for social mobility, preschool today is likely contributing to widening social stratification.

The current juncture at which preschool education finds itself is a familiar one historically. The United States was at a similar place in elementary education in the mid-nineteenth century and in secondary education in the early twentieth century: in both earlier eras, there was clear popular demand and high take-up among those with means, yet limited financial support for universal provision. Policy reforms that changed the elementary and high school landscape and expanded access to all were a key driver of U.S. industrial and financial dominance in the world economy in the twentieth century.[6]

In this chapter, we argue that given the critical importance of stimulating early childhood experiences, the growing evidence that high-quality early education improves children's school readiness and leads to better education outcomes, the current high enrollment rates of children of families with means in formal preschool, and the market-level failures to provide such opportunities to families across the income spectrum, preschool policy has moved beyond a tipping point.[7] To ensure that all children have an equal playing field for succeeding in school and reaching their fullest potential, the United States must extend access to high-quality preschool to all three- and four-year-old children.

Preschool Accelerates Children's Learning

Decades of empirical research support the high demand for preschool among families with young children. Across many programs and contexts, preschool has been repeatedly found to improve children's cognitive and socioemotional readiness for kindergarten.[8] The average effect of one year of preschool education on measures of reading, language, and math skills in kindergarten is one-quarter of a standard deviation, or about four months of additional learning for children at this age, across dozens of rigorous evaluations conducted since the 1960s.[9] This is an average of the gains across all programs of varying quality that have been evaluated. Evaluations of high-quality demonstration and high-quality at-scale programs have shown larger gains for children. In practical terms, gains from the high-quality programs represent between a half to a full year of extra learning, beyond the natural gains that children make as they grow older.

Although children from families of all income levels appear to benefit from preschool, the fact that those from lower-income families appear to benefit more represents a key opportunity to reduce achievement gaps at kindergarten entry. The extra learning from high-quality universal programs in two recent evaluations equates to closing between 38 and 77 percent of the gap in kindergarten reading and math skills between children with family incomes at the top and bottom quintiles.[10] Although there is no clear pattern of differential benefits by race or ethnicity (for example, children of all racial-ethnic backgrounds benefit to similar degrees), recent studies show that there are also advantages for children in families who speak a language other than English at home. Children from dual-language learner backgrounds experience cognitive benefits that are particularly strong, and in some cases even stronger, than those experienced by their native-speaker peers.[11] Three studies show that children with special needs experience cognitive benefits from inclusive (that is, not special education only) preschool programs such as Head Start and public prekindergarten.[12]

In Gallup's regular polls gauging American's top government priorities, 65 percent support new legislation to expand high-quality preschool to every child in America, and it has consistently been one of the three top priorities since President Barack Obama called for universal preschool education in his 2013 State of the Union Address.[13] Since 2013, a bipartisan opinion research team has regularly polled Americans and found that large and growing majorities (including majorities of respondents who identify their party affiliation as Republican or Democrat) want the federal government to help states and local communities build better preschool services and improve access to preschool.[14] Overwhelmingly numbers of parents with means and of those who live in places with free universal preschool send their children to preschool.

THE PRESENT PRESCHOOL LANDSCAPE

Preschool education in the United States relies on a mix of public and private provision. In 2014, approximately 4.7 million (more than half of all) three- and four-year-olds attended preschool, with 2.7 million attending publicly funded, center-based preschool programs and 2.0 million in private preschools (see figure 4.1). This represents a remarkable tenfold increase from 1964, when fewer than half a million three- and four-year-olds were in preschool. Growth was rapid and consistent for much of this period, accelerating in the 1990s when many states began or increased investments in preschool programs and the number of children in public preschool more than doubled across the decade. Prior to that, most of the growth had been in private preschool, fueled by early adoption and increasing use by higher-income families who could afford to pay for preschool as an educational investment for their children. Since 2000, the growth in preschool enrollment has actually slowed considerably, because most of those who can afford to pay for private preschool are close to fully enrolled and the rate of new public investments has declined.

Public preschool is comprised of Head Start (a federally funded program) and public pre-K (typically funded by states and local municipalities). Head Start, the largest and oldest such program, serves nearly 800,000 children ages three and four for one or two years, and it offers families full- and part-day options. Eligibility is restricted primarily to families in poverty. Approximately 12 percent of all four-year-olds and 9 percent of all three-year-olds attend Head Start, representing approximately 40 percent of all preschool-age children below 100 percent of the FPL. The Head Start program (as discussed in

Figure 4.1 *Three- and Four-Year-Olds Enrolled in Center-Based Early Care and Education in the United States, Selected Years, 1965–2014*

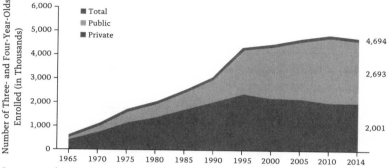

Source: Authors' compilation of CPS data, October supplements (1965–2014).

greater depth in chapter 5) has historically taken a comprehensive approach to services for young children: education is its core mission, but it also offers a range of family support, health and mental health, nutrition, and family engagement services.

There are public preschool programs in forty-two states and the District of Columbia, serving more than 1.3 million children in 2014, the large majority of them four-year-olds (1.2 million).[15] The number of children served in public preschool nearly tripled between 1990 and 2005 and has since increased only minimally. There is wide variation in the size and availability of programs across states and cities. Eight states still have no state prekindergarten, and twelve others serve fewer than 10 percent of their four-year-olds. Eight states and the District of Columbia serve more than 50 percent of four-year-olds in public preschool, accounting for 33 percent of all four-year-olds enrolled in state preschool nationally.[16] Unlike Head Start, public preschool is not a single program with common standards or largely consistent spending levels per child, but varies a great deal depending on state and locality. These programs differ in eligibility criteria (for example, targeting low-income families versus more universal programs with broader or no income eligibility), the ages of the children served, coverage, and program standards.

There are large gaps in preschool access by family income (see figure 4.2). At age four, 84 percent of children from families with incomes above 400 percent of the FPL (approximately $97,000 for a family of four in 2015) attend preschool, compared to 67 percent of

Figure 4.2 *Three- and Four-Year-Olds in Center-Based Preschool, by Family Income Level and Child Age, 2013*

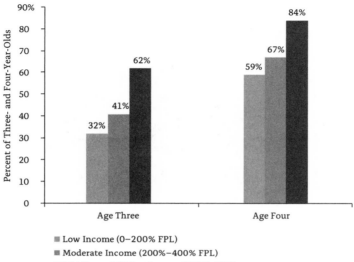

Low Income (0–200% FPL)
Moderate Income (200%–400% FPL)
Middle- and Higher-Income (400%+ FPL)

Source: Authors' analysis of data from the 2013 CPS.

those between 200 and 400 percent of the FPL and 59 percent of those below 200 percent of the FPL. At age three, these disparities are larger: 62 percent for those above 400 percent of the FPL versus 41 percent for those between 200 and 400 percent of the FPL and 32 percent for those below 200 percent of the FPL.

These gaps are not surprising, given the cost of preschool. Using a range of data sources, we estimate that, on average, preschool costs between $7,000 and $15,000 per year per child in different parts of the country; these estimated costs do not cover the summer and before- and after-school wraparound child care that many working families need. These costs frequently are borne by families and represent more than one-quarter of household earnings for families in the lowest two income quintiles.[17]

The lack of public support for preschool extends to lack of support for equitable pay for preschool teachers. Low pay for preschool teachers is a major problem that contributes to the dearth of highly qualified individuals entering the field and fuels turnover. In real dollars, preschool teacher wages have increased by 15 percent over the last twenty-five years, but only to an average of $15.11, compared to $25.40

for kindergarten teachers (both in 2013 dollars). The wage penalty for teaching preschool versus kindergarten amounted to approximately $21,000 in 2013—on average, teachers of five-year-olds made 68 percent more than teachers of four-year-olds.

Not surprisingly, given this low level of pay and the pay disparity, average yearly worker turnover in the early care and education field was 13 percent in 2012.[18] In K–12 public schools, by contrast, turnover was 8 percent.[19] In centers that experienced any turnover in 2012, the turnover rate was 50 percent on average, and as high as 84 percent in for-profit franchise centers.[20] Turnover undermines teacher training and quality improvement efforts, which are then akin to adding water to a leaky bucket. High turnover also deprives children enrolled in early care and education programs of the secure bonds with a consistent caregiver that are vital for their optimal development.

Preschool Quality Matters

The evidence is clear that high-quality preschool programs have larger positive impacts on children's development than lower-quality programs. The best preschool programs are characterized by sound *structural quality*—safety, nutrition, low teacher-child ratios, small class sizes, and qualified and trained teachers. They also have high *process quality*—rich teacher-child interactions that support learning in specific domains, a warm emotional climate, and an evidence-based curriculum. Both aspects of quality are important, and they are linked, though their association is not very strong.[21] Structural quality sets the stage for higher-quality interactions, or may serve as a prerequisite for those interactions, but it does not guarantee them.[22] Structural features alone show little or no association with improvements in child outcomes in the United States.[23]

Traditionally, early care and education regulations have focused on structural quality, which is easier to measure, regulate, and enforce. As the demand for out-of-home child care grew rapidly in the 1960s and 1970s, more states developed structural child care regulations focusing on minimum standards.[24] Structural quality dimensions in these decades were often referred to as the only "regulable" aspects of quality. Process features such as the quality of interactions between caregivers and children were assumed to be much more difficult to measure, regulate, and enforce. More recently, however, ratings of program process features have been incorporated into some state quality rating systems.[25] The Head Start program now regularly rates the classrooms of every grantee on its process quality, and these ratings are used to determine which grantees are required to recompete for continued funding.[26]

Measures of process quality have focused on general emotional climate or behavior management, general instructional skills, and indicators of the organization of the classroom. In empirical research, process quality measures are consistently, though modestly, associated with higher rates of growth in children's skills, across a wide range of cognitive and socioemotional domains.[27] Associations are somewhat stronger at higher levels of process quality.[28] Associations between process quality in programs serving children birth to age five and measures of children's skills persist at least to age fifteen.[29]

In the preschool years, as children's skills become more sophisticated, complex, and differentiated, process quality can be further distinguished according to the dimensions that support specific domains of skills, such as language and literacy, math, socioemotional development, self-regulation, and executive function. Accordingly, measures of domain-specific instruction have been developed for the preschool years in areas such as language (for example, ELLCO) and math (for example, COEMET).[30] Across child ages and program types, we define high-quality care as classrooms and programs that have high ratings on observational measures of both structural and process quality.

What do we know about the role of quality in promoting children's gains in preschool? We see in the preschool evidence base that higher-quality programs tend to have initially larger and more lasting benefits for participants. For example, Tulsa public preschool programs, both Head Start programs and those in the public schools, are known for their high quality and have been shown to produce a large boost in children's literacy and mathematics readiness for kindergarten.[31] The Tennessee voluntary prekindergarten program, in contrast, has relatively lower quality scores on quality measures, with smaller, though still positive, initial impacts on children's kindergarten readiness.[32] Rigorous evidence, using propensity score analyses for Tennessee and Tulsa, shows that benefits for Tennessee participants disappeared quickly, while benefits for Tulsa participants were still evident in elementary and middle school.[33] In older studies of both small- and large-scale preschool programs, we see a similar pattern—larger long-term payoffs in higher-quality versus lower-quality programs. (Although most rigorous studies that have followed preschool participants into adulthood have found long-term benefits such as increases in college enrollment, decreases in incarceration rates, and decreases in teen pregnancy.)[34]

To be sure, pathways by which preschool effects persist or do not persist are complicated and not entirely understood.[35] Some work suggests that persistence depends on elementary school quality—effects may persist in higher-quality but not lower-quality subsequent environments.[36] Other work suggests that the preschool boost persists only if kindergarten instruction is aligned with preschool instruction so that content repetition is minimized.[37] The focus of the preschool program also might matter. If preschool instruction focuses on skills that almost all children would develop anyway later in schooling, like alphabet recognition and sound-symbol correspondence, the initial positive boost may quickly fade. If preschool instruction focuses on more fundamental or broad-based skills, such as vocabulary, effects may be more likely to persist.[38] There are still more questions than answers in the persistence literature to date. The current evidence base suggests that a primary way to ensure lasting gains from preschool is via high-quality programs that produce larger impacts on children's kindergarten readiness during the preschool years.[39]

Given the importance of quality, how do existing public preschool programs perform? Existing process quality is mixed: *emotional support is good, but instructional quality is poor.* Programs in the United States tend to score quite well on emotional climate, meaning that programs are often successful in providing children with warm, caring interactions with their teachers.[40] Figure 4.3 displays average emotional support scores that range from 5.2 to 6.1 (on a scale of 1 to 7) across a study of eleven state prekindergarten programs, Head Start grantees, Boston's prekindergarten program, and Tulsa's prekindergarten and Head Start programs.[41] These scores all reflect good to excellent quality, in about the same range across the programs studied. Standard deviations for emotional support scores in these studies were likewise quite similar (0.34 to 0.78) and reflect a small amount

Figure 4.3 *Average Preschool Process Quality in Large-Scale Preschool Systems*

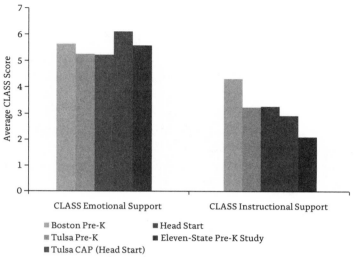

Source: Authors' compilation.

Notes: Boston data were collected in 2010 (N = 83 classrooms; Weiland et al. 2013); Tulsa data were collected in 2006 (N = 77 pre-K classrooms, N CAP = 28 classrooms; Phillips, Gormley, and Lowenstein 2009); Head Start data were collected in 2014 (N = 404 grantees; U.S. DHHS/ACF/OHS 2014); eleven-state pre-K data were collected in six states in 2002 and in five additional states in 2004 (N = 671 classrooms; Mashburn et al. 2008). The eleven-state study reported results using an older version of the CLASS than the other studies included here. Data from the eleven-state study accordingly are approximately, but not exactly, comparable to those of the other studies shown.

of within-program variation—an indication that emotional support quality levels are similar across most centers for the Head Start and prekindergarten programs that were studied.

Programs, however, more often fail to adequately support the learning needs of young children. Specifically, they fail to provide them with intentional, play-based, and scaffolded learning opportunities that are tailored to their interests and developmental level and that provide just enough help to support growth in their conceptual thinking and cognitive skills without frustrating them. This failure has been well documented in the preschool period. Average preschool instructional quality is below adequate across different types of non-parental care settings.[42] Within center-based programs, figure 4.3 also shows that average instructional quality scores ranged from a low of 2.08 to a high of 4.30 across the eleven-state prekindergarten, Head

Start, Boston, and Tulsa studies. (A score of 3 indicates adequate quality and 5 indicates good quality.) This range of 2.7 standard deviations in effect size (using the standard deviation from the eleven-state study) is very large. Within programs, standard deviations were considerably larger for instructional quality than for emotional support (21 to 63 percent larger), demonstrating that instructional quality varies more across the programs studied than it does for emotional quality.

Underscoring these findings, a time-use study of public preschool classrooms in eleven states found that children spent a large portion of the day (44 percent) not engaged in a learning activity (for example, in transitions or meals with no learning activity or unoccupied).[43] Children from higher-income families spent somewhat more time in learning activities, but overall, children of all income levels spent a considerable portion of the day not engaged in activities that promote early learning. Furthermore, when children were engaged in learning, child-teacher interactions were three times more likely to be didactic or rote rather than scaffolded. In 2013, among Head Start grantees, even those at the top 10 percent of the quality distribution were just above the adequate benchmark (3.3 out of 7) on instructional support, though 2014 data showed progress in this area (3.65 out of 7 for the top 10 percent).[44] Adequately supporting young children's conceptual development tends to be a particular problem.[45]

Certain types of instruction tend to be almost entirely lacking in existing programs. For example, math instruction is typically limited to counting, rudimentary addition, and identification of basic shapes, rather than support for the much greater range of math skills that preschoolers can learn, including magnitude, spatial skills, geometry, and arithmetic.[46] In the domains of literacy and language support, most preschools do an adequate job teaching the very basics of literacy. For example, a recent meta-analysis found that preschool raised emergent literacy measures, such as letter-word identification, by an average of 0.27 standard deviations.[47] However, the impacts of preschool on broader language outcomes that are more predictive of later reading comprehension, such as oral language and vocabulary, are not as evident. Studies typically find that the most effective approaches to early-childhood vocabulary instruction—for example, including more complex words, returning to words over time and linking them in different ways to children's lives and everyday situations, moving beyond simple definitions to broader conceptual links, and encouraging elaborated and extended conversations—are lacking in most preschool classrooms.[48]

There is evidence that higher instructional quality is possible to attain in larger-scale programs, with the right investments in professional development and proven curricula (described in more detail later).[49] Few programs to date, however, have made these investments.

LARGE GAPS IN EXPERIENCED
QUALITY BY FAMILY INCOME

Figures 4.4 and 4.5 present data on income-based gaps in experienced structural and process quality from a sample of prekindergarten classrooms. We use two metrics in these figures: overall average scores (figure 4.4) and a standard-deviation difference measure of the gap in quality experienced between children in each quintile and children in the top quintile (figure 4.5).

In figure 4.4, there is a fairly consistent income gradient, or step function, across the quality types—quality is higher with each incremental increase in income. In figure 4.5, we see that differences in quality experienced by children in the top income quintile versus the bottom quintile are as large as 0.8 standard deviations.

PROVEN PATHWAYS TO INCREASING
PRESCHOOL QUALITY

Recent research across more than a dozen randomized controlled trials indicates that the combination of developmentally focused curricula and integrated, in-classroom professional development has the largest effects on children's school readiness.[50] Developmentally focused curricula target language or literacy, math skills, or socioemotional outcomes such as reduced behavior problems. In the most successful examples, implemented across various systems such as Head Start and public prekindergarten programs, intensive mentoring or coaching conducted in the classroom helped teachers implement these curricula.[51] Such coaching typically included direct observation of instructional practice and provision of feedback in the context of

Figure 4.4 *Overall Average Process and Structural Quality in a Sample of Prekindergarten Classrooms for Four-Year-Olds Across Six States, by Family Income Quintile*

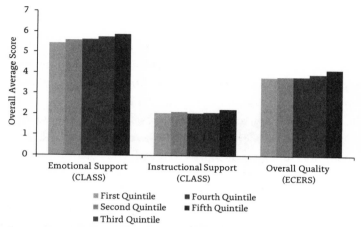

Source: Ana Auger's unpublished analysis and compilation of data from the National Center for Early Development and Learning (NCEDL).
Note: ECERS = Early Childhood Environment Rating Scale.

Figure 4.5 *Gaps (in Standard Deviations) in Experienced Quality Between Children in the Lower Four Income Quintiles Relative to Children in the Top Income Quintile*

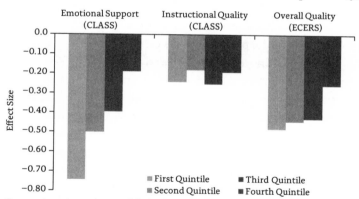

Source: Ana Auger's unpublished analysis and compilation of data from the NCEDL.
Note: ECERS = Early Childhood Environment Rating Scale.

a supportive working relationship (usually twice a month or more across these studies). Randomized trials of different curricula that included only training and no coaching found few impacts of these curricula on children's developmental outcomes at the end of preschool and into elementary school.[52]

The majority of publicly funded preschool programs, rather than using developmentally focused curricula, use what are called "whole-child" or "global" curricula.[53] These curricula tend to have a very wide scope, providing activities that are thought to promote socioemotional, language, literacy, and mathematics skills and knowledge about science, arts, and social studies. However, they do not have a specific scope and sequence designed to match the natural development of children's skills in the preschool period. Global curricula have not often been evaluated rigorously. Existing evidence from independent evaluators suggests no or small gains associated with their use when compared with pedagogy developed by individual teachers or with other commercially available or researcher-developed curricula.[54]

The combination of developmentally focused curricula and coaching can but does not always work. For example, evidence on the "Tools of the Mind" curriculum, which focuses on addressing children's self-regulation skills through coaching and training, has shown mixed results: one small study in preschool and one large study in kindergarten showed substantial positive effects on kindergarten readiness, and two large studies in preschool showed no effects.[55] The latter result may have had something to do with the implementation challenges presented by the "Tools" curriculum, given its many components and design. Some curricula have produced more consistently positive effects. The socioemotional-focused "Promoting Alternative Thinking Strategies" (PATHS) curriculum, for example, produced consistent gains in children's socioemotional skills in two randomized controlled trials relative to "business-as-usual" classrooms.[56] More curriculum trials and trial replications like these are needed, particularly ones that pay attention to the dosage and fidelity of coaching across all the domains of children's skills development. Currently, however, the weight of the evidence points to this combination as our most proven pathway for improving instructional quality and children's outcomes.

Box 4.1 *What Is a Developmentally Focused Curriculum?*

Douglas Clements (2007) has provided a definition of a developmentally focused curriculum in early childhood. First, the subject matter of the curriculum must be matched to the child's developmental stage. Second, the curriculum must be based on strong evidence of the effectiveness of particular instructional strategies and pedagogy. Third, the set of teacher activities and materials must follow evidence on skill growth across the targeted developmental period. Sets of activities are sequenced in ways that build and foster specific trajectories of skill development. For example, a learning trajectory identified by Clements in geometry consists of a progression from lack of competence in composing geometric shapes to (a) composing individual shapes; (b) combining shapes into pictures; and (c) synthesizing combinations of shapes into new shapes. At each stage, a set of tasks is designed to help children transition to the next stage. These tasks, which solicit original input from children, are accompanied by probing of children's thinking and reasoning as they solve problems. The following example from Clements and Sarama's (2007) "Building Blocks" math curriculum shows specific activities linked to a learning trajectory:

Level	Behavioral example	Instructional task	
Nonverbal Addition. Children reproduce small (< 5) sums when shown the addition of subtraction of groups of objects (Baroody, 2004; Mix, Huttenlocher, & Levine, 2002).	After watching 2 objects, then 1 more placed under a cloth, children choose or make collections of 3 to show how many are hidden in all.	Two pepperoni slices were shown on the pizza on the right; at this point, the child sees 1 more moving out of the tray onto the pizza. Children put the same number of slices on the left pizza.	
Small Number Addition. Children solve simple "join, result unknown" problems with sums to 5, usually by subitizing (instant identification of small collections) or using a "counting all" strategy (Baroody, 1987; Fuson, 1988).	"You have 2 balls and get 1 more. How many in all?" Child counts out 2, then counts out 1 more, then counts all 3.	The customer wants his order in one box; what should the label for that (rightmost) box be?	
Find Result. Children solve "join, result unknown" problems by direct modeling—"separating from" for subtraction or counting all for addition, with sums to 10 (Carpenter et al., 1993; Clements, Sarama, et al., 2004; Fuson, 1992a).	"You have 3 red balls and then get 3 blue balls. How many do you have in all?" Child counts out 3 red, then counts out 3 blue, then counts all 6.	Children play with toy dinosaurs on a background scene. For example, they might place 4 tyrannosaurus rex and then 5 apatosaurus on the paper and then count all 9 to see how many dinosaurs they have in all.	
Find Change. Children solve "change unknown" word problems by direct modeling. For example, they might "add on" to answer how many more blocks they would have to get if they had 4 blocks and needed 6 blocks in all (Clements, Sarama, et al., 2004).	"You have 5 balls and then get some more. Now you have 7 in all. How many did you get?" Child counts out 5, then counts those 5 again starting at one, then adds more, counting "6, 7," then counts the balls added to find the answer, 2.	Children are shown a pizza with 4 toppings but should have 7. They are asked to "make it 7."	
Counting On. Children continue developing their counting methods even further, often using objects to keep track. Such counting requires conceptually embedding the 3 inside the total, 5 (Baroody, 2004; Carpenter & Moser, 1984; Fuson, 1992b).	"How much is 4 and 3 more?" "Fourrrrr . . . 5 [putting up one finger], 6 [putting up a second finger], 7 [putting up a third finger]. Seven!"	Children use cutout "pizzas" and disks for toppings. The teacher asks them to put 5 toppings on their pizzas, and then asks how many they would have in all if they put on 3 more. They count on to answer, then actually put the toppings on to check.	

Source: Clements and Sarama 2007, 141.

This suggests that an effective, developmentally specific curriculum is not simply a set of positive teacher practices, but a structured and sequenced set of activities designed to foster specific trajectories of growth during the preschool period. Curricula that do not specify such sequences, or that fail to rely on research-based understanding of the learning trajectories of specific skills, may be less likely to produce positive impacts on the development of these skills. Research suggests, in fact, a weaker evidence base for the success of more general curricula than for those that are developmentally specific.[57]

Importantly, developmentally appropriate curricula in preschool are both play-based and intentional. A false dichotomy—that learning is either play-based or academic, but not both—is common in the early childhood field and in the media.[58] Designers of successful, developmentally appropriate preschool curricula recognize that young children learn best through play and make play central to instruction.

Box 4.2 *What Does the "Proven Pathways" Model Look Like Implemented at Large Scale?*

The Boston Public Schools prekindergarten program uses two domain-specific curricula: the language- and literacy-focused curriculum "Opening the World of Learning" and the math-focused curriculum "Building Blocks." District leaders chose these two curricula after evidence early in the program's history suggested that the quality of instruction was mediocre. Both curricula are play-based: instruction is intentional and rigorous, but is experienced by children as fun, hands-on learning.

Implementation of the curriculum was supported by thirteen days of training across summer and the school year and by weekly to biweekly in-classroom coaching by an expert mentor. Mentors coached teachers on curriculum implementation and on any other weaknesses in their practice, including classroom management and addressing challenging child behaviors. Coaches also created an integrated curricular guide for teachers—for example, teachers were not expected to juggle two different curricula without support. They also ensured that teachers had the many materials necessary for fully integrating the curriculum, so that they did not skip crucial parts of the curriculum because of resource or logistical difficulties.

Within two years of implementing this model, Boston's programs showed the highest level of instructional quality observed in any large-scale prekindergarten study and showed some of the largest impacts on children's kindergarten readiness skills from any large-scale preschool program.

Universal Access to High-Quality Preschool

The benefits of high-quality universal preschool education have been demonstrated at scale in recent evaluations. An analysis focusing on potential earnings impacts has found that the Tulsa program in particular has had significant benefits relative to costs.[59] In addition, universal access can reduce barriers for children experiencing the highest levels of adversity, as well as for those whose parents are unlikely to enroll them in preschool or apply for means-tested child care subsidies (for example, children whose parents have unstable employment, children who are dual-language learners, or children from immigrant families).[60] Universal access also has the potential benefits of greater public support, political sustainability, and reduced stigma for families compared to a targeted approach.

We propose a universal preschool plan in which state departments of education would work with local districts to roll out full-day, eleven-month programs for three-year-olds and four-year-olds. For states that are ready, we propose that universal access begin at age three. It is clear that, developmentally, three-year-olds are ready to learn and can benefit—cognitively, socially, and emotionally—in an organized group learning setting.[61] Ages three and four are a time of particularly rapid development for children's language and social skills, and children can make enormous strides at this age given two years of high-quality learning opportunities. Research further shows that two years of preschool has greater benefits beyond a single year of preschool, especially for the most at-risk children.[62] The benefits of one year of early childhood education are comparable at age three to gains at age four.[63] In addition, the disparities in children's access to preschool are actually larger and have been growing for three-year-olds relative to four-year-olds.

Although we would like to see most states establish preschool education for all children starting at age three, ultimately that is a decision that states will make, and we think that states will vary in their readiness to establish or expand their preschool services. Some states might prefer to establish or achieve universal access for all four-year-olds, while others will want to implement universal services for all three- and four-year-olds, particularly those states that currently offer services to both age groups or are serving most of their four-year-olds already. And even with a funding incentive, some states may not choose to provide universal early education in the near term.

For states interested in expanding to three-year-olds, we suggest the threshold of having 50 percent of four-year-olds enrolled in public preschool—or 70 percent of all four-year-olds in the state enrolled in any preschool (including private preschools)—and ensuring that existing programs for four-year-olds in the state are of sufficient structural and process quality, as determined by assessing a random sample of programs within the state. Adopting the threshold of 50 percent of four-year-olds in public preschool or 70 percent in any preschool is meant to ensure that states have developed adequate coverage for four-year-olds; if set any higher, the threshold might build into a state's universal preschool program a perverse incentive for public preschool to crowd out private preschool before incorporating expansions to three-year-olds. The quality provision and others that we discuss later are necessary to ensure that states deliver on quality before undertaking extensive expansion.

Under our proposed plan, states would be the primary agents in funding, developing, and implementing universal early education, much as they are today with K–12 education. This approach takes advantage of existing state prekindergarten structures that have been developed in forty states already. It also honors the importance of local control in American education.

The federal government would provide vital support for states, with three primary roles: (1) providing ramp-up matching funds to accelerate the development and integration of universal early education with K–12 education, ensuring that all parts of the country create a shared common starting point for education; (2) prioritizing access to very low-income children, children in low-income, newcomer immigrant families, and others who are currently least likely to have preschool access; and (3) providing a shared research and development framework to support the adoption of best-evidence models (for example, domain-specific curricula supported by coaching) and to evaluate new models for testing and scaling innovations. We also propose that some significant initial federal investments be used to support capital development and other onetime costs, such as support for preschool teacher higher education, to facilitate faster ramp-up. These investments would be based on what each state proposes for universal preschool provision within a ten-year time frame and the net number of children who would be newly served. We suggest that the federal share of matching funds to support operating costs during the expansion period be no more than 50 percent and ultimately phase down to no less than 25 percent in continuing matching funds, ten years into implementation. This match-rate system balances initially incentivizing states to implement expanded preschool programs with not putting them in a precarious or unstable financial position as the match rate drops over time. Our match-rate proposal is considerably higher than the current federal share of 7 to 8 percent of K–12 spending. A larger proportional federal investment would incentivize states to invest in public preschool and to prepare public schools to meet the needs of younger children.

We suggest a flexible federal role that meets states where they are and that rewards rather than punishes states that have already made significant investments. An increased match level could be offered to states that are already well on their way to offering universal early education to their preschool-age children—such as Oklahoma, which first moved to establish universal preschool in 1998 and now offers free preschool to all four-year-olds. We propose that such states be offered an enhanced or less-decelerated match rate (for example, an initial 60 percent match rate or a slower phasedown in the match rate over ten years), which would allow them to use some of their current investments and matching funds to expand their coverage to three-year-olds or improve the quality of their services while ensuring that they maintain their current expenditure levels.[64]

Some states might decide not to provide universal preschool despite federal supports, and possibly regardless of the generosity of the initial matching funds. Cities or local education agencies (LEAs) within such states, however, might still want to offer universal preschool. Cities have in fact been leading the way just as often as states in the movement toward universal preschool (for example, Boston, Denver, New York City, Philadelphia, Seattle, San Antonio, and Washington, D.C.). We propose that states, cities, and LEAs all be eligible to apply directly to receive federal funds for universal preschool expansion, as long as they are seeking to ensure universal access to the educational system for which they have responsibility. This expansion strategy would require tailored outreach and communication to LEAs to guide them through the process.

MIXED-AUSPICE APPROACHES

States and localities should be free to pursue the provision of early education in public school or community-based settings. A mixed-auspice approach provides states with the flexibility to retain existing high-quality providers and ensure that services are located in areas where they are needed. As long as an LEA is responsible for policies and practices, quality standards, and oversight, states, localities, and districts are best equipped to make decisions on the location of services and timing the growth of services.

Despite the reasons for a mixed-auspice system at the outset, we expect that over time the primary settings for expanded universal preschool programs, like kindergarten programs, will become public elementary schools. A primary locus in public schools supports many of the other key elements of our vision and rationale for universal early education support. In this setting, the preschool years would be clearly viewed as part of every child's educational career. Educators would be able to align transitions and pedagogy across the preschool through third-grade years. Finally, a public school–based system would facilitate the staffing of these programs with teachers as professionally trained, credentialed, and compensated as other teachers in the system.

CONSISTENT STRUCTURAL QUALITY STANDARDS ACROSS SYSTEMS

Our proposal addresses the challenges of achieving both structural and process quality in preschool systems. It is clear that some states, like Oklahoma, have already done so. Our goal is to spread successful approaches and continue to identify and improve achievable levels of quality through the federal matching incentive and federal research and development resources for preschool. Federal matching funds should be set at a level sufficient to incentivize the adoption of high-quality standards. We recommend a national framework for structural quality standards aimed at establishing the key elements in ensuring a common, minimum floor for program quality. Regardless of auspice, programs would be expected to meet the same standards in order to qualify for federal matching funds.[65] At a minimum, programs would offer: a full school day (for example, the same hours as K–12); student-teacher ratios of no more than one-to-ten; comprehensive services for families and children, including screening for developmental delays, special needs, and health problems; teacher pay scales, benefits, and educational requirements consistent with those in the public schools; and transportation. These features are characteristic of the universal preschool programs with the largest positive impacts on children, such as those evaluated in Tulsa and Boston. Teachers should have at least a bachelor's degree and training in early childhood development, and paraprofessionals should have at least a child development associate (CDA) degree.[66]

CURRICULAR AND MENTORING SUPPORTS TO PROMOTE HIGH PROCESS QUALITY

We recommend a research-based combination of evidence-based curricula and on-site coaching and mentoring supports as the principal route to ensuring process quality, which is most directly tied to improved child outcomes. Universal early education programs would be incentivized to use evidence-based curricula, and a list of those curricula would be supplied by the federal government according to the standards for demonstrated effectiveness of the What Works Clearinghouse.[67]

Teachers would be supported in their implementation of evidence-based curricula through curricular trainings as well as through biweekly to monthly on-site visits and observations of teacher practice by early childhood coaches. Part of the federal match would cover the cost of the implementation of new curricula and more labor-intensive coaching. Early childhood coaches would be expected to hold at least a master's degree, to have at least three years of early childhood teaching experience, and to have a proven track record in promoting the school readiness of young children. Comprehensive family-support workers likewise would receive the professional development they need from experienced mental health consultants, and training and supportive coaching on a monthly basis would be available to help them refine their skills and improve their effectiveness in working with families. In addition, pre-service programs would be encouraged via a monetary incentive to incorporate on-site mentoring and coaching, so that teachers have this experience of observation and feedback in the classroom during their practica.

FULL SCHOOL DAY, LONGER SCHOOL YEAR, AND WRAPAROUND CARE OPTIONS

The large majority of public preschools in the United States provide a nine-month program, mirroring the tradition of a long summer break in the K–12 public education system. Hours vary between half-day programs as short as three hours and "full-day" programs (most commonly six to seven hours). In contrast, we propose at least six and a half hours per day of preschool—for example, from 8:30 AM to 3:00 PM. Recognizing that continuity of care is especially important for young children and that most young children have employed parents, we also propose that preschool programs offer at least an eleven-month school year as well as wraparound care services, preferably on-site. For example, as is often the case now in K–12 programs, there could be on-site wraparound care from 7:30 to 8:30 AM and from 3:00 to 6:00 PM for the large subset of parents who need such care. Local districts would be free to choose how to use this before- and after-school time. Funding for the extended day and extended year could be based on a progressive income sliding scale for parents, including the use of the Assurance subsidies (explained in chapter 3) for eligible low- and moderate-income families and eligibility for tax credits for all families. Successful out-of-school-time programs often focus on providing students from low-income families with enrichment activities that mirror those accessible to their peers from more affluent families, including music lessons, sports, and academic enrichment. Gaps in access to out-of-school activities during the academic year and summers have grown over time and may be a factor in the widening of the achievement gap as children progress through school.[68]

An additional month of time for summer also represents an extension of learning time, with opportunities to offer enrichment options and avoid the often substantial summer learning loss. Similar to teachers in many K–12 systems, regular-year preschool teachers would have the option of working an additional month, with additional pay. This month could also offer a unique opportunity for building the human capital of providers; new teachers, coaches, and paraprofessionals could undergo further training in preschool settings.[69]

PHASE-IN CONSIDERATIONS FOR
GETTING TO SCALE WITH QUALITY

There is a risk in expanding preschool access too quickly. Localities need time to grapple with the complexities of providing access to high-quality programs, including systems for quality monitoring and improvement. To date, states, cities, and countries that have implemented universal preschool have done it in different ways, and at varying speeds. Some have chosen to prioritize low-income communities first, while others have increased access across the income continuum simultaneously, even in the initial phases.[70] Some systems have expanded from a public school base (such as Boston and Tulsa). Others have expanded in a mixed-delivery system, including public school–based prekindergarten, community providers, and Head Start.[71]

These approaches have trade-offs. Initially excluding children from higher-income families or excluding higher-income communities may limit the potential positive effects of mixed-income classrooms.[72] On the other hand, effective targeting may lead to less crowd-out or net gain in access to early education, offering opportunity to the population that is least likely to access high-quality programming. In any event, approaches are likely to vary by context.

In our proposal, states would build from their existing capacity in stages. Within ten years, each entity would have reached universal coverage for all four-year-olds or all three- and four-year-olds in preschool.[73] States would be allowed flexibility in reaching this goal, but would be required to show that their expansion plans have adhered to the following principles:

1   The rate of expansion should be consistent with the ability to ensure that the educational services being implemented are of high quality and meet the key common standards.
2   Populations with low access to preschool (such as newcomer immigrants, homeless families, migrants, and families with heightened risks) should be prioritized.
3   For states proposing to build toward universal services for three-

and four-year-olds, the primary service model should be two years of preschool, beginning at age three, and those for other states should allow for eventual expansion to include two years of preschool.

4 As much as possible given local demographics and policies, classrooms include children with different characteristics (for example, children from families of different income levels and inclusive settings for children with and without disabilities).

5 States and localities should roll out new programs in ways that facilitate rigorous evaluation and learning.

Currently, many states do not require districts to offer full-day kindergarten; several other states provide for full-day kindergarten but do not require it.[74] Overall, 77 percent of kindergarteners are enrolled in full-day programs, and 23 percent are in half-day programs.[75] Half-day programs can place stress on working families. Transitions from full-day preschool—as we propose—to half-day kindergarten should be avoided. To be eligible for federal preschool funds for younger children, states should be required to offer full-day kindergarten.

Although we propose universal preschool starting at age three, we expect that many states would choose to begin with universal preschool for four-year-olds because it would easier to implement and also because the current evidence base and models for public preschool have been better established for services aimed at four-year-olds.[76] The states that choose to implement both three- and four-year-old preschool would provide an opportunity to test elements of a two-year sequence of public preschool. Such elements could include sequenced curricula and coaching over two years, as well as greater understanding and testing of curricula for three-year-olds, the development of which lags behind those for the older age group. Programs in these "laboratory" states could be designed, for example, as formal preschool-university partnerships that are part of a national learning network and research clearinghouse on program development and effectiveness.

ALIGNMENT OF PRESCHOOL WITH K–3

From the very outset of a path to universal preschool, providers should try to align their services with the K–3 system so that gains from preschool are built upon over time. At present, there are no proven, sequenced curricula across the three-, four-, and five-year-old years. Consequently, children who attend preschool often repeat the same material over two years in preschool and then again in kindergarten. Therefore, it is not surprising that the academic gains of preschool fade out (or converge with those of children who have not repeated the same material) at a rate of approximately 0.03 standard deviations per year.[77] Under our proposal, states and local providers would be expected to develop explicit alignment plans and show steps toward alignment to receive funding. These steps could include adoption of consistent curricula across preschool and primary education; joint professional development and planning time with preschool and K–3 teachers, including visiting and observing each other's teaching practice; meetings between preschool directors and K–3 principals or instructional leaders; and aligned parent engagement across this grade span.

OTHER CONSIDERATIONS

Providing high-quality preschool at a large scale will also require particular attention to the needs of the changing demographic groups in the United States, particularly dual-language learners. (Children of immigrants are currently one-quarter of children in this country.)[78] For preschool specifically, several studies have found that dual-language learners are less likely to be enrolled in preschool, compared to their monolingual peers. As mentioned previously, these children also stand to benefit disproportionately from high-quality preschool. Issues of access and quality for this group are crosscutting for birth-to-age-five policies; we return to this issue in the conclusion of the book.

Another important element that should be available to families enrolled in public preschool programs as needed is on-site support services—comprehensive screening of parents as well as children and referral to IDEA (Individuals with Disabilities Education Act) services, as well as mental health, domestic violence, substance abuse, or other services in the community or in the program itself. Besides making support services available to parents, steps should also be taken to monitor and improve the quality of these services. At present, there is considerable range in the quality of such services as offered through preschool programs and little to no quality oversight. Head Start has a more comprehensive set of standards covering health, mental health, and other social services than most state public pre-K programs, and it also screens for disability.[79] We envision a coaching system for the providers of these support services as a key mechanism to improve and monitor quality. In chapter 5, we discuss how a community hub model can provide locally sourced and evidence-based professional development and training for a range of services.

States should form councils at multiple levels, with representation across health, public school, community provider, and Head Start program administrators, teachers, and parents. These state-level councils would be similar to those integrated into the Head Start reauthorization of the Race to the Top Early Learning Challenge grants. Finally, a standardized data system should be created to track program operations, quality, and child outcomes across auspices.[80]

A POLICY- AND PRACTICE-BASED RESEARCH AGENDA FOR ACHIEVING QUALITY IMPLEMENTATION AT SCALE

As states and LEAs scale universal preschool programs, there is a tremendous opportunity to add to the evidence base on how to best improve children's school readiness skills; how to best train and support teachers; and how to sustain children's learning gains after preschool. The field has learned much from previous expansions, including those in Georgia, North Carolina, and Oklahoma, and in Boston and Tulsa. The greater the specificity in studies regarding curricula, fidelity of implementation, more general classroom quality, and supports like professional development, the greater the knowledge gained.

Accordingly, similar to, and perhaps built on, the current Early Learning Network established by the Institute of Education Sciences in 2015, we propose a national network of place-based preschool researchers who collaborate to answer the field's most pressing questions, using a mix of experimental and quasi-experimental evaluation methods as well as implementation research. These questions would include (but not be limited to): the best balance between native-language and English instruction for dual-language learners;

the best curriculum sequence leading up to kindergarten entry; optimal pathways and approaches to attracting, training, and retaining highly qualified teachers, particularly in bilingual and inclusive settings; and curriculum alignment from preschool to third grade, so that children's early elementary experiences build on their early learning. Such a network would advance the science of early childhood development and learning, while also informing improvements in preschool and early primary-grade policy and practice.

Trade-Offs and Alternatives

As with any policy, there are trade-offs and alternatives to be considered. First, as we detail in the appendix, we estimate that the program will cost approximately $33 billion, or in the range of $29 billion to $37 billion (see table A4.1). Preschool programs have been shown to generate savings over time that exceed their costs. In the short run, however, these funds would be spent on preschool instead of other policy priorities and additional revenues may be required, particularly at the state or local level.

In addition, there are market-level effects to consider when expanding preschool to all three- and four-year-olds. In centers that serve children across the early childhood age spectrum, tuition for preschool-age children may currently help support the provision of center-based care for infants and toddlers, and expanding preschool could draw resources away from these early childhood services. Our plan is unlikely to substantially change this older-to-younger subsidization in mixed-auspice systems, since preschool-age children will continue to enroll in centers that also serve children under age three. However, market-level effects in localities that pursue a public school–based approach could be larger. The recent finding by Daphna Bassok, Maria Fitzpatrick, and Susanna Loeb that no crowd-out of private child care providers occurred in Georgia and Oklahoma after the advent of universal preschool suggests that market-level effects may not threaten the supply of birth-to-age-three center-based care.[81] Also, the ACE subsidies we propose in chapter 3 would help to mitigate these market-level effects by making center-based care more affordable for the parents of children under three. Nonetheless, further study will be necessary to understand these effects.

There are several alternatives to our proposal. First, we could wait for states to cover all preschoolers using their own dollars, given that forty states do already have public prekindergarten programs. We would advise against this option because states vary widely in their funding levels and program requirements and most programs are mediocre. The preschool period is too important developmentally not to raise the bar on quality nationally and serve children more equitably.

Second, the overall initiative and the federal role could be limited to support only lower-income families, avoiding the provision of a universal, free education service to families who are already paying for preschool. This could be accomplished through a program that is universal for up to a targeted level of family income, with a sliding scale to determine family payments. Some localities have implemented a sliding-scale payment system (including Denver and Seattle). Federal funds could also be targeted to poor and lower-income families through guaranteed subsidies for care and education, as outlined in our ACE subsidies proposal. We believe, however, that such approaches ultimately do not accomplish the goal of universality in public education for an age at which all children can learn in center-based settings. The benefits of greater socioeconomic diversity in early education are also increasingly evident.

Third, the federal incentive could be structured to explicitly require a state to provide universal access for both three-year-olds and four-year-olds in order to qualify for matching funds, since the gaps in access are actually greater for children in low- and middle-income families at age three than at four. However, given the highly variable levels of coverage across states for four-year-olds, we expect that some states would view high-quality coverage for three-year-olds as unrealistic in the near future. When the country of Mexico mandated coverage for three- and four-year-olds simultaneously, enrollment of three-year-olds actually declined as the Mexican states first turned to increasing coverage for four-year-olds. Our proposal acknowledges these pragmatic concerns and expects states to have the opportunity to design services that best meet their capacities.

A final alternative is to focus initially on access rather than quality. It is true that moving children from home-based to center-based or preschool education does result in better quality relative to the alternative care that some children receive without universal access. Regulating only access is also simpler from a policy perspective. However, we believe that current levels of quality in many large-scale systems are much too low. Raising quality is difficult at scale, and investments to raise quality do not always pay off. Expanding access without paying attention to quality could lead to intractable quality issues in the longer term as well as massive losses in potential learning and development for our nation's children.

Summary and Conclusion

A new common starting point for our public education system is necessary as a smart economic investment that will advance the nation's overall interests in fostering individual and economic growth and increasing the country's human capital. The evidence base for public demand for preschool, gaps in preschool access by family, and widening achievement gaps all converge to a singular conclusion: it is time for an earlier common starting point for children's formal education.

Our proposal emphasizes that universal preschool is an *education initiative*. Americans have long seen education as a public good worthy of public investment and a preferred form of support for addressing inequality. Although we advise developing new programs that are responsive to the needs of working families in terms of length of the school day and year, the primary purpose of this part of our proposal is to increase children's early learning and thus their long-term success. For the same reason, our proposal emphasizes *how* young children learn best—through the kind of intentional play advanced by proven domain-specific curricula and delivered by well-trained and well-supported teachers.

Our proposal also addresses the disparity in status and compensation between preschool teachers and their K–12 counterparts. We propose that teachers who have the same educational background and training and do the same job should be paid equally. The proposal also allows for flexibility to meet local needs. Local control in education is a time-honored American value. Our proposal honors the fact that local communities know their needs and priorities best.

Our vision of universal preschool connects the best current research to policy and practice in a plan that is achievable at scale. The benefits of the plan for children and their families would outweigh its costs. At its center is a science-based conviction that access to high-quality learning opportunities in early childhood is too important, to society and to individual children and families, to be left up to accident of birth.

A NEW HEAD START 5

The policy components proposed in the previous three chapters would help to better meet the early needs of most American children so that many more are ready to learn and succeed when they reach kindergarten. But what about the most disadvantaged? A critical pillar in our comprehensive approach is targeted, intensive, and early support for children in the most disadvantaged circumstances. Those born into the most concentrated, long-term poor communities experience some of the most severe educational and economic inequality.[1] Assuring high-quality early care and education may not be enough to enable this group to reach their full potential, particularly those whose parents may not be working consistently enough to benefit from parental leave and access to child care subsidies or tax credits. For these children, a vigorous and well-coordinated response from the earliest point is needed and is likely to be much more effective than addressing the consequences of concentrated disadvantage in later years.

In this chapter, we propose a comprehensive approach to meeting the needs of the most disadvantaged with a "reinvention" of one of the nation's most important antipoverty programs: Head Start. Head Start has an infrastructure of programs across the country in areas of concentrated disadvantage and a history of providing services to children from early in life. Our reenvisioned Head Start would focus on the prenatal period to three years of age by providing intensive, coordinated services to those growing up in the most-disadvantaged communities, as well as those in other communities who experience high levels of family adversity.

Meeting the Needs of the Most Vulnerable Families

Research across several decades has documented how severe poverty and very low levels of family resources in early childhood lead to much worse child health, education, and behavior outcomes.[2] Several studies using rigorous empirical methods (experiments and quasi-experiments) have found that even modest income differences among families at very low incomes have significant effects on children's academic performance, eventual educational attainment, and criminal activity.[3] Indicators of adversity that affect family functioning, parent and child stress, and quality of caregiving are more common in contexts of poverty.[4] Poverty and low family income contribute to parental stress and compromise parents' capacity to engage in the responsive interactions that are needed to support children's early development.[5] As such, early childhood programs must engage with these families from the earliest possible point in their children's development and focus more explicitly on supporting parenting within a comprehensive two-generational framework that addresses children's development and creates greater stability in their lives.

The importance of continuity in early services and supports for the most disadvantaged is highlighted by the instability in employment, families, housing, and related factors that are much more common for children in these families. For example, shifting household composition as parents repartner, new adults and children enter and leave the household, and parents are incarcerated or released from incarceration can make for complex and interrupted relationships for children, and frequent disruptions can contribute to household stress and worse child and adult outcomes.[6] Housing instability and residential moves are also common among poor families with children, owing to factors that include formal evictions and homelessness, and this instability often triggers school changes and has been found to affect children's academic and behavioral outcomes.[7] Low-wage jobs are often very stressful as well as unstable; more frequent job losses and longer spells of unemployment among parents are associated with less responsive and engaged parenting practices and worse school outcomes for children, including higher rates of placement in special education, grade retention, and school dropout.[8]

Research further shows that opportunities and outcomes are considerably worse for children in poor families who are also growing up in areas of concentrated poverty than for poor children as a whole.[9] Living in severely disadvantaged communities is associated with lower levels of early cognitive development, poorer reading and math skills at kindergarten entry, worse health, a lower likelihood of high school completion, and lower social mobility, including into the next generation.[10] As an indicator of the power of neighborhood-level risk, young children in nonpoor families in these communities actually fare much worse than poor children from neighborhoods of less-concentrated poverty across a range of child and adult outcomes, including much lower levels of early reading and math skills and twice the likelihood of dropping out of high school or becoming teen parent.[11] Several aspects of communities can contribute to these powerful effects, including low-quality schools, high levels of joblessness and incarceration, neighborhood violence, lack of positive peer influences, and low levels of collective monitoring and watching out for neighbors and children.[12]

It is unlikely that the ACE subsidies proposed in chapter 3 would be sufficient to address the level of needs faced by families in communities with high concentrations of poverty while addressing the developmental needs of young children. Areas of concentrated disadvantage have a very limited supply of early care and education.[13] Even when fully implemented with the expected increases in the supply of early care and education, the Assurance might not produce substantial effects on the availability of good-quality care in the most economically distressed communities. With higher levels of joblessness in these communities, fewer parents will be eligible for this new source of support. In addition, families exposed to severe stress are likely to require more extensive assistance. Research shows that effective programs serving families with these levels of stress directly address the source of the stress, whether it be deep poverty (defined as income less than half the federal poverty threshold), homelessness, violence in the home, or community violence.[14] We argue that intervention is needed to establish or strengthen neighborhood-based centers that offer comprehensive early learning and well-targeted intervention services to children and their parents, protecting the most vulnerable children against the risk factors present in their early environment and offering much-needed stability.[15]

As discussed in chapters 1 and 2, developmental science shows that early learning and development disparities begin much sooner than the preschool years. However, we currently lack the specific programs at a sufficient scale that could tackle the most severe and chronic sources of family stress to fulfill the promise of development during the earliest years of life. Not only are existing programs limited in scale, but they tend to be uncoordinated and scattershot, reaching only some families. These vital child development and family support needs ought to be addressed more comprehensively well before age three or four to give these children a fair shot in school and in life. We propose a *targeted intensive and comprehensive child development initiative* for the child population who begin life in concentrated poverty and need more focused attention and services to overcome significant developmental challenges. Fortunately, we have a national program that can be built upon and reimagined to serve in this role: Head Start.

Why Head Start?

Head Start has a long-standing mission to serve the most disadvantaged children and families with a comprehensive model of services. Head Start was launched fifty years ago, in 1965, as part of President Lyndon Johnson's War on Poverty. At the outset of the War on Poverty, nearly half of the nation's poor were children. Sargent Shriver was director of the Office of Economic Opportunity (OEO), which was newly established to manage the new initiatives in the War on Poverty, and he wanted a program that would offer positive developmental opportunities to improve the early intellectual capacity and school performance of children born into poverty.[16] The committee that initially developed Head Start ensured that it would be far more than just a preschool program.[17]

The initial program guidelines required not only attention to the core educational experience of a half-day preschool in the classroom, but also provision of access to basic health care (immunizations and dental and regular medical care) and social services, family engagement, and community participation in governance. This approach was unusual for early education at the time and has since served as a model for preprimary education worldwide.[18] The early emphasis on health services contributed to Head Start's impact in its early years in reducing childhood mortality and the occurrence of some early childhood health conditions.[19]

Over the years Head Start has experimented with new models of service.[20] Most notable among these has been Early Head Start, the prenatal-to-age-three program initiated under the Clinton administration. A committee of experts on infant and toddler programs helped design Early Head Start, and the first grants for this program were awarded in 1995. Early Head Start has grown over the years, but it remains much smaller than the Head Start program and still reaches a relatively small share of eligible children: just 4 percent of low-income families with children age prenatal to three and meeting the program's income guidelines were served in 2013.[21] Head Start, by comparison, serves many more children in its program for three- and four-year-olds, reaching 42 percent of eligible children with family incomes below the poverty level in 2013.[22]

HEAD START: A LEADER IN PROVIDING COMPREHENSIVE SERVICES, SETTING STANDARDS, AND SERVING VULNERABLE POPULATIONS

Head Start's comprehensive services model of promoting child development across multiple domains within the ecological contexts of poor families and children offers a unique and adaptable foundation for addressing the complex challenges of children in the most-disadvantaged communities. In its first decades, Head Start helped to both set and raise the bar for expectations of all children's preschool education—not just programs aimed at poor children. Serving as a base that spurred advancement and research in early childhood development and education, Head Start framed much of the state preschool expansion that followed over time.[23] Among the innovations it introduced were performance standards for quality that were designed to offer detailed direction for programs to create consistency at scale and guide program monitoring. The performance standards have since served as a template for other state and private preschool programs.

Another pioneering aspect of Head Start has been its responsiveness to vulnerable populations such as children with special needs, children of diverse cultural and linguistic backgrounds, migrant children, children in tribal communities, homeless children, and children at risk of abuse and neglect.[24] For example, Head Start led the way in many places on models of inclusion for children with special developmental needs within regular classrooms, setting a minimum percentage (10 percent) of inclusion of children with disabilities for all Head Start grantees.

THE POSITIVE BUT COMPLEX EFFECTS OF HEAD START

Head Start has been the subject of more research on its effectiveness than any other large-scale early childhood program. Systematic reviews of the evidence in the 1980s and 1990s consistently found positive effects across multiple developmental outcomes for program participants.[25] Several studies that tracked children also documented what has been termed a "fade-out," or reduction in the relative gains of participants, compared to nonparticipants on later cognitive test measures after they left the program across the kindergarten to third-grade years.[26] However, long-term studies that exploit longitudinal data and use quasi-experimental designs have shown significant impacts on important later outcomes—reduced placement in special education, reduced grade repetition, increased high school completion, and reductions in criminal behavior.[27]

In 1999, Congress mandated the first randomized national evaluation of the Head Start program: the Head Start Impact Study (HSIS). Results from the experiment, carried out with a cohort of three- and four-year-olds in 2002 and 2003, show an overall pattern of positive effects during the program for participants on school readiness across cognitive, language, and socioemotional skills. However, these effects were modest in size and smaller than the benefits that had been found in prior nonrandomized studies. In addition, these effects had largely disappeared by the first-grade follow-up.[28]

A significant complication in interpreting the results of the Head Start Impact Study is that approximately 60 percent of the study's control group were also participating in center-based preschool programs, including other Head Start centers, when they were not offered a place in the experimental study site; thus, the small overall effects found for those who participated in one year of Head Start are compared to a control group in which many also participated in Head Start or a similar center-based program. In fact, the positive effects for Head Start are concentrated in the comparison of Head Start children to those not in other centers or preschools (that is, children at home or in informal care).[29] Jens Ludwig and Deborah Phillips have estimated the impact of actual Head Start participation (rather than the primary experimental question of the impacts relative to the control group) and find that overall impact is 50 percent greater than the experimental impact across a range of cognitive and social emotional measures.[30] Other important findings from studies of variation in Head Start impacts have found that the program has larger impacts for children with lower levels of initial cognitive skills, for dual-language-learner children, and for those who received full-day programming.[31]

The HSIS and other studies have found wide variation in the quality of Head Start programs across sites, indicating that, like other early care and education programs, some Head Start programs are much better than others at producing positive effects.[32] In fact, overall, as indicated earlier, no difference has been found in the outcomes for children in Head Start relative to comparison-group children in alternative center-based programs, including a large share of children in state-funded prekindergarten programs of comparable quality. Observational assessments of the quality of caregiving and education provided by Head Start teachers show overall levels of quality that are adequate or better in the areas of classroom organization and classroom climate, but low levels in instructional quality—which, as discussed in chapter 4, is the case not only with Head Start but with other public prekindergarten programs (See figure 4.3).[33] Research showing that higher-quality Head Start and pre-K programs yield greater learning gains points to the need to invest in the Head Start workforce to promote improved child outcomes.[34]

Longer-term studies of Head Start's impacts using the available national data sources demonstrate positive results on important and tangible measures of economic and social outcomes for children. Notably, several of these studies show positive long-term impacts while also demonstrating patterns of convergence between Head Start and control-group children's test scores during the early elementary school years.[35] One recent study found that participation in Head

Start had significant positive effects across a series of young adult outcomes, including higher levels of high school graduation and reduced delinquency and teen pregnancy. Head Start reduced approximately one-third of the gap between lower-income children and those at the median across these long-term outcomes.[36] These effects are similar to the scale of the positive long-term effects that were identified in two earlier cohorts of Head Start participants in analyses of long-term effects of the program as experienced in the 1970s and 1980s.[37] Together, the studies using all of the available national data sources that permit causal analysis of long-term impacts have found evidence of positive effects in the majority of outcomes analyzed. It is likely that, as with the long-term effects of smaller demonstration projects like the Perry Preschool Project, other mechanisms are responsible for these long-term effects besides those that account for the convergence of scores on primary-school achievement exams.[38]

Despite the longer-term benefits that have been found, the disparities are so large at the outset that it is not reasonable to expect that participating in a single program for one or two years will eliminate the gaps in important outcomes between children from poor families and those from middle- or higher-income families. As discussed earlier, these wide disparities emerge very early in young children's lives—in fact, in the first year of life. When we then consider the ongoing influence of the persistently great disadvantages of growing up in poverty and in low-resourced communities and the poor quality of the schools these children move on to in kindergarten, we could not expect a high-quality preschool intervention to be a silver bullet: it may reduce but cannot eliminate disparities. Our plan seeks both to intervene even earlier to mitigate the emergence of the learning gaps and to build a comprehensive and well-integrated set of supports for young children and their families to further narrow these disparities.

In contrast to Head Start and the HSIS, the national Early Head Start was evaluated during the first few years of the program's implementation. Families at seventeen sites among the first round of grantees were randomly assigned to an offer of an Early Head Start slot or to a control condition. Results showed a pattern of small short-term positive effects on parenting and child cognitive and social development but also, as in the HSIS, a rapid decline in the size and significance of these effects such that by age five the control-group children had largely caught up to the program participants on most outcomes.[39] Larger positive effects were found in the sites that had fully rather than partially implemented the program.[40]

HEAD START: PIONEERING THE LOCAL GOVERNANCE MODEL THROUGH STRONG TIES TO COMMUNITIES

Head Start was one of the earliest, and is still the largest, federal education program that funds local communities directly. Along with the creation of Title I in the War on Poverty, Head Start represented a greater federal involvement in education, which had long been under the full purview of states, with the express purpose of leveling educational opportunities across the nation.[41] The establishment of a Head Start center was a direct investment in poor communities where early childhood program services often did not exist. Head Start helped set anchor institutions within poor communities and introduced a strong model of local governance, including parent involvement in program management and decision-making.

Harkening back to Head Start's origins, we are reminded that it was a cutting-edge concept at the time because it sought to build on emergent developmental science to address the condition of children living in poverty. Its early emphasis on providing critical links to non-educational resources, such as regular immunizations and preventive and curative medical care, resulted in reductions in childhood mortality in its early years.[42] Head Start's unique features make it the most suitable platform for targeting the most disadvantaged much earlier in life with the appropriate mix of the parenting, health, early intervention, and early learning resources they need. With realignment and strengthening, Head Start could be on today's cutting edge in providing children in the most-disadvantaged circumstances with a sound foundation for early development, growth, and learning.

Repositioning Head Start at the Cutting Edge of Scientific and Program Innovations

Several major changes in the landscape of early childhood education and advances in research on neighborhood effects provide reason to reenvision Head Start. The first change is the large increase in access to public prekindergarten programs in the last twenty-five years. Evaluations of universal prekindergarten have shown benefits for the nonpoor as well as the poor, suggesting that these programs may offer a suitable alternative to Head Start for three- and four-year-olds.[43] Such an alternative could be designed to offer better pedagogical opportunities and to be practically integrated with K–12 education. Second, evidence has amassed that intervening in the prenatal-to-age-three period can improve children's developmental trajectories.[44] What Head Start has uniquely offered to poor communities prior to primary schooling—a comprehensive approach focused on health, child development, and family supports—is needed as much as ever today, especially now that we know that much earlier interventions provide children with a true head start. Third, new research on social mobility in the United States and community characteristics suggests that certain neighborhoods are associated with not only higher levels of disadvantage but much lower rates of social mobility across generations than other neighborhoods.[45] This suggests the urgent need to target neighborhood factors in programming that is intended to foster children's learning and development and reduce educational and economic inequality in the United States.

What is the role of Head Start in a future in which public preschool programs in the United States serve a substantially larger proportion of three- and four-year-olds? While Head Start continues to be an important source of preschool education for children living in poverty, it still reaches just a minority of eligible children.[46] Children from advantaged families are now participating in preschool education at far higher rates and are enrolled in preschool education programs at even younger ages, so the program no longer offers much of a "head start" relative to the educational opportunities enjoyed by many other children. As states implement universal preschool initiatives, these services will ultimately reach a much larger proportion of children across income groups throughout the country. Given the enormous size of the income-based disparities that are present at kindergarten entry, a true head start for children from the most-disadvantaged backgrounds needs to begin much earlier and offer more continuous services.[47] Taking these bold steps would allow Head Start to fulfill its mission of giving children living in poverty a better chance to develop early learning skills and a better opportunity to succeed in school.

A New Vision for Head Start

We propose that Head Start be reimagined and reinvigorated by building off its core mission and existing resources to realign it toward three crucial roles moving forward:

1 *Targeting the youngest children in areas of concentrated poverty and those who face significant family adversities with services starting before or at birth:* The new Head Start would provide more intensive and specific program components to address the sources of stress in the most vulnerable families. In addition, it would provide early child development and family-focused services primarily from the prenatal period to age three, with some continuing to receive services for ages three to school entry. Existing federal funding sources for home visiting would be integrated into this new Head Start program, building off existing support for evidence-based models, and home visiting would be offered as a core element of Head Start together with center-based early learning and comprehensive services.

2 *Creating strong links between early health and development by integrating pediatricians and early intervention services providers into comprehensive services hubs:* In addition to providing comprehensive learning and intensive support to parents and families, Head Start facilities would serve as community hubs. In this role, the programs would not only link participating families to community services (as they have done historically) but also provide training and support for other community-based service providers in their area (for example, early care and education programs). This support would focus on evidence-based and curricular interventions to address sources of severe stress and disadvantage.

3 *Generating innovations in the birth-to-age-three field:* With the greater focus on early learning services starting at birth and further development as community hubs, Head Start programs would serve as innovation laboratories for the integration of

scientific knowledge, experimentation, and innovation in program service models that serve the continuum of children from birth to school entry—particularly those models focused on sources of severe stress, such as parent mental health issues, deep poverty, substance use, or interpersonal conflict and violence.

Several aspects of Head Start make it uniquely suited to filling these three critical programmatic roles. First, Head Start facilities are well equipped and widespread, with most already located in the highest-need areas. In addition, Head Start has high name recognition and generally enjoys the trust of residents and leadership in low-income communities. Further, all three of the roles involved in reinvigorating Head Start are grounded in long-standing tenets of the program, which would be updated and strengthened to meet the contemporary needs of children, families, and low-income communities. Finally, Head Start has always had a highly dedicated staff, many of whom are rooted in the community.

In recent years, Head Start has made strong advances in the educational training and credentialing of staff and leadership (for example, the 2015 revised performance standards). When Head Start was last reauthorized in 2007, several important changes were included for Early Head Start, and more than half of all new program funding was targeted to Early Head Start expansion. In addition, some centers have sought to convert more slots from Head Start to Early Head Start. The new program direction we propose here is consistent with and would accelerate the direction in which Head Start has already been heading.

Focusing on the Most Vulnerable Children from the Earliest Years

We propose eliminating the distinction between what is now Early Head Start and Head Start. There would simply be one Head Start that serves children from the prenatal period to the point of universal school entry in an area. Evidence-based service models would be developed and implemented that are based on the primacy of working with children from the most-disadvantaged circumstances starting as early as possible in their lives and continuing for their first few years.

We propose two sets of targeting criteria: one at the community level and the other at the family level. Together, these criteria would provide a consistent approach to targeting intensive services in the prenatal-to-age-three developmental period. Currently, the patchwork of home-visiting and parenting programs and specialized services for families with high levels of adversity does not utilize consistent criteria for identifying and serving the most vulnerable.

TARGETING CHILDREN GROWING UP IN COMMUNITIES OF CONCENTRATED DISADVANTAGE

Children growing up in areas of concentrated poverty experience heightened and multiple risks and limited opportunities. Nearly 600,000 children, or 5 percent of all children under age three, live in such areas.[48] The overall child poverty rate in these communities is over 60 percent, and more than 80 percent experience child poverty during their first five years. The powerful predictive relationship between neighborhood poverty during childhood and both childhood well-being and adult social mobility provides a strong rationale for neighborhood-based targeting.[49]

We propose universal site-level eligibility for all children residing in a designated high-poverty area whose overall concentrated poverty level is above a defined threshold (such as a household poverty rate of 33 percent or higher).[50] Market-based early care and education services, especially programs serving young infants and toddlers, are often in especially limited supply in such communities. Our proposal would shift the primary eligibility criteria for Head Start in these areas to community poverty rather than family poverty. Levels of community-level poverty would need to be updated periodically (for example, every ten years or at some other appropriate time interval), with community-based eligibility revised accordingly, and new service opportunities would be prioritized in areas where poverty is newly becoming concentrated. If and when areas of concentrated poverty change over time, the thresholds for community-based poverty could be revised (for example, from 33 percent community-level poverty to 30 percent) or individual-based eligibility could be ex-

panded to those living in a broader geographic area relative to existing Head Start sites.[51]

TARGETING CHILDREN IN POOR FAMILIES FACING
PARTICULARLY ADVERSE CIRCUMSTANCES

Family-level eligibility would target subgroups of disadvantaged families experiencing hardships that warrant early, intensive, and comprehensive services—for example, children with special needs, families who have had contact with state and local child welfare systems,
and families that have experienced domestic violence, parental substance abuse or mental health issues, or homelessness. These children
would benefit from a comprehensive services model that reaches
them early and serves them continuously over the early years. Although children in areas of highly concentrated poverty experience
such adversities at disproportionate levels, they are not the only children who experience them. For example, researchers have found that
rates of substantiated abuse and neglect in neighborhoods of highly
concentrated poverty are between two and eight times higher than
overall levels, controlling for other characteristics. So even though
there is significant overlap in these two groups, the majority of child
abuse and neglect cases are in fact outside the target communities
and involve children and families who might benefit from Head
Start.[52]

Head Start currently prioritizes for enrollment children and families who face many of these circumstances. For example, in the most
recent program year for which data are available, approximately
50,000 children, or 5 percent of all children served in Head Start, experienced homelessness at or during the time they were enrolled; 2
percent of enrolled children were in foster care during the program
year (and a larger share were referrals from child welfare agencies);
and 12 percent were children with special needs.[53] In the proposed
program, we would further develop channels for referrals through
primary health care systems—prenatal clinics, hospitals, and health
care settings that provide well-child care—and program sites for the
Supplemental Nutrition Program for Women, Infants, and Children
(WIC) program. WIC's program assistance to pregnant women and
young children has a very high rate of program participation by eli-

gible families, including in areas of concentrated poverty. Family-level screening systems such as those recently implemented through universal home visits in Durham, North Carolina, have been effective in identifying families exposed to high adversity before or very soon after birth.[54] Incorporating more consistent universal screenings in pediatric practices, especially in disadvantaged communities, could provide an accurate population-based approach to determining eligibility for the new Head Start, particularly for those who do not live in an area of highly concentrated poverty.

We propose that approximately half of Head Start centers would be strategically placed over time to serve catchment areas of varying population in the most-disadvantaged communities with the highest level of childhood poverty.[55] The other half would be strategically mapped and targeted to serve the maximum number of children living outside of those areas who have the adversities or developmental challenges warranting this early intervention.

Implementing these two forms of targeting together could introduce equity issues, as would be the case with any program not made available to all of the eligible population wanting to participate. Families living in areas just below the high-concentration threshold would be eligible through family-level eligibility rather than neighborhood-level criteria. There may also be large geographical areas where only a few poor families experience these adversities and so the numbers would not be high enough to warrant a local Head Start site within commuting distance. Indeed, the current program experiences equity issues in access. Head Start currently serves fewer than half of the three- and four-year-old children in poor families who are eligible for the program, and fewer than one in twenty infants and toddlers in poor families are served by Early Head Start. Moreover, it should be acknowledged that a child in a family whose income is slightly above the cutoff might have needs comparable to or greater than those of children below it.

A New Service Model for Head Start

The evidence base for birth-to-age-three program models, though not as extensive as that for quality preschool-age education, has grown considerably in the past decade.[56] Our proposal would both build on these tested models and seek to generate new innovations. As the starting point, Head Start's new services model would have a home-visiting service component; focused on child development and parenting services, this component would be strongly linked to children's primary care, beginning prenatally and extending through at least infancy. By the second year, children would transition to high-quality center-based care, where, depending on the family's needs, part-day (three hours) or full-day (six hours) services would be offered five days a week, as well as wraparound care services funded through the ACE subsidies for dual-eligible, low-income working families.

HOME-VISITING MODELS TAILORED TO FAMILY RISKS AND STRENGTHS

After enrollment, the data from the initial screening in prenatal-care and early primary-care settings on families' areas of risks and strengths would determine the content of home-visit support. Initial home visits would aim to prepare the parents for the birth of the child, ensure access to and follow-up from prenatal care visits, and support the family's planning for the period after birth, including attention to housing and other supports needed for their stability in the first months. Key core parenting behavior would be encouraged during the first six months, including responsive and stimulating parenting in the context of good nutrition and maternal and infant health.[57] In contrast to Early Head Start's inconsistent service delivery today, home visiting would be used in all Head Start programs to match individual curricula to the particular needs of each family. Core home-visiting content would be supplemented by more specific content tailored to the family's particular risks and goals, as assessed both before and after the birth.

Home visitation services could be modeled on programs that have successfully focused visits on particular sources of stress, such as maternal depression, substance abuse, domestic violence, or responsive parenting for families in significant need of parenting support in order to prevent child abuse or neglect as much as possible.[58] For example, the Nurse-Family Partnership has recently adapted its core model to address more effectively the needs of first-time mothers struggling with depression or intimate partner violence—two of the areas of focus in our proposed Head Start program.[59] This program has an extensive evidence base that consistently identifies short-term benefits, including reduced child maltreatment, as well as longer-term benefits for children's behavioral changes.[60] Other programs have used videotaped feedback mechanisms, building on strengths observed in parent-child interactions in even the highest-risk families.[61] Our proposed Head Start program would use and extend resources such as the U.S. Department of Health and Human Services' "Home Visiting Evidence of Effectiveness" reports to encourage the use and adaptation of evidence-based models.[62]

The home visits could also be used to encourage mothers to attend primary and preventive health care prenatally and during the child's first years. This approach could feature consistent communication and coordination to support mothers' utilization of well-child visits and primary care. Referrals to more specialized supports (for example, mental health care) would also be followed up and coordinated through the trusted figure of the home visitor. Recent technological innovations may enable low-cost innovations, such as tablet-based or texting support for early nutrition and cognitive stimulation, that could be integrated into the program model of parenting support.[63]

A CENTER-BASED EARLY LEARNING PROGRAM THAT INCLUDES COMPREHENSIVE SERVICES AND A HOME-VISITING SERVICE

Families with working parents would be eligible for licensed care opportunities during their children's infancy (before age twelve months) and for extended hours of center-based care (at the Head Start site if enough families are eligible), using Assurance subsidies toward the cost of care. Dual-eligible families—those who qualify for both Head Start and ACE subsidies—would be expected to participate in Head Start center-based care as a component of ongoing enrollment. As with the home-visiting model, local centers would choose from a menu of evidence-based models for early care and education provider training, including on-site observation and mentoring.[64] This program could be modeled on the Infant Health and Development Program (IHDP), which demonstrated that center-based comprehensive care, starting during the second year, was responsible for long-term academic gains among the most socioeconomically disadvantaged participants.[65]

The home-visiting functions during the prenatal and infancy period to support the family would be transferred to a well-trained family support worker based at the early learning center, who would flexibly provide center-based or home-based support to supplement the center-based learning program. This staff member would have the mental health expertise to address any continued sources of severe family stress. In addition, this staff member would continue to assess and support the family's economic, housing, nutrition, and other needs through regular contact with the family. Finally, at the program level, early intervention services to address developmental delays or disabilities could be coordinated through the center, particularly in areas with a weak infrastructure for early intervention.

Head Start Centers as Hubs for Improving Birth-to-Age-Three Service Systems

Reconceived Head Start centers would serve as hubs that create strong links between early health, child development, and family support services and a more effective early care and education workforce. As community hubs, Head Start centers would help coordinate and support the full-service needs of enrolled children and also provide family support services to children and families served by other early childhood program providers in the area, including those in ACE-funded programs and universal early education programs.

Community hubs could serve several other important functions. First, they would provide a setting for community-level support of the prenatal-to-age-three workforce. The coordinated support of caregivers, family support workers, health and mental health providers, and (when applicable) early intervention teams could benefit from regular contact and, when needed, co-location. This workforce, serving the youngest children in the United States, is perhaps the least supported among the different workforces in education. A learning collaborative approach for such interdisciplinary groups has recently shown positive impacts on outcomes in early childhood.[66]

Second, the hubs would serve as access points for a range of other programs supporting low-income families. Many Head Start families are likely to qualify for a range of safety-net programs, such as WIC, SNAP, Medicaid, the Child Health Insurance Program (CHIP), and other programs. Head Start sites could become satellite enrollment locations, as has been done with SNAP programs in many states and localities.[67]

Third, the hubs could provide professional development for a range of child care programs in their neighborhoods. Coaching and mentoring home-based child care providers, for example, has proven successful in some evaluations in improving the quality of care and could be adapted for this Head Start model, with the center perhaps serving as a location for training coaches.[68] Hub staff could perform these roles centrally (at the hub), or they could rotate across other community- and school-based early learning facilities, depending on the economies of scale and proximity.

Head Start: A National Laboratory for Model Development, Innovation, and Rigorous Evaluation of Outcomes

The new Head Start program would contribute to the assessment of what works best in early care and education. As discussed in this chapter, there have been advances in recent years, including a handful of program models for infant and toddler early education services that have been shown by a systematic evidence review of high-quality studies to have had positive impacts on outcomes, as well as programs focused on home visiting and specific areas of parenting.[69] However, more design and experimentation are needed to foster a new wave of competitive innovation, demonstration, and testing.[70] These efforts should focus on the large gaps that remain in the evidence base on prenatal-to-age-three services, particularly with respect to integrating parenting, home visitation, and early learning services as well as curriculum and professional development. This role will be especially crucial in the first decade of transition.

Experimentation would include rapid testing cycles and comparisons of benefits from multiple new models, including program components that may be directed at particular groups of vulnerable children (such as those who are in the child welfare system, those from families facing other traumas or adverse circumstances, or dual-language learners). New models would be evaluated using small-scale efficacy trials followed by large-scale effectiveness trials and scale-up—an approach that has been used successfully in educational and prevention research in the United States.[71] Rapid-cycle innovation models drawn from continuous quality improvement (CQI) would be encouraged.[72]

The Head Start program would develop an integrated large-scale data infrastructure to enable cost-effective experimentation. All Head Start centers would collect and report comparable data on teacher, family, parent, and child characteristics, and developmental and program quality assessments. The data infrastructure would be designed to allow these data to be randomized within localities or larger geographic units.[73]

Transitioning to the New Head Start

We envision that the new Head Start program would initially be developed to serve at least the number of children as the current program—between 900,000 and 1 million annually. These levels would begin to grow incrementally over the first five years as the program is expanded to focus on more very young children and, where possible, preschool-age program services are converted to serve younger children and new models of infant-and-toddler-focused services continue to be tested for efficacy.

Within ten years there would be a significant shift in the number and age distribution of children in Head Start. More than 80 percent of the children currently enrolled in Head Start and Early Head Start are ages three and four (table 5.1). Should universal early education for children beginning at ages three or four approach full implementation across most of the country within ten years, we would anticipate at that point more than 80 percent of Head Start children being under age three (scenario A in table 5.1).[74] In states that are already closer to serving many three- and four-year-olds, this broad-based shift could occur within five or six years.

In addition, some states may choose not to take advantage of even a generous federal funding incentive to build universal preschool education. Today there are twenty states that have yet to offer state-

Table 5.1 *Enrollment in Head Start in 2015 and Enrollment in the Proposed New Head Start Under Two Scenarios*

Child Age	Current Number Served (Percentage Distribution)	Scenario A: Potential Number Served (Percentage)	Scenario B: Potential Number Served (Percentage)
Pregnant women	5,000 (less than 1%)	250,000 (25%)	250,000 (20%)
Less than one	45,000 (5%)		
Age one	50,000 (5%)	275,000 (27.5%)	275,000 (22%)
Age two	70,000 (8%)	300,000 (30%)	300,000 (22%)
Age three	345,000 (36%)	125,000 (12.5%)	300,000 (24%)
Age four (and five)	425,000 (45%)	50,000 (5%)	150,000 (8%)
Total funded enrollment (number of slots)	940,000	1,000,000	1,250,000

Source: 2015 enrollment figures from U.S. DHHS/ACF/OHS 2015.

funded prekindergarten programs or that serve fewer than 5 percent of their three- and four-year-olds. As such, though we would seek to transition to our earlier-age model for Head Start gradually to coordinate with state-level variations in pace and intentions among the states expanding preschool (for example, to serve all three-year-olds and four-year-olds, or to serve all four-year-olds), the Head Start slots for three- and four-year-olds in states that are not expanding preschool would at least be maintained at their current levels. Head Start would also be expanded to serve infants and toddlers in these states, and many centers would adopt programs that serve children from birth to school entry. For illustrative purposes, scenario B in table 5.1 suggests the potential size and distribution of children by age where a significant number of states do not expand preschool and very few states reach universality for three-year-olds.

Following the transition in Head Start enrollments, children in states that have developed universal early education programs would enroll in these programs in September of the year they turn three or four, depending on the age of universal access in the state. In states that expand their preschool to serve four-year-olds but not three-year-olds, existing levels of Head Start funds for three- and four-year-olds might be used to supplement preschool funds to provide slots for all eligible Head Start children at age three so that these children who most need these services can receive them for two years of preschool before kindergarten entry.

OVERLAP WITH ASSURING CARE AND EDUCATION FOR YOUNG CHILDREN

The Head Start program would primarily serve children with the most acute needs, regardless of parental employment status. For low- and moderate-income working families with children ages zero to three, the primary system of support would be the Assuring Care and Education for Young Children subsidy system described in chapter 3. The ACE subsidies would be flexible enough to enable the broad range of working families to make early care and education arrangements consistent with their own needs. As envisioned, the children of most low-income and even very low-income families with parents who work significant hours would be served through the ACE subsidy system, though there would be overlapping eligibility for those in higher-risk circumstances, and some could be enrolled in Head Start alongside additional wraparound care services funded with the Assurance. Some families eligible for ACE subsidies might still choose Head Start because of limited early care and education alternatives in their area. Just as likely, however, is a working family with both Head Start and ACE subsidy eligibility opting to use the subsidy to purchase the available care options that best correspond with their work needs, while seeking additional early intervention or family support services through the Head Start program in its (auxiliary) hub capacity. Also, families who enroll a child in Head Start prenatally or soon after birth and later become eligible for ACE subsidies would be allowed to keep the child in Head Start, while taking advantage of the subsidy for additional hours of care that correspond to their employment needs.

Serving infants and toddlers is more costly than serving preschool- age children, because toddler care requires lower adult-child ratios. At the same time, a specialized and better-qualified workforce, in- cluding social workers to serve as family support staff, will be essen- tial to realizing the hub capacities of Head Start centers to coordinate early care and education with children's and families' health care needs and individualized early intervention services for specific children. Thus, our reenvisioned Head Start will require gradually increased funding levels.

Head Start would continue to be a federal government-to-grantee program, with states being eligible grantees, as is currently the case for Early Head Start but not Head Start. The program would retain its current funding and governance structure: primarily federally funded with grantees expected to contribute 20 percent of total resources either through matching dollars or in-kind resources. The existing federal Mother, Infant, and Early Childhood Home Visiting Program would also be fully integrated into the new Head Start program. In addition, the program would continue to be offered at no cost to highly disadvantaged families with children. Families who are in Head Start and getting ACE subsidies for extended-hours care would be expected to contribute their parent share of the costs for the extended hours, but not for the core Head Start program services.

Hubs would, at minimum, employ a core staff of full-time, master's-level social workers and case managers to work with families and children, as well as child development specialists to screen, identify, and diagnose children in the poorest communities for early intervention needs. The centers would also employ health and mental health professionals, whose services would be billed through families' health insurance. Some Head Start programs are already providing early intervention services to address special needs and developmental delays, and with increased coverage by Head Start of infants and toddlers, more centers may be able to do so in the future.[75]

As public preschool is expanded, Head Start programs would shift to serving the birth-to-age-three population. There are several ways to sequence this transition. For example, when existing Head Start grants come up for renewal in five-year cycles, new grant opportunities could be targeted for services to younger populations depending on the preschool services available or under development in the community. In states and areas that do not create or expand preschool within ten years, birth-to-age-five and preschool-only Head Start service models may persist past the ten-year implementation and scale-up of this proposal. For details on the cost of the changes to Head Start see table A5.1.

As part of the evaluation goals for Head Start, existing and new service models will be tested at scale. While encouraging the use of common service approaches (for example, the sequence of home visitation and center-based early care and education), these R&D initiatives would encourage the development and testing of different curricula, staffing requirements, and other elements. Planned variation studies could answer questions about the appropriate intensity and dosage of particular components. In addition to a gradual rollout and expansion of the core Head Start service model, hub services would similarly be developed and expanded over ten years and would include their own R&D efforts. All of these initiatives would build on recent efforts to innovate within Early Head Start and the birth-to-age-three field, such as the Early Head Start–Child Care Partnerships and Educare.[76]

OPPORTUNITIES FOR CURRENT AND NEW HEAD START PROVIDERS

Many of the Head Start centers could be built around existing high-quality Early Head Start and Head Start programs, particularly those located in areas of concentrated disadvantage. These would become some of the baseline Head Start centers serving children from birth. New entrants into Head Start could be identified through competitive grants targeted to currently underserved locations. Some existing programs that are early intervention services providers or community health centers could become new Head Start program centers.

Alternatives and Trade-Offs

Our proposal for Head Start as a program serving infants and toddlers from the most vulnerable families in the United States represents a major change to the current program. There are several possible alternatives to making such a shift. First, Head Start could continue as the federal portion of preschool education in the United States, focusing on the poor. As states expand prekindergarten programs, Head Start could continue to primarily serve preschool-age children under the federal poverty line. We believe that simply continuing Head Start's current mission in this way, however, is no longer aligned with developments in early childhood education given the widespread gaps in access for a wide range of low- and middle-income children.

Our proposal for universal preschool sees the federal role as incentiv-izing states to expand their programs as the country moves toward preschool for all three- and four-year-olds.

Another alternative might be for Head Start to primarily serve children from birth to age three, but without focusing on the most vulnerable children. We believe that the lifelong consequences of se-vere early adversity in education, health, and circumstances warrant an intensive focus on identifying children exposed to these condi-tions as early as possible. Although the current proposal might not cover all of this population, particularly during the transition period, we believe that a sustained national effort to reduce the effects of toxic stress on the youngest Americans is critical for both develop-mental and long-range policy goals.

Summary and Conclusion

The prenatal period and the first 1,000 days of a child's life are critical for establishing a positive trajectory of health, learning, and behavior and have long-term implications for later child and adult outcomes.[77] Yet with a patchwork of early care and education policies that are even more threadbare than programs for preschool-age children and their families, this period is the least consistently supported in the United States. Concentrating support on those families who most need it, our proposal for Head Start would advance the field by real-izing the unfulfilled promise of Early Head Start and leveraging the expansion of universal prekindergarten at the state level. This fun-damental revision of Head Start would offer an opportunity for greater innovation in birth-to-age-three services, while also provid-ing greater and more consistent coverage to the most vulnerable fam-ilies. Building the next generation of interventions at scale to address sources of severe adversity at the family and community levels would powerfully complement the more widely targeted supports we pro-pose in family leave, child care, and preschool education.

CONCLUSION: NO MORE TINKERING AT THE EDGES

6

In chapter 1, we introduced two families whose struggles in providing for their young children's care and learning were emblematic of our country's inadequate infrastructure for early care and education. In both Benji's and Adrienne's families, the parents were unable to access and arrange the early care and education that they wanted for their children's development, and the limited supports left them unable to adequately meet their work and family needs. Both families would have fared much better under our proposed approach to integrated early childhood policy, as presented in chapters 2 to 5. Benji's parents would have had twelve to sixteen weeks of paid parental leave, instead of the unpaid month his mother took off for Benji and the two weeks she took off after the birth of his brother. Benji's grandmother would still have been able to provide the earlier care for both him and his brother, but she could have felt more comfortable accepting some payment from her daughter, knowing that a significant share of the costs would be offset through the expanded Child and Dependent Care Tax Credit. Most importantly, Benji could have been enrolled in an early care and education setting at age two, when his parents believed he was ready to receive such early enrichment. He could have then transitioned to free, high-quality preschool by age three or four.

Adrienne's parents also would have had up to sixteen weeks of paid leave following her birth, which would have provided considerable benefit over the seven unpaid days her mother actually took. They would have received subsidies for higher-cost, higher-quality, and potentially more stable infant child care, an improvement over the series of short-term arrangements in providers' homes where Adrienne essentially was left to watch television. As the value of the subsidy phased down, her family's share would have increased as their income rose, preventing Adrienne from being kicked out of her care arrangement at that point. Adrienne's mother, Diane, would have had access to stable, reliable, and high-quality care, which probably would have increased her job stability and boosted, rather than threatened, her children's early learning. This outcome would have been a stark contrast to the job transitions and twenty-five different arrangements she had to make for her children. Finally, stress levels regarding child care and finances for both Benji's and Adrienne's parents would have been dramatically reduced, with potential benefits for the well-being and learning of their children.

This book argues for more equal opportunity beginning at birth. We argue that a nation with the resources of the United States has a responsibility to give all children a fair chance at the best start in life, so that where an individual begins due to the lottery of birth does not control his or her destiny. We also believe that the common good is served when individuals can make the most of their own abilities in the pursuit of their dreams—economically, with greater wealth for the nation and an improved standard of living; socially, with a fairer and more just society; and politically as we move toward a more perfect union.

We began this book describing the large disparities in early childhood development and learning that exacerbate rather than remedy the inequality crisis in the United States. Economic inequality has surged as real wages have remained stagnant or declined for the majority of workers over the last four decades and the growth in Americans' levels of educational attainment has slowed. The United States has become more unequal by income than at any time in its history, and more unequal by wealth than it has been for the last eighty years.[1] Moreover, income inequality in the United States is higher than in any other advanced economy in the world today.[2] Educational inequality in the United States, as measured by disparities in children's skills across levels of parent education and family income, is also among the highest of the OECD countries. Most of this skill gap is already apparent at school entry and does not grow substantially across childhood and adolescence.[3]

Addressing economic and educational inequality requires public and private investment across the life cycle, from birth through adulthood. In our existing system, we rely heavily on families' own private investments during the birth-to-age-five period. Families bear responsibility for the costs of raising children precisely during the years when those costs are highest and when their children's brain development is most sensitive to environmental influence. The result is that children born into families in less-advantaged circumstances have the least access to resources and services that can support development and learning, a pattern that increases rather than reduces disparities across the life course. Addressing inequality from the first day of life—by effectively investing more public resources in early care and learning—is among the most necessary and effective steps for narrowing social and economic inequalities and promoting long-term economic growth for the nation.

The current early childhood policy landscape in the United States has piecemeal elements of the service systems that we propose in chapters 2 through 5: many state prekindergarten programs that cover a varying share of preschool-age children; paid leave laws in a few states; a child care subsidy program; and a federal Head Start program. While each of these elements provides services to a segment of the population, each is underdeveloped and underfunded and fails to reach most of the children and families who could potentially benefit. Further, these elements often operate in parallel or in isolation from each other, with little coordination and no seamless handoffs for children and families. Moreover, the evidence that we have reviewed in these chapters suggests that most of these systems provide services of minimal to mediocre quality, particularly with respect to interactions between children and their adult teachers and caregivers—a key factor that spurs children's learning in the early years. Central contributors to the low levels of quality are poor compensation and the lack of the training and mentorship that could otherwise boost the skills of the early care and education workforce.

Nearly all past early childhood policy efforts have addressed only a piece of what is needed for a comprehensive and coordinated birth-to-age-five policy in the United States. Each incremental step has focused on one service system (for example, pre-K), one narrow age group or population of children (for example, children of working parents or four-year-olds), or one problem component of existing services (for example, low-quality care or equity of access), often in isolation. All of these efforts are important. There has been growing momentum to address the long-standing challenge of inadequate infrastructure to support children's early care, development, and education. Yet there is little or no articulation of what the end-goal looks like and how these efforts could work together to form a single coherent policy that raises the quality of early learning for young children and reduces early inequality. If they remain piecemeal, these burgeoning policy efforts could risk further fragmentation and an inadequate response to the wide disparities that such concerted action is intended to address.

In chapters 2 to 5, we described the elements of a bold strategy of coherent, coordinated investments to build an early childhood infrastructure that provides:

· Federal paid parental leave for all employed parents of newborns for the first twelve to sixteen weeks of life
· Expanded subsidies and tax credits for care and education between birth and age five that together provide reliable and meaningful help for working parents to support high-quality care and education for their young children
· An earlier common starting point for universal public education—at age three—with universal access to state-administered, high-quality early education
· A reinvented Head Start, focused primarily on ages birth to age three, that would provide more intensive services to children and families who live in concentrated poverty and experience multiple adversities

This comprehensive approach builds on current evidence about what works; invests in higher-quality services while expanding access; and provides continual investments in research and development to build the evidence base and further improve outcomes over time. Taken together, this plan would offer all children the developmental and early learning opportunities they need, lay a strong foundation for our nation's economic future, and improve social mobility.

In this chapter, we discuss our plan as a whole, projecting its potential benefits, providing an overview of the investments that would be required, and describing how this comprehensive vision can be realized.

A Balanced Plan for Meeting Young Children and Families Where They Are with What They Need

A key challenge discussed throughout this book is how to make the public investments in early care and education that will help parents support their children's development in the early years while also supporting families' private responsibility, autonomy, and formative role in their children's lives. We seek to balance public investments in opportunities for children's early learning with parents' responsibility to care for their children consistent with their needs, preferences, and circumstances. The questions of whether, how much, and when each parent works represent choices and conditions within labor markets that we do not directly address in our proposed plan. Each of our proposed policies allows for flexibility in parents' choice of the right balance between work and direct caregiving in the early years. For example, paid parental leave would allow for more flexibility and security for parents to time their return to employment in ways that support child-rearing. When parents return to work, they would have access to financial assistance to use a range of early care and education options, based on their own employment demands, family needs, and choices for their children. Parents would share the financial responsibility for many of their children's services, from receiving partial pay during their parental leave period to making payments toward their share of the costs for early care and education services based on their family income.

Our plan calls for a substantial increase in public funding, but it also relies on parents and the private market to choose and provide high-quality early care settings. These settings would be subsidized with funding at levels adequate for providing high-quality services. Our subsidies for children's care and education would be available for eligible families to use at private, not-for-profit, and public early care and education centers and licensed family child care homes, while expanded tax credits would help support the costs of child care for all families, including home-based care by relatives or family friends. Similarly, we expect that some employers could offer additional or more generous paid leave benefits to their employees or provide on-site child care when family costs are being subsidized, building on the proposed public investments.

We recommend devoting substantial public investments to broad-based services for paid leave and preschool because the need for these services is widely shared and middle-class families struggle with the lack of infrastructure for them. For preschool, the evidence suggests that all families would benefit, with the less-advantaged benefiting more. There is widespread demand and ample evidence to support the need for high-quality universal preschool education, and having all families invested in the programs and broadly sharing their services raises the potential for higher quality.

The more targeted aspects of our plan address specific sources of need—such as the needs of working parents who disproportionately use infant and toddler care, or the needs of those living in concentrated-poverty areas or adverse household circumstances. Our plan would ensure a more effective use of the resources needed to serve those with the greatest disadvantages, who may need services that differ in focus, content, or intensity. There is little evidence, for example, to support the provision of ongoing, intensive home visiting to all families regardless of their level of risk. Among the downsides of such targeting is the possibility of isolating the population served; as a result, the services they receive may not be comparable to the services available to families who can afford to pay for them. This is one reason why we have proposed the national Head Start program—which is generally regarded as successful and not as stigmatizing—as the platform upon which to build a carefully targeted set of supports to reduce high levels of adversity.

In our effort to broaden opportunities in early care and education, we pay special attention to the potential tension between greater access and quality. Rather than examine access and quality as two separate issues in early care and education, we jointly examine the current state of access and quality across income groups. We observe that although the overall quality of early care and education settings is distressingly low—particularly for instructional quality, which predicts cognitive development—children whose families are in the two lowest income quintiles (annual incomes of less than $42,000) fare even worse than the general population. These children are the least likely to have access to early care and education, and when they do, they are the most likely to experience low quality. This double whammy relegates children in disadvantaged families to lower opportunities for early learning and reduced social mobility.

Our proposal pairs investments in quality with expanded access. Research strongly indicates that higher-quality care and education provides substantially greater and more lasting benefits for children, particularly those who face the most limited access.[4] The magnitude of the income gaps in achievement and development call for significant public investments to narrow the gap in high-quality care and education opportunities. For both our Assuring Care and Education for Young Children proposal and universal preschool education initiatives, we emphasize ensuring that funding is adequate to support hiring well-trained staff, and that on-site coaching and mentoring support is paired with evidence-based curricula to enhance quality. We also encourage innovation in the content of such quality supports through monitoring and evaluation.

Following the U.S. federalist tradition, public investment and responsibility in the early childhood field is shared across the federal, state, and local levels. In elementary and secondary education, states and localities have long had primary responsibility, and passage of the Every Student Succeeds Act in 2015 reinforced this historic trend. In that sector, the federal government's role has often been to supplement funding for vulnerable children, including those with low incomes or special needs, in order to provide more equity in access and quality. Disagreements remain, however, about the size and scope of the federal role in public education and about the policy areas and tools that should be in its purview. The distribution of roles and responsibilities in early care and education contrasts with that for elementary and secondary education. Federal supports, such as Head Start and the Child Care and Development Block Grant, have been a more significant source of funding for young children for a longer time. Also, as in many other areas of social policy, such as supports to low-income families for food assistance, housing, and health insurance, the federal government has initiated policy interventions and provided the lion's share of the funding. Some state governments have provided matching funds, and in most cases state and local providers have taken the lead on implementation.

Our plan relies on a combination of state, federal, and local governance. In universal preschool education for ages three and four, for example, the federal government would play a larger role during the transition period and scale back its efforts over time as states take on primary responsibility for these systems and create stronger ties with K–12 education. For paid parental leave, the federal government would have primary responsibility, much as with Social Security. Head Start would continue to have a federal-to-local finance and administrative structure, one that has historically ensured high community buy-in and ownership.

Getting from Here to There

Building a coherent system requires a phased approach to building systems and governance capacity, thereby ensuring that new program investments are effective. To do this well will require sequencing component changes and expansions; enhancing workforce capacity; aligning across systems; and supporting a coherent research and development strategy.

We propose sequencing component expansions incrementally over a ten-year period, laying the foundation for steady development of high-quality services. For example, we envision that the ACE subsidies would create additional consumer demand, driving incremental growth over time in new market supplies of center-based care and licensed high-quality home-based care. States and localities would supplement this process by using contracted care in locations, such as rural areas, where these market forces may fail to materialize. Similarly, our proposal would provide federal funding to help public education systems shift to an earlier beginning and gradually shift Head Start resources away from preschool education in the process.

Possibly the greatest challenge to the success of our proposal, and a major reason to implement the expansions gradually, is the need for a vastly larger and more skilled workforce for the early childhood system. Given that caregiver- or teacher-child interactions are the key element to higher quality and improved child developmental outcomes, the success of this plan will depend on a prepared workforce. Early care and education providers will need to be adequately compensated if high-caliber staff are to be attracted, rewarded, and retained. High-quality education opportunities in early childhood at two- and four-year colleges should incorporate on-site practica with mentoring, as well as career ladders and continuing education opportunities for professionals to move up from assistants to lead teachers, to mentors or coaches, to program leadership. Coaching and in-service training should be offered to educators and others, such as home-based child care providers, who have had little access to quality professional development. Our plan would make reenvisioned Head Start centers key hubs for supporting this role of generating a more skilled workforce.

We seek to align more closely the service systems for children and families that currently operate quite separately. Millions of American families have great difficulty constructing a manageable and affordable sequence of quality care and learning settings for their children's first years that aligns (rather than conflicts) with their work hours and careers. Several aspects of our proposed policy aim to increase this alignment. First, some programs would build on familiar systems in Americans' lives. For example, we propose making paid parental leave a federal social insurance program like Social Security, which is already familiar to many families. In addition, we would put local elementary schools in the driver's seat for families accessing public preschool even when schools are working in concert with community-based providers, allowing families to use the most familiar entry point. Accessing universal preschool will be on par with enrolling in local kindergarten, a common experience across all communities.

Second, we promote better, more seamless transitions across services. A working mother who has a young infant and is returning to work from paid parental leave will be able to enroll in early care and education with Assurance subsidies prior to the week she plans to return to work, even if she chooses to return to work before the full leave period is up. In the infant-toddler years, children's health and early learning services often operate in separate spheres with little coordination. Our proposal would deepen the integration that often occurs within Head Start by expanding this program's family support staff to include providers qualified to offer or manage services across mental health, physical health, and child development and developing their capacities to make stronger ties to primary care settings.

Finally, we propose the pursuit of research-based innovation to continuously improve early childhood policy. Early childhood development programs and policies in the United States have benefited from one of the longest-standing research programs in any educational or social sector, with the first experimental evaluations occurring in the early 1960s. The field now has a database of hundreds of program evaluations across the areas of early education, family support, and health interventions.[5] Yet the research question driving much of this literature—does early care and education "work" compared to no early care and education?—is no longer adequate to meet the goal of building a coordinated and single birth-to-age-five early care and education policy that can test and scale innovative approaches to improving quality.

We believe the next stage of research should focus on new questions in order to drive policy choices and decisions. Among the most urgent is how to improve quality at a large scale. In the large systems that we propose, it is critical to improve assessments of quality, support the early childhood workforce, and better integrate pre-service and in-service training for teachers that is effective at scale. Second, the sequencing of learning supports across ages three to eight would benefit from a robust research agenda focused on intentionally sequencing two years of public preschool education and better aligning pedagogy in the preschool and early elementary school years. Third, the reenvisioned Head Start program will critically require the development and evaluation of new models and testing innovations to address extreme poverty, mental health issues, domestic violence, and substance abuse in the context of very early development. Finally, our integrated proposal covering paid leave and child care through preschool education and beyond will require strong data systems, beginning at birth and allowing for continuous evaluation and research.

Probable Impacts of the Plan

We expect that our plan will substantially increase children's skills by reducing inequities in access to quality early learning, with a range of positive short- and long-term outcomes for both children and their parents.

Universal paid leave starting at birth would benefit all families, with low- and moderate-income families benefiting the most in some respects. These families are currently the least likely to have sufficient leave time to care for their newborns, the least likely to have high-quality alternatives to parental care, and the least likely to have access to unpaid or paid leave.[6] As we showed in chapter 2, those in the lowest quartile of earnings are just one-fourth as likely as those in the highest quartile to have access to any paid leave. Yet even among that highest quartile of earners, just one-fifth have access to paid leave through an employer.[7] Our proposal of up to sixteen weeks of paid leave (and up to forty weeks of job-protected leave per child if both parents maximized paid and unpaid leave allotments through FMLA in addition to their paid leave time) would provide flexibility during the critical early weeks of children's lives for all families, including the well-off, and greatly ease financial pressures, especially for less-well-off families.

Our proposed ACE subsidies and reformed CDCTC policies would replace the current inadequate child care funding streams with a single and powerful guarantee to the nation—that no family will have to spend more than 10 percent of their household income on child care and that all children will have access to high-quality early care and education. Our proposal would address the huge disparities in access to center-based care. In chapter 3, we showed that by age two, children in higher-income families (above 400 percent of the federal poverty line, or $97,000 for a household of four in 2016) were nearly three times more likely to be enrolled in center care than children from low-income families (below 200 percent of the FPL, or $48,500 for a household of four in 2016). In addition, the plan would improve the economic resources and stability of the workers who care for our nation's most precious resource.

Our proposal focuses on reducing the inequalities in access to high-quality preschool that are experienced by three- and four-year-olds in low-income families as well as those from racial and ethnic minority groups and low-income immigrant families. Children from high-income families are currently twice as likely to be enrolled in center-based preschool at age three, and 40 percent more likely to be enrolled at age four, than their counterparts in low-income families (again comparing families with incomes of 400 percent of the FPL or greater with those at 200 percent of the FPL or lower). Research shows that universal, high-quality preschool can benefit both non-poor and poor families, but that the more disadvantaged benefit more; as a result, socioeconomic disparities in school readiness are reduced.[8]

Finally, for the most vulnerable infants and toddlers in our country, we propose a reenvisioned Head Start with a suite of powerful, evidence-based strategies to tackle the sources of severe adversity: deep and persistent poverty, parent mental health or substance abuse, and exposure to family and neighborhood violence. Our vision for Head Start is to greatly strengthen its impact on families who experience toxic stress and subsequently incur a disproportionate share of the costs of social and educational remediation services and involvement in the criminal justice system later in life. Taking an intensive preventive approach early in childhood could result in substantial savings for both these families and society.[9] We would return Head Start to its historic role as a source of innovation in family support and early care by applying new models of parenting support; offering dual-generation programming to enhance parents' education and job skills; and providing family-based prevention and promotion programs to enhance early socioemotional, cognitive, self-regulation and executive function skills among infants and toddlers living in neighborhoods with concentrated disadvantage and family stress.

SHORT- AND LONG-TERM BENEFITS FOR CHILDREN AND PARENTS

We believe that the benefits of this plan would significantly outweigh the costs of investment for generations of American children to come. During the early childhood period, the paid parental leave and Assurance components of the plan would jointly support parents' employment stability, thus increasing families' financial resources. As discussed in chapter 2, the birth of a child can trigger poverty or a substantial loss in income.[10] In our current system, the care of young children falls disproportionately on women. In the absence of adequate public support, juggling work and child care often leads to disruptions in women's work lives or requires a switch to part-time work, both of which can reduce long-term wages and aggregate productivity.[11] Paid leave would provide financial resources to bridge the time needed to care for new children between work periods, and the availability of affordable, high-quality early care and education would increase the likelihood that mothers would return to the workforce (and to their previous employer). Our Assurance system and universal preschool proposals allow families to better afford the hours of care they need, in higher-quality settings, so that more parents can work full-time if they wish. Increased employment rates and long-term wages would raise incomes and payroll tax revenues. Among low-income and single mothers in particular, paid leave may also reduce the use of some means-tested benefits over time, such as SNAP benefits (food stamps).

Increased support for parental leave and child care would also improve children's short- and long-term outcomes. Paid leave across the income span would reduce socioeconomic inequalities in the amount of time parents spend with their newborn children, providing families with greater opportunities to develop strong lifelong bonds. Given the research on paid leave in the states that have implemented it or in other countries, we can expect universal paid leave to result in improved maternal and infant health and improved educational outcomes in the long term.[12] A consistent finding from the early care and education literature is the boost in early cognitive skills from increased access to center-based care for infants and toddlers from low-income families.[13] And consistent with studies of the impact of universal high-quality preschool, our proposed preschool plan for three- and four-year-olds, implemented with quality provisions, would increase children's cognitive skills at school entry, reducing both income-based disparities in school readiness and disparities between dual-language-learner children and other children.[14] Finally, the implementation of evidence-based parenting and family supports through the new Head Start program would reduce the severe stress on both parents and children that is linked to a wide variety of later health, mental health, and learning problems.[15]

Our proposed plan should have long-term benefits as well. Economic evaluations show that high-quality preschool education can have significant benefits on life-course outcomes such as increasing high school graduation and earnings and reducing crime and early childbearing. Studies of the high-quality Tulsa prekindergarten program, for example, as well as both large- and small-scale preschool programs, show benefits that outweigh the costs.[16]

The glaring disparities in earnings across child care and public school workplaces, as well as between preschool and kindergarten teachers and staff, would also be reduced in our plan, and these improvements would translate into higher overall quality levels and lower disparities in the quality of early care and education. All components of the proposal would promote increased support and recognition of the early childhood workforce as a more important and consequential (rather than marginal and underpaid) sector among American workers.

Investments in Young Children

We expect our plan to have strong, sustained impacts worthy of a strong investment. However, these benefits will require an ambitious, comprehensive plan for services for children from birth to age five, and substantial new investments will be needed to truly meet the needs of young children—in large part because existing public investments start from such a low level relative to need.

Current spending on early care and education is very low by several benchmarks: other areas of social-sector spending in the United States; spending on older children; and spending in other high-income nations on young children's development. According to an analysis by the Urban Institute, all federal spending on children in 2014 amounted to $354 billion—10 percent of the $3.5 trillion that the U.S. government spent in that year.[17] This expenditure represented just 2 percent of the U.S. GDP.[18] When we add state and local spending on children—primarily on elementary and secondary education—the proportion of our GDP spent on children increases to just 6 percent.[19]

Very little of this federal, state, and local spending on children is devoted to young children (under age five). We estimate that expenditures in federal and state funding for child care subsidies and tax credits for children under age five, state and local spending on prekindergarten programs, and the federal Head Start program amount to $29.1 billion annually, which is less than 0.2 percent, or one-five-hundredth, of the nation's GDP. Even adding an estimate of what is privately spent by families themselves on early care and education in the United States brings the total to just 0.5 percent, or one-two-hundredth of the nation's total economic resources.[20] Raising public spending for early childhood development and education programs to the roughly $12,400 that was spent on education for each child for K–12 education in the 2011–2012 school year would require spending an additional $220 billion annually, or 1.3 percent of GDP. Our proposal does not approach this level.[21]

We estimate that our proposed plan would require as much as $70 billion per year in new investments from federal, state, and local governments. Together with the $29 billion in current annual spending from similar existing programs, total annual public expenditures across all levels of government would be $99 billion per year. (See table 6.1 and the appendix tables for greater detail on how we estimated the costs for the plan's components.) These costs represent less than 0.5 percent of GDP and a fraction of the spending that has gone for other relatively large new areas of public expenditures in recent years.[22] As a comparison, a twenty-seven-country report showed that European Union nations spend an average of 0.49 percent of GDP on preprimary education alone.[23]

These estimates are based on what we believe would be the likely maximum level of investments required for the overall plan by the tenth year if each component of the plan is fully implemented within that time frame. Lower levels would be required in the prior nine years as the program grew to scale. These estimates are based on all components of the plan being implemented and high levels of participation that may take longer than ten years to reach. In reality, any reduction in the scale or pace of implementation would result in lower costs overall. Furthermore, these are just the gross total public expenditures for the key components and do not take into account possible changes in other public program spending or revenues (for example, from increased labor force participation or from cost savings to families), which we believe could substantially reduce these costs.

For paid parental leave, we estimate annual costs of $18–20 billion per year once fully implemented. Our estimate is based on assumptions of very high rates of participation: we estimate that 4.1 million workers each year (100 percent of eligible women and 50 percent of eligible men with recent or aggregate work histories) would take paid leave time. Actual take-up is likely to be less than full participation or maximum durations of leave. Parents may continue working, or

Table 6.1 *Total Annual Investment Required for Proposed Plan After Full Implementation*

	Total Investment Required (in Billions of Dollars)
Program component	
Paid parental leave	$19.0
Assuring Care and Education for Young Children (ACE)	22.2
Child and Dependent Care Tax Credit (CDCTC)	8.0
Universal early education (state-administered, center-based programs for three- and four-year-olds)	33.0
New Head Start program focused on infants and toddlers	17.2
Total	99.4
Current sources of spending or savings	
Child Care and Development Block Grant (CCDBG) and other block grant spending for children's care from birth to age five (of total) (2013)[a]	7.9 (of 11.3)
CDCTC spending (2015)[b]	4.5
Dependent care flexible spending accounts (FSAs) (2012)[b]	1.5
Total spending for state-administered prekindergarten programs (2014)[c]	6.2
Head Start spending (2014)[d]	8.6
Mother, Infant, and Early Childhood Home Visiting Program spending (2014)[d]	0.4
Total	29.1
Net new investment required	70.3

Source: Authors' compilation.

Notes: The $70.3 billion in new investments would include increases in federal, state, and local government annual spending. When fully implemented in the long term (at the end of ten years), an estimated $52 billion would be new federal investments, which would include all of the costs for implementing paid parental leave, the additional costs for the new Head Start investments, almost all new costs for child care, and one-quarter of the total costs for universal preschool. State and local governments would incur approximately $18 billion in increased costs, primarily for the expansions to preschool education ($24.2 of the total costs less the $6.2 billion that states currently spend).

[a] U.S. DHHS/ACF/OCC 2015; Schmit and Reeves 2015; for more detail, see chapter 3, note 28, and notes to table A2.1.

[b] Tax Policy Center 2015.

[c] Barnett et al. 2016.

[d] U.S. DHHS/ACF/OHS 2015.

they may return to work sooner, because their earnings are only partially replaced or for other reasons. We make no assumptions about how private employers or states that currently offer benefits may change their policies; we expect that many might continue providing primary or supplemental benefits.

For the Assurance and the expanded Child and Dependent Care Tax Credit, we estimate that an additional $16 billion would be required. For the Assurance, we estimate that total public investment of $22.4 billion would provide subsidies to support the higher-quality early care and education of 2.5 million children with working parents between birth and age five in low- and moderate-income families. If all of the estimated $7.9 billion currently spent on children from birth to age five through Child Care and Development Block Grants and other block grant spending is used to fund the Assurance, the net increased cost would be $14.3 billion in new public spending. The current federal spending for school-age child care could be separated and remain block grant funding to states and combined with other afterschool funding, or it could be devoted to supporting the costs of the new ACE subsidies, which would further reduce the costs from our estimates.

All or most of the net increase in expenditures in the initial phase-in years of the Assurance could be structured so that the federal government covers all or most of the new costs, with state spending remaining close to current levels. Upon full implementation, the $3.8 billion that we estimate would be the states' share of the $22 billion in total expenditures would be nearly the same as what states currently contribute in the aggregate to federal-state funding streams for child care. In addition, parents would be responsible for copayments totaling $4 billion (or $1,600 per child served).

During the years when states are expanding public preschool programs, families with eligible three- and four-year-olds would probably utilize ACE subsidies for market-based preschool services for full-time primary arrangements, and there would be a gradual shift in the use of ACE subsidies to secondary or wraparound services as universal preschool and reenvisioned Head Start move to full implementation. In states where implementation of preschool education may remain limited, the Assurance would continue to cover low- and moderate-income families with three- and four-year-olds, an expense we account for in the estimates.

Even with a generous cost-sharing structure and most administrative control remaining under state purview, some states might choose not to establish the Assurance.[24] We expect that making the federal share generous enough and the additional state costs modest enough could encourage most states to move to the Assurance. However, in the event that not every state takes up the program in the ten-year time frame, there should be a backup strategy to help ensure that at least the lowest-income families with children receive needed assistance to access early learning opportunities. The need for a backup strategy is underscored by the already wide disparities across states in assistance for child care, access to public preschool, and a host of other benefit programs.[25]

For the expanded Child and Dependent Care Tax Credit, we estimate that an additional $2 billion would be required beyond what is currently spent, combined on the credit and the dependent care assistance program accounts—$4.5 billion on the CDCTC and $1.5 billion on the DCAP accounts for child care costs administered through employers. Flexible spending accounts would be eliminated, with those families expected to use the CDCTC program instead. With the more generous proposed CDCTC for children from birth to age five, the shift to making the credit refundable, and elimination of the FSAs, total costs would increase to approximately $8 billion compared to the recent $6 billion.

We estimate total annual costs (federal and state) upon full implementation at year ten of universal early education of $33 billion (or between $29 and $37 billion). We built our estimate beginning with the average per-child, per-year costs for children in K–12 spending ($11,101 in 2014–2015).[26] We assumed that the average take-up during the years of state implementation of preschool expansions with federal matching funds will increase by three to five percentage points each year, until reaching 50 to 60 percent of four-year-olds enrolled in public preschool and 15 to 20 percent of three-year-olds enrolled by year ten. We expect that other children will be residing in states that do not significantly expand preschool during this time, particularly three-year-olds but also four-year-olds in some states; we also expect that sizable shares will be attending private preschool, including with ACE subsidies, and that others will be enrolled in Head Start where public preschool capacity has not been developed. This would nevertheless represent more than a doubling of the number of four-year-old children in state public preschool and triple the current number of three-year-olds in public preschool, with growth likely to continue beyond the ten-year time frame. Our plan would include a 50 percent federal share (match) for new preschool expansion costs in years one to four, decreasing to 40 percent for years five through seven, 30 percent in years eight and nine, and 25 percent in year ten and thereafter.[27] Currently state spending for universal prekindergarten programs is estimated to be $6.2 billion, and the bulk of expenditures for preschool education and care are made by parents.

The reimagined Head Start program's services would be targeted to approximately 825,000 children from before birth to age three, and a residual number of three- and four-year-olds that could range from 175,000 to 425,000, depending on how many states establish universal preschool for three- and four-year-olds. We estimate a need for approximately $8 billion in new investments to increase total annual expenditures from the $9 billion for Head Start and the Mother, Infant, and Early Childhood Home Visiting Program expenditures today to meet the estimated annual costs of $17 billion that will be required once many of the existing services are converted to serve younger children. This would include $11.1 billion for the primarily child development and center-based services for children enrolled in the prenatal-to-age-three Head Start program. We assume that the costs associated with the program needs of younger children would be greater ($13,500 per child compared to $8,500 per child for Head Start program services for three- and four-year-olds). Between $1.8 billion and $4.3 billion would be needed for Head Start for three- and four-year-olds. The range represents the different scenarios for how many preschool-age Head Start slots would need to be maintained, which would depend on the extent to which states expand public preschool. The total figure also includes $2.5 billion for broader community hub services for health and development screenings and ongoing service for an additional 1.5 million children not enrolled in Head Start. Finally, the program would also include $500 million for model development, research, and evaluation to generate innovation in birth-to-age-three services. With all of the current $8.6 billion in Head Start spending and $400 million in the federal Mother, Infant, and Early Childhood Home Visiting Program funding repurposed to support the new model for Head Start, the net cost would be $8.1 billion in additional public spending.

There is some reason to believe that the actual costs of these plans might be lower. If, as we expect, some states choose to establish broadly available, universal, full-day, full-year preschool just for four-year-olds, while a smaller number of states do so for three-year-olds as well, actual costs will be lower. In that scenario, most income-eligible working parents would be able to use the Assurance for full-day, full-year services on a sliding scale, with higher-income families not eligible for the ACE subsidies continuing to pay out-of-pocket but recovering a bit more of their spending through the more generous tax credit. This change would shift the amount of funding among these components and in net raise the overall private share of early care and education costs, but reduce the overall public spending required.

Pathways for Moving Forward

Building the comprehensive, high-quality early care and education system that we envision will require substantial investments in funding and time. These investments will pay off in the medium and long term, but we cannot ignore the political and policy realities that make new short-term investments difficult. We are aware that in the current political and budget climate, it might seem naive and impractical to believe that the national and state governments will soon achieve a new consensus to devote the resources to a plan of this scope and magnitude. However, we believe that these changes are not only achievable but also necessary to secure a bright economic future for our children and the nation. Here we highlight some of the practical challenges and provide some thoughts on how this plan might become a reality.

Although we envision the final stage as a cohesive early childhood care and education system, the path to that stage may involve several phases of potentially fragmented implementation. First, the components require statutory authority, entailing the drafting and passage of legislation at the federal level within the jurisdictions of several different congressional committees.[28] New laws or reauthorizations of existing laws are likely to involve considerable deliberation, along with the addition of new programs or spending and the streamlining of others. All of this will take time. Our preschool proposal also requires action and investment from states, which in many of them will also require legislation.

Once passed into law, each component will have unique implementation challenges. Paid parental leave, if based in the Social Security system (as we recommend), would be advantaged in its use of an existing infrastructure and more centralized implementation and could probably be fully implemented within two years after becoming law. Similarly, the CDCTC could be expanded (and the DCAP flexible spending accounts eliminated) as soon as the next full calendar (tax) year following the change in law. By contrast, the ACE subsidies would require time after passage and initial implementation to ensure that early care providers meet quality standards, markets have a chance to respond to the availability of subsidy support to increase the supply of quality care settings, and investments are made in workforce development. Further, although we propose that all eligible working families up to 250 percent of the FPL be supported on a sliding scale once fully implemented, the ACE subsidies could also follow a phased-in approach, initially targeting families up to 200 percent of the FPL or beginning the guarantee with a new birth cohort and thereby expanding the eligible child population over five years.

Our proposal develops and integrates an effective array of early childhood supports for the long term. Because funds may be limited for the foreseeable future, we recommend starting with the greatest needs and the most readily achievable investments to serve as platforms for further investments. Federal resources could be devoted initially to implementing universal preschool for children in low- and moderate-income families and then expanded later to include higher-income families.

Even with the seemingly paralyzing levels of polarization in American politics today and the fiscal squeeze that has severely cramped the U.S. domestic policy agenda, we sense that opportunities may emerge for a cohesive, well-articulated vision for better shaping young children's future prospects. As we discussed in chapters 2 to 5, we have seen a few factors that offer real hope for making this plan a reality.

First among these factors is that most of the ideas we offer are not new or wholly original and in fact have been a growing part of the policy discourse in the national and state capitals. Policies that seek to provide equal opportunities for success in childhood have long enjoyed bipartisan support, from the creation of Head Start in the 1960s and expansions through the 1990s, to enactment of the Children's Health Insurance Program in the 1990s, to reauthorization of the Every Student Succeeds Act in 2015. A type of child care guarantee was seriously considered as far back as the Nixon administration.[29] In recent years the Obama administration has proposed both a child care guarantee for working families with young children and a reformed child care tax credit that together would provide greater support to families across the income spectrum in dealing with the high costs of child care.[30] After expansions in state prekindergarten programs stalled for several years following the Great Recession, some states began modest expansions in the reach of their prekindergarten programs, and several governors from both parties have called for universal programs in their states. Even more boldly, and with the intention of accelerating the pace of action in the states, President Obama advanced a proposal, not unlike our own, for universal preschool for all American four-year-olds through increased federal financing to support the states.[31]

Importantly, we have often seen more concerted support across the political spectrum for policies to better meet the needs of working families, particularly when the proposal is to achieve these goals through the tax system. The expansion of child care tax credits for families with young children is currently being debated in both political parties. Such an expansion, and even some variation of our paid parental leave proposal, could advance as part of a national package of tax reforms or adjustments that will be required to strengthen the long-term financing of Social Security. There also may be broad political appeal in our proposal's substantial streamlining of the existing piecemeal systems in early care and education and expansion of access to high-quality services.

Second, public attention to rapidly growing inequality and declining social mobility has strengthened the appeal of early childhood investments. President Obama proclaimed that income inequality is "the defining challenge of our time" in very clear and resonating terms in December 2013:

> [The] American people's frustrations . . . [is] rooted in the nagging sense that no matter how hard they work, the deck is stacked against them. And it's rooted in the fear that their kids won't be better off than they were. . . . They experience in a very personal way the relentless, decades-long trend . . . [of] a dangerous and growing inequality and lack of upward mobility that has jeopardized middle-class America's basic bargain—that if you work hard, you have a chance to get ahead.
>
> I believe this is the defining challenge of our time . . . [and] that the decisions we make on these issues over the next few years will determine whether or not our children will grow up in an America where opportunity is real.[32]

This issue was the focus of intense debate in the 2016 presidential campaign, and it particularly animated the surprising strength of the campaign of Senator Bernie Sanders, especially among adults under age forty-five. Public concern about income inequality has increasingly been linked to the rationale for early investment. The campaign of New York City mayor Bill de Blasio in 2013 showed that framing investment in children as an approach to reducing inequality can lead to electoral success. Beyond New York City's rapid preschool expansion for four-year-olds, there have been lopsided electoral victories when ballot efforts have included preschool expansion, even when voters were asked to agree to increased taxes to pay for expansions.[33] Broader national polling shows that majorities of voters in both major parties support using federal funds to ensure that high-quality preschool education is available to every child in America.[34] And as of this writing, there have been new advances at the edges of this plan. Just in the last year, New York State and San Francisco have passed more expansive paid parental leave programs, and legislation has been introduced in more states in the last two years compared to prior periods.

The passage and implementation of many elements of this plan will require a strong and vocal coalition of supporters, made up of state and federal policy leaders, advocacy organizations, employers, and the public. Of course, parents and their young children stand to benefit directly from our proposal. However, while today's parents of young children do not constitute a dominant voting bloc in elections, they are not the only constituency who would benefit from our proposal. Many employers—the majority of whom employ parents—are likely to support their employees' greater access to affordable, reliable child care and publicly supported paid parental leave because these benefits can promote productivity and reduce turnover. In the long term, employers and the economy benefit from their future workforce's greater financial security and access to high-quality early care and education because these programs better prepare children for success in school and the labor force. Additionally, most people have been or will become parents at some point during their lives. Although being the parent of a young child is a temporary condition, the experience touches the lives of the majority of Americans in important and lasting ways.

The evidence accumulated over decades of experience and study is unequivocal. Our nation needs a stronger and more comprehensive framework of support for early care and education. All this knowledge tells us that early investments in human development must be a key part of any strategy to tackle the crisis of economic inequality, provide the educated labor force needed for sustained economic growth, and ensure social progress in this century.

The United States cannot simply tinker at the edges of its current investment in the early years. A patchwork system that leads to vast geographic differences does not meet the nation's long-term interests. A family moving from Oklahoma to Arkansas should not face the loss of good-quality preschool opportunities for a job change to better support their family. A baby born to Pennsylvania parents has as much need for uninterrupted early parenting time as a baby born in New Jersey. All American children should have robust and equal opportunities to thrive, learn, and grow. In choosing this future, we can invest in a more economically productive and socially just nation for us all.

APPENDIX: ESTIMATES AND ASSUMPTIONS FOR INVESTMENTS IN THE COMPONENTS OF OUR PROPOSED PLAN

Table A2.1 *Estimates for Investments in Proposed Paid Parental Leave Plan*

Policy	Current Expenditures	Estimated Costs Under Plan
· Parents are eligible for up to sixteen weeks of job-protected paid leave per child, supported by a public social insurance (for example, Social Security) system. Both parents are eligible, with eight weeks reserved for mothers, four weeks for fathers, and four weeks for either parent. · Each parent is eligible for an additional twelve weeks of job-protected unpaid leave. · Wage replacement for the first $25,000 in annual earnings is 80 percent, and 60 percent wage replacement for earnings between $25,000 and $75,000, after which the benefit amount is capped. · Private employers, states, and localities can provide additional benefits separate from federal public paid parental leave (for example, providing the full wage replacement, providing the difference in pay between the public amount and 100 percent of wages, or extending periods of job-protected paid or unpaid leave).	*Federal expenditures: $0* · FMLA, administered by the U.S. Department of Labor, provides for unpaid leave and job protection for twelve weeks. *State expenditures:* · Three states have public parental leave systems: California ($614 million in 2014), New Jersey ($82 million in 2013), and Rhode Island ($194 million projected for 2016). · New York State is implementing paid leave to begin in 2018; Washington State has paid leave in law but has not funded or implemented the program; and Hawaii, the District of Columbia, and Puerto Rico have TDI systems that cover the period following childbirth for biological mothers.[a] *Financing:* · California: Each employee pays an average of $30 per year into the paid leave fund. · New Jersey: Each worker contributes 0.09 percent of the taxable wage base ($32,000), to a maximum of $29 per year.[a] · Rhode Island: Each worker contributes 1.2 percent of first $66,300 in wages. *Participation levels:* · *California:* Up to six weeks of leave can be taken at 55 percent of earnings, up to a maximum of $1,104 per week in 2015; estimated take-up in 2009 was 30 per 100 live births[b] (0.9 percent of all eligible employees in states).[c] · *New Jersey:* Up to six weeks of leave at two-thirds of earnings, up to a maximum of $595 per week (averaged $561 in 2010); take-up rates were less than 1 percent (0.6 percent) among all eligible workers.[d] · *Rhode Island:* Up to four weeks of leave can be taken, with the average weekly benefit rate of 4.6 percent of wages paid during the highest quarter of the worker's base wage (maximum of $795 per week; average $519 in December 2015). Less than 1 percent (0.7 percent) of private-sector workers took bonding leave in 2014 (the first year of the program).[e]	*Federal costs: $19.0 billion per year[f]* · We estimate that the minimum benefit of $160 per week and maximum of $962 per week, taken for up to sixteen weeks, would result in an average expenditure per birth of $4,700. *State costs:* · States may choose to augment or extend parents' paid leave wage replacement or extend the job protection period.

Source: Authors' compilation.

[a] U.S. Social Security Administration, Office of Research, Evaluation, and Statistics 1997.

[b] Bartel et al. 2014.

[c] National Partnership for Women and Families 2015b.

[d] Lerner and Appelbaum 2014; National Partnership for Women and Families 2016. Wen-Jui Han, Christopher Ruhm, and Jane Waldfogel (2009) estimate that there is a high degree of overlap among those who take both the resources eligible under the state's TDI program and the additional paid leave time, with an estimated 42 to 82 percent of new mothers eligible for TDI taking paid leave.

[e] Eileen Appelbaum and Gayle Goldin, "Paid Family Leave Should Be for Everyone," *Boston Globe*, May 14, 2015.

[f] A 2012 survey of employees and employers for an evaluation of FMLA showed that 2.8 percent of all workers (including both those eligible and not eligible for FMLA) were found to have taken *any leave* (even one day) related to having a new child in the prior twelve months. The rate of any leave-taking related to having a new child was 3.6 percent among all female workers and 2.5 percent for all male workers (Klerman, Daly, and Pozniak 2014). The average duration of parental leaves was fifty-eight days for women taking leaves and twenty-two days for men who took leaves; the survey also found that 21 percent of women and 13 percent of men taking leave were paid during the leave. In addition, according to BLS data, 62 percent of women who gave birth in 2013 were in the labor force during the prior year, and this was true for 90 percent of new fathers who lived with their children, suggesting a universe of potential leave-takers of 2.5 million women and more than 3 million men annually. We expect the take-up rates of paid leave available to all workers with a work history as defined by Social Security (including the self-employed, those at small firms, and so on) to be higher than rates for unpaid leave.

Using these 2012 estimates, if every parent who takes any leave from employment after having a child takes at least some paid leave under our proposed plan, this will amount to approximately 2.5 million mothers and 1.6 million fathers. This estimate assumes that 100 percent of women who are eligible and 50 percent of men take some leave. A total of 4.1 million workers taking leave for the birth of a child is roughly consistent with the number of annual births in the United States (just under 4 million in 2014 [Hamilton et al. 2015]), assuming that many newborns will have both parents taking leave, whereas others will have only one parent taking paid leave.

We model an average leave-taking duration across all births of ten weeks divided between parents to account for a significant number of families in which two parents will take the maximum amount of leave allowed under our plan of sixteen weeks per child, some families in which neither parent will take leave, and many cases in which one or both parents will take some leave but less than the allowable maximum for a two-parent family. If we assume that, overall, women take three times the duration of leave as men (as found in Klerman, Daly, and Pozniak 2014), the overall average would include seven and a half weeks on average for mothers and two and a half weeks on average for fathers who take leave. From CPS data we determine average earnings of parents of approximately $770 per week ($557 per week worked for women and $1,147 per week worked for men) in a household that has had a newborn in the previous year. Using these average earnings levels, we calculate an average benefit per family of $4,700, totaling $19 billion per year.

Given the temporary nature of parental leave and the partial wage replacement it would offer, we recommend that these benefits be exempt from calculations of eligibility or amounts for public programs, including SNAP, SSI, WIC, Medicaid, health insurance tax credits, and child care benefits, so as not to discourage the use of the benefit by those using these other programs around the time of birth.

Table A3.1 *Estimates for Investments in the Assuring Care and Education for Young Children Subsidy to Support the Financial Costs of High-Quality Early Care and Education for Low- and Moderate-Income Families with Children Under Age Five*

Policy	Current Expenditures	Estimated Costs Under Plan
· Parents in eligible families live in the same household with a child under age five, are both employed (working an average of at least twenty or more hours per week), and have family income below 250 percent of the FPL ($60,750 for a family of four in 2016).	· Total annual federal and state costs for Child Care and Development Block Grant (CCDBG) subsidies, Temporary Assistance for Needy Families (TANF), and Social Services Block Grants (SSBGs) amounted to $11.3 billion in FY2013.[a]	· Estimated total annual public cost at full implementation: $22.4 billion, which includes $19 billion as the cost of direct subsidy payments. (The 80 percent federal share is $15.2 billion and the 20 percent state matching share is $3.8 billion.)[c]
· Subsidy provides direct financial assistance toward the cost of a state-licensed nonparental care provider of the parents' choice, with the amount of assistance being based on the cost of care (by child age, type of care, number of children in care, and hours in care).	· Of this total, an estimated $3.4 billion was for the cost of child care subsidies for school-age children ages six to twelve. The average cost per child (ages zero to five) served with subsidies for twelve months in FY 2013 was $5,270.[b]	· For the cost of quality support and monitoring, administration and oversight, and evaluation: $3.4 billion. Parents' total copayments tied to subsidies: $4.0 billion.
· The family contribution to the cost of care is based on a sliding income scale, with copays representing a higher percentage of family income, such that families spend between 3 and 10 percent of their total annual income on child care and all families contribute a minimum amount (for example, $10 weekly for families at 100 percent of the FPL). States can provide subsidies up to higher levels of family income, up to a maximum of 400 percent of the FPL, at the same federal match rate to account for the wide differences in the cost of care across states and areas within states.	· For the 34 percent of children ages six to twelve receiving child care subsidies, the average cost of the subsidy over twelve months was an estimated $3,640.	· Average total cost of care: $9,100 per child for 2.5 million children in subsidized care; $10,300 per infant or toddler (the majority of whom are in full-time licensed care); and $7,800 per preschool-age child (some of whom are in part-time licensed arrangements).[d] Parents' share of total cost averages $1,600 annually (or $31 per week), and the difference funded through ACE subsidies averages $7,500.

Source: Authors' compilation.

a U.S. DHHS/ACF/OCC 2015; Schmit and Reeves 2015; see also chapter 3, note 28.

b Cost per child calculated from data reported by U.S. DHHS/ACF/2015.

c Estimating that between 1.8 million and 3.2 million children (ages zero to five) would be in ACE-subsidized arrangements annually at full implementation, we use 2.5 million, the middle of the range, as our estimate. We determine that potentially eligible children would be 5.2 million of the 22 million children under age five plus half of five-year-olds, who may not be age-eligible for kindergarten. We develop low- and high-participation estimates for each child age in the range of 25 percent to 75 percent among families with children under age four (with increasing participation rates by child age): 25 percent (lower-bound participation rate) to 40 percent (upper-bound participation rate) for children under age one; 35 percent to 50 percent for one-year-olds; 45 percent to 60 percent for two-year-olds; and 50 percent to 75 percent for three-year-olds. For four-year-olds and some five-year-olds, since we assume that a large proportion will be in public preschool, we assume that between 25 and 50 percent will also access subsidies, most for part-time care after preschool hours and to pay for summer preschool. We assume that families use a mix of state-licensed care types—center-based care and family child care—for children receiving ACE subsidies (with increasing percentages in center-based care by child age): 40 percent of infants in centers and 60 percent in licensed home-based care; 50 percent of one-year-olds in centers and 50 percent in licensed home-based care; 60 percent of two-year-olds in center care and 40 percent in licensed home-based care; and 90 percent of three-year-olds in center care and 10 percent in licensed home-based care. We assume that 80 percent of subsidies are for full-time care for children under age four and 20 percent are for part-time care, and that 80 percent of subsidies for four-year-olds, many of whom are enrolled in universal public preschool in their states, are for part-time care.

d Based on 2013 CPS data, there are approximately 20.3 million children under age five (22.4 million children if we include half of five-year-olds who may not be age-eligible for kindergarten) in the United States. Approximately 5.2 million children are in families with incomes below 250 percent of the FPL with both parents working twenty or more hours per week and therefore eligible for ACE subsidies (and 7.9 million children have both parents working twenty or more hours per week and family income levels up to 400 percent of the FPL).

Table A3.2. *Estimates for Investments in the Expanded Child Care Tax Credit to Provide Financial Assistance for a Broad Range of Paid Early Care and Education for Families at All Income Levels with Children Under Age Thirteen and Expanded Support for Families with Children Under Age Five*

Policy	Current Expenditures	Estimated Costs Under Plan
· Tax credit can be taken for a proportion of costs for all types of paid care (licensed and unlicensed). · The annual cap is increased to $5,000 (from $3,000) in child care expenses for children under age five for one child and to $7,500 (from $6,000) for more than one dependent; these caps are indexed for inflation. · The maximum percentage of expenses eligible for the tax credit is increased from 35 percent to 50 percent of expenses for families with children under age five. (The 35 percent maximum remains for children five and older.) The maximum percentage credit is applicable over an increased range of family income (up to $60,000) with more gradual phase-down as income increases (1 percent for every $1,500 increase) to a minimum credit level of 20 percent of expenses for all incomes above $105,000. · The tax credit is refundable for any family for whom the credit exceeds their total tax liability. · With all families having access to the tax credit, flexible spending accounts (FSAs) for dependent care expenses will be eliminated.	· In 2015, $4.4 billion in credits were taken by 6.6 million families (tax filers) and 1.2 million tax filers reported reducing their taxable income with FSAs, costing an estimated $1.5 billion in tax revenue.[a] · The average CDCTC benefit was $538 per family in 2012. The average salary reduction for FSAs was $3,456 per return, indicating a salary reduction for the FSA that translates into an estimated $900 benefit per family with an FSA.[b]	· Total costs increase by an estimated $2.0 billion to $8.0 billion, which accounts for increases in the number of households receiving the credit, increases in the number of those families with children under five receiving the maximum amount of the credit, and families who currently receive FSAs receiving the tax credit instead.[c] · The benefit for families with children under age five increases significantly, with the maximum credit increasing from $600 to $3,000 for one child and from $1,200 to $4,500 for two children under five.

Source: Authors' compilation.

[a] Office of Management and Budget 2016, 230 (training, employment, and social services section); Tax Policy Center 2015.

[b] Office of Management and Budget 2014; Tax Policy Center 2015.

[c] This estimate is based on the cost of the components of similar proposals and accounts for differences between proposals. For example, the Tax Policy Center (TPC) in 2009 estimated the cost for a proposal that would make the CDCTC refundable to all families with children under age thirteen (just as we propose); increase the maximum expenses subject to the credit from $3,000 to $5,000 for one child and from $6,000 to $10,000 for two or more children and index these limits to inflation (we increase the maximum eligible costs to $6,000 and $9,000 for one and two children, respectively, but only for children under age five); increase the maximum credit rate to 50 percent, increase the income level at which the tax credit begins to phase down to $30,000, and index for inflation the income threshold above which the credit rate phases down (our higher income level at which we begin to phase down the credit rate for families with children under age five is higher). When fully implemented, the TPC estimated that this proposal would cost $3.3 billion annually (in 2009 dollars). Since our proposal includes similar components but primarily for children under five, we roughly estimate the cost as half the TPC estimate, or $2 billion (updated to 2016 dollars). See Williams and Gleckman 2009; Maag et al. 2014.

Table A4.1 *Estimates for Investments in Universal High-Quality Preschool for Three- and Four-Year-Olds*

Policy	Current Expenditures	Estimated Costs Under Proposal
· States and/or local school districts develop plans to expand access and improve quality provision of preschool for three- and four-year-olds, or just four-year-olds, with the goal of reaching universal provision for at least four-year-olds within ten years; states can seek federal matching funds for new state spending to expand access and improve quality. · States are eligible for federal matching funds for 50 percent of new expenditures in years one through four, 40 percent for years five through seven, 30 percent for years eight and nine, and 25 percent for the tenth year and thereafter (or approximately 40 percent overall across the ten years of expansion). · States or localities that are already serving a significant share of four-year-olds in public preschool (more than 50 percent of four-year-olds in the state or relevant jurisdiction), or jurisdictions where more than 70 percent of children are in center-based preschool (public or private), or jurisdictions that are already serving a significant number of three-year-olds (more than 10 percent of three-year-olds are in public preschool) would be most likely to expand their services to provide universal access for all three-year-olds and four-year-olds within ten years.	· Overall, an estimated $6.2 billion was spent for public preschool in the states in 2015.[a] · States spending varies widely—from eight states spending $0 and another six states spending less than $10 million annually to four states that spend between $600 million and $800 million per year.[b] · Forty-two states and the District of Columbia spent an overall average of $4,489 per child, with a great deal of variation among state preschool programs in services offered, the number of children served, and quality standards. Per-child expenditures among the states with any state preschool range from eight states in which annual spending per child served was less than $3,000 to two states in which it exceeded $12,000.[c] · In addition to the approximately 1.35 million children (5 percent of all three-year-olds and 29 percent of all four-year-olds nationally) who are in state prekindergarten programs,[d] there are 770,000 preschool-age children in Head Start[e] and 400,000 in center-based preschool arrangements subsidized by the Child Care and Development Fund (CCDF).[f] · An additional 2 million three- and four-year-olds are in private preschools, for which families pay an average of $12,770 per child per year.[g] · Altogether, approximately 4.7 million three- and four-year-olds attend preschool.[h]	· Costs would total $33 billion by year ten, including 3 percent of total costs for quality monitoring per year.[i] · The average cost per child for full-day preschool for the traditional (nine-month) school year would be $11,011, which is the average recent spending per pupil in K–12 education plus a supplemental amount for classroom coaching.[j]

Source: Authors' compilation.

[a] Barnett et al. 2016.

[b] Idaho, Indiana, Montana, New Hampshire, North Dakota, South Dakota, Utah, and Wyoming have no state preschool and $0 in expenditures. Alaska, Delaware, Hawaii, Mississippi, Nevada, and Rhode Island spent less than $10 million in state expenditures for preschool in 2015. The four states that had the highest expenditures—California, New York, New Jersey, and Texas—all spent between $600 million and $800 million on their state's preschool education programs in 2015 (Barnett et al. 2016).

[c] Estimate from Barnett et al. 2016. The eight states where per-child expenditures are less than $3,000 are Florida, Iowa, Kansas, Maine, Mississippi, Nebraska, Nevada, and South Carolina, and the two states where per-child expenditures are the highest, at more than $12,000 per child, are the District of Columbia and New Jersey.

[d] Barnett et al. 2016.

[e] In the 2014–2015 program year, Head Start had a funded enrollment of 771,049 (U.S. DHHS/ACF 2015).

[f] In 2014, 1,406,000 children were served in CCDF programs nationally, of which 28 percent were children ages three and four (U.S. DHHS/ACF/OCC 2015).

[g] Two million children ages three and four are enrolled in private preschool, according to data from the Current Population Survey (U.S. Census Bureau 2014). Data from the 2012 National Household Education Survey indicate that among families with children ages three to five who had not yet entered kindergarten and whose family paid for preschool, the average expenditure was $246 per week in 2012 (Mamedova and Redford 2015). Multiplying this by 52 gives us a $12,770 per year estimate for what families spend overall for full-year preschool and center-based care, which, for 2 million children, would equal $25.5 billion.

[h] There are approximately 4 million four-year-olds and 4 million three-year-olds in the United States; 42.6 percent of three-year-olds and 66.3 percent of four-year-olds attend preschool (U.S. Census Bureau 2014).

[i] Assumptions for this estimate include that after ten years between 50 and 60 percent of all four-year-olds would be in public preschool, which would have become universal in most, but not all, states. (For estimation purposes, we assume that between thirty and forty states would seek federal matching funds for development of a universal program to include at least all four-year-olds, and that in states that reach universal preschool for four-year-olds, 75 to 85 percent of four-year-olds would be in public preschool and 15 to 25 percent would be in other private preschool arrangements, which parents might prefer, either for their continuity with the center-based care in which their children had been enrolled already or for other reasons.) We assume that between 15 and 20 percent of all three-year-olds would be in public preschool within ten years. (For estimation purposes, we assume that between five and fifteen states seeking to establish universal preschool for four-year-olds within ten years would also propose to expand preschool to include three-year-olds; as of 2015, eleven states (the District of Columbia, Florida, Georgia, Iowa, New York, Oklahoma, South Carolina, Texas, Vermont, and West Virginia) had at least 45 percent of their four-year-olds in state-funded pre-K, and three of these states (the District of Columbia, Vermont, and West Virginia) plus four others (Arkansas, Illinois, Nebraska, and New Jersey) were serving more than 10 percent of all three-year-olds in state preschool. Among these fifteen states, there may be greater interest in or likelihood of establishing universal preschool for three- and four-year-olds, though some states may choose to use federal matching funds to support higher-quality care provision for four-year-olds rather than or at least before expanding preschool for three-year-olds. (Three- and four-year-olds would also be attending preschool through Head Start and ACE subsidies in those states that do not provide universal access to children at those ages.) We assume that overall take-up in public preschool would increase gradually with state expansions by three to five percentage points each year, until reaching between 15 and 20 percent of all three-year-olds and 50 to 60 percent of all four-year-olds enrolled in public preschool nationally by year ten.

[j] The base cost is the K–12 average per pupil spending nationally for nine months, or $11,011 for the 2012–2013 school year, in 2014–2015 dollars (Kena et al. 2016, 134).

Added to this would be an average coaching cost of $400 per child per year and curricula costs of $50 per child per year (\$1,000 per classroom, with an average of twenty children). For assumptions using ranges of 15 to 20 percent of all three-year-olds and 50 to 60 percent of all four-year-olds multiplied by the per-child spending of $11,411, we calculate the range of total annual costs for year ten as $29 billion to $37 billion for three-year-olds and federal matching funds combined, with a midpoint estimate of $33 billion. The extended-year costs for eleven-month programs would be funded on a sliding scale using ACE subsidies for those eligible and parent fees for those not eligible.

Table A5.1 *Estimates for Investments in a New Head Start Comprehensive Services Program to Target the Most Disadvantaged Children from Birth to Age Three*

Policy	Current Expenditures	Estimated Costs Under Proposal
· Through the transition to new service models and expanded focus, Head Start continues to serve at least the current number of children enrolled (approximately 925,000) as it shifts more services, starting before or at birth, to the youngest, most vulnerable children in areas of concentrated poverty and those facing significant adversities. The new service models for younger children combine home-visiting services specifically targeted to family needs from prenatal to infancy and center-based care for children until age three or when they are eligible for public preschool. In addition to existing federal Head Start funding, existing federal resources for the Maternal, Infant, and Early Childhood Home Visiting Program would be integrated into the new Head Start program.	· Total federal funding for Head Start was $8.6 billion in FY2014 and funding for the Maternal, Infant, and Early Childhood Home Visiting Program was $400 million. · Approximately $8,500 per child (per enrollment slot) was spent for all children served in the 2013–2014 program year: $8,000 per three- or four-year-old in Head Start, and $12,500 per child age birth to three in Early Head Start.	· The estimated total cost is approximately $17.1 billion. · Of the total, $11.1 billion is spent for children age prenatal to age three in Head Start, and $1.75 million to $4.25 million (an average of $3 billion) for three- and four-year-olds continuing in Head Start. · The average annual total cost is $13,500 per child for 825,000 children served in birth-to-age-three Head Start and $10,000 per child for 175,000 to 425,000 three- and four-year-olds continuing in Head Start.
· Head Start centers serve as larger community service hubs that provide initial comprehensive home visits, developmental screenings, and assessments following all births in high-needs communities, creating stronger links between the centers and the early health and development needs of the children they serve. In addition to providing comprehensive learning and supports to Head Start families, Head Start centers as community hubs link a larger group of children and families to services and provide training and coaching support for other community-based services providers in their area (for example, other area early care and education providers).		· Broader hub services for health and development screenings and coordination of ongoing services for identified child and family needs cost $2.5 billion.[a] · The average annual cost for 1.5 million additional children age prenatal to five receiving hub services (postpartum developmental screenings and referrals and follow-up for comprehensive services) and continued services on-site for Head Start enrollees who have transitioned to preschool is $1,700 per child.

- The new Head Start program rigorously tests service models, identifies evidence-based approaches targeted to family needs, and serves as an innovations laboratory for the integration of scientific knowledge, experimentation, and innovation in program service models, particularly those focused on sources of severe stress, such as parent mental health issues, deep poverty, substance use, and interpersonal conflict or violence.

- Funding for model development, research, evaluation, and service innovation is $500 million.[b]

Source: Authors' compilation.

[a] We calculate $700 annual cost per child multiplied by 1.8 million children for comprehensive nurse home visits, with identification of child and family needs, referrals for services, and follow-ups for the initial time period; plus $1,000 multiplied by 1.8 million children for ongoing case management and core hub services (such as parenting classes). The 1.8 million children would be from a broader catchment area and not enrolled in the birth-to-age-three Head Start program and would include children ages three to five, including those who have transitioned from Head Start to preschool.

[b] Research costs would be for experimentation and innovation within and across new Head Start program models in the first ten years. In most cases, core direct service costs would be covered by program funds, with research funds available for studying effects for service recipients and control groups and building data infrastructure to support research and evaluation.

NOTES

Chapter 1: Introduction

* We have given pseudonyms to research study participants.

† This family's story comes from *Child Care Choices of Low-Income Working Families* (Chaudry et al. 2011), a research study on how families consider their choices for the early care and education of young children. The family was interviewed twice, once in the winter of 2008–2009 and once in the winter of 2009–2010.

‡ This family was part of the study sample for *Putting Children First: How Low-Wage Working Mothers Manage Child Care* (Chaudry 2004). The family was interviewed four times between the spring of 2000 and the spring of 2002.

§ Throughout the book, we use the term "early care and education" to refer to the wide range of nonparental care settings for young children under age five, including both center-based and home-based settings.

1. U.S. Census Bureau 1982.
2. U.S. DOL/BLS 2016.
3. Chaudry 2004; Yoshikawa, Weisner, and Lowe 2006; Chaudry et al. 2011.
4. For example, census data from the Survey of Income and Program Participation (SIPP) show that families with employed mothers with children under age five spent an average of $179 per week (or $9,300 per year, or 10.5 percent of family income) on child care. Families with incomes below $43,000 per year (or twice the federal poverty level in 2011) with working mothers on average spent three times the share of their income on child care relative to those with family incomes above this amount: 21 percent of their income compared to 7 percent (Laughlin 2013).
5. A poll conducted in 2015 by Hart Research and Public Opinion Strategies asked 800 registered voters to rate the importance of a list of policy topics, and 89 percent said that children getting a "strong start in life" is "extremely" or "very" important; that policy topic was tied for first with "improving public education" (Tully 2015). For information on other polls, see Public Opinion Strategies and Hart Research 2013, 2014.
6. Cunha and Heckman 2007.
7. OECD 2014, 2015; NCES 2015a.
8. According to data from the 2014 Current Population Survey (CPS), in 2014 15.4 million (64 percent) of the 23.9 million children under age five in the United States lived with

their married parents, and more than 5 million children had parents who had both attained a bachelor's degree or higher and were in the labor force.

9. According to our calculations based on data from the 2013 and 2014 CPS, among families with two college-educated, full-time working parents, 64 percent of three-year-old children were enrolled in preschool or other center-based care and education in October 2013; those who remained in the CPS rotation sample the following October 2014 were also enrolled at age four. Similarly, in the Early Childhood Longitudinal Study–Birth Cohort (ECLS-B) data, as far back as 2003, 33 percent of children at twenty-four months whose mothers had a college degree or higher and worked full-time were in center-based care in 2003 and were in center care continuously through ages forty-eight to fifty-seven months. These data suggest that among children with working parents with higher educational attainment levels, one-third are getting three or more years of center-based care and education, and approximately two-thirds are getting two or more years.

10. Heckman 2006; Magnuson and Duncan 2006, 2014; Halle et al. 2009; Duncan and Magnuson 2011; Reardon and Portilla 2016.

11. Reardon and Portilla 2016. Sean Reardon (2011) analyzed data from nineteen national studies of U.S. children's test scores, using nearly sixty years of comprehensive data for children of all ages. The gap in academic skills between the highest- and lowest-income groups is the equivalent of a difference of one year of learning at age five, or all of the learning that might occur in a full year of kindergarten or first grade. This difference between children in the highest and lowest quintiles of family income increased by almost 40 percent between 1970 and 2000. Another way to describe this gap in terms of SAT-type test scores is that it represents an increase from an already high 80–90-point gap in the 1970s to a 120-point gap in the 2000s.

12. Reardon 2011.

13. Ibid.

14. Greg Duncan and Katherine Magnuson (2011) have found that in addition to these large gaps by family income in cognitive skills, there are also smaller gaps in children's socioemotional and self-regulation skills at kindergarten entry. The National Education Goals Panel described five dimensions of school readiness that are important to children's educational and long-term success: (1) physical well-being and motor development; (2) social and emotional development; (3) approaches to learning; (4) language development; and (5) cognition and general knowledge (Kagan, Moore, and Bredekamp 1995). Of these, language development, cognition, and general knowledge—the "academic readiness" skills—are typically measured using cognitive tests that assess children's literacy and language skills, numeracy and premathematical skills, and general knowledge. These cognitive measures are stronger predictors of later academic achievement (Duncan et al. 2007) and adult earnings (Chetty et al. 2011), but other dimensions of school readiness, including social, emotional, and behavioral skills, also affect success in school and later life (Grissmer and Eiseman 2008).

15. Halle et al. 2009; Fernald, Marchman, and Weisleder 2013.

16. Reardon 2011; Reardon and Portilla 2016.

17. Bassok and Latham 2016, referenced with the permission of the authors.
18. Cunha and Heckman 2007; Duncan et al. 2007; Duncan and Magnuson 2011.
19. Duncan et al. 1998; Currie 2009; Shonkoff, Boyce, and McEwen 2009; Duncan, Ziol-Guest, and Kalil 2010; Chetty et al. 2011; Duncan, Morris, and Rodrigues 2011; Dahl and Lochner 2012. These studies use rigorous research designs to demonstrate causal relationships between early economic disadvantages and long-term outcomes, including natural experiments and experimental studies that have taken place in recent decades.
20. Duncan and Sojourner 2013; Bartik 2011.
21. Gormley et al. 2005; Magnuson, Ruhm, and Waldfogel 2007; Duncan and Magnuson 2013; Weiland and Yoshikawa 2013.
22. Deming 2009.
23. See, for example, Stiglitz 2012; Pew Research Center 2009.

Chapter 2: Paid Parental Leave

1. Laughlin 2011; Washbrook et al. 2011. In 2015, 58 percent of mothers with infants under age one (57 percent of married mothers and 59 percent of unmarried mothers) were employed at a point in time (U.S. DOL/BLS 2016).
2. The American Academy of Pediatrics recommends exclusive breast-feeding for the first six months of life.
3. Waldfogel, Han, and Brooks-Gunn 2002; Brooks-Gunn, Han, and Waldfogel 2002, 2010; Berger, Hill, and Waldfogel 2005; Hill et al. 2005; Lombardi and Coley 2014.
4. Berger, Hill, and Waldfogel 2005; Guendelman et al. 2009; Heymann, Raub, and Earle 2011; Daku, Raub, and Heymann 2012.
5. Berger, Hill, and Waldfogel 2005; Guendelman et al. 2009.
6. Kalil and Ziol-Guest 2005; Hardy 2014; Gennetian et al. 2015; Wolf and Morrissey 2015.
7. Heymann, Raub, and Earle 2011.
8. Daku, Raub, and Heymann 2012.
9. Ruhm 2000a; Tanaka 2005. A study of the effects on U.S. children of the 1993 Family and Medical Leave Act (FMLA), which provides unpaid, job-protected leave to eligible workers, found modest increases in children's birth weight and decreases in the likelihood of premature birth and infant mortality in the years following FMLA among women likely to have taken leave (Rossin 2011). Earlier studies in other countries have found no associations between unpaid leave and infant mortality.
10. New York State has passed a paid family leave law that will provide twelve weeks of paid leave, beginning in 2018, and is also built off the state TDI system.
11. Appelbaum and Milkman 2011; Mathur 2015.
12. Breast-feeding rates increased from five to eleven weeks for women in higher-quality jobs and from five to nine weeks for those in lower-quality jobs (Appelbaum and Milkman 2011).
13. Klevens et al. 2016. Paid family leave decreased hospital admissions for pediatric abusive head trauma an estimated 2.8 to 3.2 per 100,000 children under two years of age.
14. Waldfogel 1998; Chatterji and Markowitz 2012; Wiese and Ritter 2012.

15. McKernan and Ratcliffe 2005.

16. Research suggests that relatively brief periods of leave (three months) have little effect on women's wages compared to no leave, but longer durations (nine months or longer) are associated with relative wage reductions in the 2 to 3 percent range (Ruhm 1998; Waldfogel 2001a).

17. Kennedy and Bumpass 2008; Martin et al. 2015.

18. Brooks-Gunn and Duncan 1997; Duncan and Brooks-Gunn 2000; Carlson and Corcoran 2001; Lichter, Graefe, and Brown 2003; Child Trends 2015a. Unmarried mothers have lower incomes and educational attainment, on average, and are more likely to receive public assistance (Thomas and Sawhill 2005).

19. Parker and Wang 2013.

20. Huerta et al. 2013.

21. Nepomnyaschy and Waldfogel 2007; Huerta et al. 2013.

22. Parker and Wang 2013; Pew Charitable Trusts 2015a.

23. Seward, Yeatts, and Zottarelli 2012.

24. Evaluations of the provision of unpaid leave in the United States through the FMLA indicate that the law did not affect fathers' leave-taking (Han and Waldfogel 2003; Zigler, Muenchow, and Ruhm 2012). Men's share of claims for paid leave in California, however, did increase in the initial years after the California paid leave benefit was instituted, from 17 percent in 2004–2005 to 29 percent in 2011–2012 (Appelbaum and Milkman 2011).

25. Prior to the implementation of Quebec's law, Quebec parents, like all Canadian parents, could claim gender-neutral parental leave—which is paid up to 55 percent of income to a strict cap—but fewer than 20 percent of fathers participated, for an average of two weeks, and many men transferred their benefits to their female partner. Quebec increased the income replacement to 70 percent, increased the maximum benefit level (from $412 to $767 per week), and created a five-week, nontransferrable leave benefit (a "daddy quota"). These changes increased fathers' participation rate by 250 percent (from 20 percent to 50 percent), and the average duration from two weeks to five weeks. As a result of expanded paid leave to both parents, mothers' participation also increased by 16 percent, but the father-specific set-aside led to a much greater increase in fathers' use of the benefit program. Over the long term, mothers spent more time in paid work following these changes and fathers spent more time engaged in child care or housework (Patnaik 2015).

26. Policies that provide for long leaves (twelve months or more) or work-family benefits offered or used by women can reduce their promotion opportunities relative to men (Fernández-Kranz and Rodríguez-Planas 2013).

27. Thomas 2015.

28. Pew Charitable Trusts 2015a.

29. Waldfogel, Higuchi, and Abe 1999; Baker and Milligan 2008; Appelbaum and Milkman 2011; Houser and Vartanian 2012.

30. Claire Cain Miller, "In Google's Inner Circle, a Falling Number of Women," *New York Times*, August 22, 2012.

31. Heather Boushey and Sarah Glynn, "Protecting Workers and Their Families," *Michigan Chronicle*, April 8, 2012.

32. Institute of Leadership and Management 2014.

33. Appelbaum and Milkman 2011. Similarly, a 2012 study of New Jersey's leave system, which began in 2009, found that a minority of employers report negative impacts. Of employers with workers who have used the leave system, 31 percent report a negative effect on business profitability or performance, and 42 percent report a negative effect on employee productivity. In contrast to the findings from California, smaller businesses in New Jersey are more likely to report negative effects on productivity or performance than large businesses. Smaller businesses tend to report higher administrative costs resulting from the law, whereas larger firms report higher costs due to greater overtime pay (Ramirez 2012).

34. For example, Ruhm 1998; Zigler, Muenchow, and Ruhm 2012; Boushey, O'Leary, and Mitukiewicz 2013.

35. Blau and Kahn 2013.

36. Ruhm 1998.

37. Carneiro, Løken, and Salvanes 2011.

38. Zigler, Muenchow, and Ruhm 2012.

39. Gornick and Meyers 2003; Waldfogel 2001b.

40. In 2012, 59 percent of the U.S. labor force worked for employers covered by the FMLA and met the FMLA's eligibility requirements for length of service and hours (Klerman, Daly, and Pozniak 2014).

41. Han, Ruhm, and Waldfogel 2009; Council of Economic Advisers 2014a; Winston 2014.

42. Gault et al. 2014.

43. Appelbaum and Milkman 2011; Houser and Vartanian 2012; Gault et al. 2014; Klevens et al. 2016.

44. Council of Economic Advisers 2014b; Boushey and Mitukiewicz 2014; Winston 2014.

45. The term "family leave" includes maternity and/or paternity leaves, long-term leaves for a personal illness, and leaves to care for an ill or disabled family member (U.S. DOL/BLS 2014). Recent studies using nationally representative data from the ECLS-B found that overall mothers in the United States take an average of nine weeks of leave, with wide variation (a standard deviation of more than eight weeks). On average, only five of these weeks were paid (Chatterji and Markowitz 2012; Han et al. 2008).

46. A 2014 survey found that Google provides eighteen weeks of paid maternity leave and twelve weeks of paid paternity leave. Yahoo, Facebook, and Reddit are close behind at sixteen or seventeen weeks of paid maternity leave; Facebook and Reddit offer fathers the same amounts of paid leave as mothers (Grant 2015).

47. U.S. DOL/BLS 2014.

48. Winston 2014.

49. Ariel Edwards-Levy, "Most Americans Support Paid Sick Days, Parental Leave," *Huffington Post*, February 4, 2015, available at: http://www.huffingtonpost.com/2015/02/04/sick-leave-poll_n_6616566.html (accessed August 22, 2016); Boushey and Mitukiewicz 2014; Lake Research Partners and Chesapeake Beach Consulting 2013.

50. Johnson 2016.

51. S. 786, Family and Medical Insurance Leave (FAMILY) Act, 114th Congress, 2015–2016.

52. Winston 2014.

53. "The Pentagon's New Parental Leave" (editorial), *New York Times*, February 2, 2016.

54. Bryce Covert, "Why Marco Rubio's New Family Leave Plan May Only Help the Well-Off," ThinkProgress, September 25, 2015, available at: http://thinkprogress.org/economy/2015/09/25/3705535/rubio-paid-family-leave/ (accessed August 22, 2016); Danielle Paquette, "What Clinton's and Trump's Child-Care Plans Mean for Parents," *Washington Post*, September 15, 2016.

55. Family and Medical Insurance Leave (FAMILY) Act, 114th Cong., S. 786 (2015); see also Boushey 2009.

56. Patrick McGreevy, "Brown Signs California Law Boosting Paid Family-Leave Benefits," *Los Angeles Times*, April 11, 2016. In April 2016, California increased its paid leave benefits such that workers earning close to the minimum wage would receive 70 percent of earnings while on leave, and those with higher pay (up to $108,000 annually) would receive 60 percent of wages.

57. Boushey and Mitukiewicz 2014.

58. For example, the leave benefit could be divided proportionally to the custody arrangement, or a default formula could be used, such that the custodial parent uses twelve weeks and the noncustodial four weeks.

59. Patnaik 2015.

60. Given the temporary nature of parental leave, we suggest that these benefits be made exempt from calculations of eligibility or amounts for public programs such the Supplemental Nutrition Assistance Program (SNAP), the Supplemental Nutrition Program for Women, Infants, and Children (WIC), Medicaid, health insurance tax credits, and child care benefits.

61. For the parent making $25,000 annually, the benefit would be the weekly income ($25,000 divided by 52) times the benefit replacement rate of 80 percent (for the first $25,000 in income), which equals $385. For the parent earning $37,500, the benefit would be income above $25,000 ($12,500) divided by 52 times the benefit replacement rate of 60 percent plus $385 (the benefit level for the first $25,000 in income), which equals $529.

62. See Boushey 2009. This definition of eligibility for benefits would include the currently employed, the long-term unemployed, and stay-at-home parents who have work histories, but not certain other groups, including most teen parents. In families with one stay-at-home parent without a work history, the employed parent would be eligible for parental leave benefits. Alternatively, eligibility could be determined using the SSA's disability threshold triggers. The excluded groups would continue to have access to other income supports, including SNAP and Temporary Assistance for Needy Families (TANF) benefits.

63. Boushey 2009; Boushey and Glynn 2012a; Winston 2014.

64. Boushey and Mitukiewicz 2014.

65. Winston 2014.

66. According to the Abt Associates report on family and medical leave prepared for the

U.S. Department of Labor (Klerman, Daly, and Pozniak 2014), besides the 21 percent of FMLA leaves taken for pregnancy or a new child, 18 percent of all leave events in 2012 were related to the illness of a qualifying relative, 55 percent were for an employee's own illness or medical need, and 2 percent were for other qualifying events. See also Klerman, Daly, and Pozniak 2013.

67. Waldfogel 1999; Winston 2014; U.S. DOL/BLS 2015a.

68. Dahl et al. 2015.

69. For example, the average Social Security monthly benefit for a retired worker in 2015 was $1,335. To fully pay for this benefit, the child would delay his or her future retirement by four months (not adjusting for inflation and discount factors).

70. Boushey 2009.

71. National Partnership for Women and Families 2015a. Prior proposals estimated that larger payroll taxes would be needed, approximately 0.3 percent in total (Boushey 2009). The proposal that has been debated in Massachusetts is estimated to cost $159 per worker each year ($3.05 per worker per week) (Johnson 2016; Albelda and Clayton-Matthews 2016).

72. State of California Department of Workforce Development Agency 2014; Zigler et al. 2012.

73. Boushey 2009.

74. U.S. DOL/BLS 2015b.

75. Boushey and Mitukiewicz 2014.

76. Zielewski and Waters Boots 2010; Boushey and Mitukiewicz 2014; Winston 2014.

77. For in-depth analyses of two alternatives, see Boushey and Glynn (2012b) on the Center for American Progress's Social Security Cares system, and Berkeley School of Law and Georgetown Law (2010) on the policy collaboration between the Berkeley Center on Health, Economic, and Family Security (CHEF) and Georgetown Law's Workplace Flexibility 2010 (WF2010).

78. Mathur 2015.

79. Independent Women's Forum 2014.

80. Kaiser Family Foundation 2016.

81. Isabel Sawhill, "Is It Time for a Shorter Workweek?" *Washington Post*, May 13, 2016.

82. Appelbaum and Milkman 2011.

83. Institute of Leadership and Management 2014.

Chapter 3: Affordable, High-Quality Care and Education

1. Lawrence Katz and Alan Krueger (2016) recently documented a 50 percent increase in just ten years in the proportion of American workers in temporary, contract, freelance, or on-call work—from 10.1 percent of all U.S. workers in 2005 to 15.8 percent in 2015.

2. Shonkoff and Phillips 2000; Center on the Developing Child at Harvard University 2009.

3. Center on the Developing Child at Harvard University 2007; Nelson et al. 2007.

4. Toxic stress has become widely used to describe the effects of prolonged and intense

stress experienced by children, particularly when they experience many adverse risk factors simultaneously (for example, chronic exposure to neighborhood violence combined with the accumulated burdens of the family's financial strain). Toxic stress can have pronounced negative effects on how children learn, develop, and grow, with lasting effects into adulthood. Research has shown that one way to minimize the negative effects of toxic stress on children is to ensure that they have nurturing and responsive relationships with supportive caregivers (National Scientific Council on the Developing Child 2004).

5. Blair and Raver 2012; Shonkoff et al. 2012.

6. Heckman 2007, 2008; Knudsen et al. 2006.

7. Laughlin 2013. For the 1965 figure, see U.S. Census Bureau 1982. We use multiple national data sources in this book to describe current levels of use of early care and education by type and family income, including the SIPP, the Current Population Survey (CPS), and the National Household Education Survey (NHES). These national surveys have differences in question wording, but overall their results are roughly similar. For example, the 2012 NHES reported that 13.1 million children (60 percent) under age five who had not started kindergarten were in nonparental care arrangements, of which 10.5 million came from households in which both parents were employed. This is roughly comparable to the results of the 2011 SIPP. The CPS, an annual survey, provides the most consistent data over time for the number of children ages three and four in center-based care and education settings, and we rely more on the CPS when focusing on preschool-age care, as in the figures in chapter 4.

8. Laughlin 2013.

9. Ibid.

10. Han 2004; Morrissey 2009; Chen 2013. Multiple care arrangements among families in which mothers work extended or nontraditional work hours have also been associated with poorer child behavioral and health outcomes (Morrissey 2013; Ros Pilarz and Hill 2014).

11. Laughlin 2013.

12. Chaudry 2004; Chaudry et al. 2011.

13. The 2012 NHES found that the average hourly cost of center-based care was $6.70, or $258 for forty hours in a week (Mamedova and Redford 2015).

14. Child Care Aware of America 2015.

15. Including Ohio, Rhode Island, and Washington State (Alliance for Early Childhood Finance 2016).

16. Laughlin 2013.

17. Gordon and Chase-Lansdale 2001; Bassok and Galdo 2016.

18. As rates of center care use have consistently and gradually increased across the age spectrum, there has been a corresponding and steady decline in the use of noncenter care for all ages of young children during the period from 1995 to 2011 (Burgess et al. 2014).

19. Family child care refers to care by a provider in a home (most often the provider's home) of a small group of mostly unrelated children (most often three to six), usually as a small business enterprise. Although states define subgroups of home providers

in highly varying ways, family child care homes are generally the only type of home-based care arrangement that most states regulate. Other home-based care arrangements—for example, by a relative, friend, or other "informal" care provider who provides care to one or two children (in either the child's or provider's home)—is most often not subject to any kind of licensing or regulation, even though these other home-based care arrangements are the primary source of care for millions of young children.

Findings from the National Survey of Early Care and Education (NSECE) indicate that states define subgroups of home-based providers in highly varying ways. The clearest way in which the most formal home-based providers were distinguished was according to whether they were both paid and appeared on state or national lists of early care and education services as licensed, regulated, license-exempt, or registered. The NSECE found that only a small fraction of home-based providers were on any formal national or state list of providers; the fact that the vast majority of home-based providers, which includes both paid and unpaid, were unlisted poses challenges for monitoring and supporting the quality of care (NSECE Project Team 2016).

20. Authors' analysis of 2008 SIPP panel data for primary arrangements in 2011.

21. Research using data from the nationally representative ECLS-B found that, at two years of age, most children in nonparental care were in settings rated as medium quality (61 percent), with smaller numbers in settings rated as high quality (26 percent) or low quality (13 percent) (Ruzek et al. 2014). An earlier National Institute of Child Health and Human Development (NICHD) study of early child care found that, across all nonparental care settings, positive or high-quality caregiving was highly characteristic of 12 percent of care for toddlers, somewhat characteristic for 32 percent, somewhat uncharacteristic for 51 percent, and highly uncharacteristic for 6 percent (NICHD Early Child Care Research Network 2000). Research using the Fragile Families Study, conducted with a higher-risk, urban sample, found that informal care arrangements scored the lowest in terms of quality, followed by family child care homes and then center-based care, with nonprofit centers scoring higher than for-profit centers (Rigby, Ryan, and Brooks-Gunn 2007). Although recent studies indicate that low-income children are the most likely to experience low-quality care (Rigby et al. 2007; Ruzek et al. 2014), some prior research suggests that children from both lower- and middle-income families—the latter without access to child care subsidies or public programs and lacking the economic resources to pay for high-quality care—are both more likely to experience low-quality care (Phillips et al. 1994; Hofferth et al. 1998).

22. In contrast, structural features of quality were related in a curvilinear fashion or U-shaped pattern for toddlers, such that children of families in the lower-middle range of the income distribution experienced caregivers with lower education and training than those with either the lowest or the higher incomes (Dowsett et al. 2008). This may reflect the fact that public investments in early care and education are concentrated among very low-income families, while higher-income families can afford to pay more out-of-pocket for higher-quality care.

23. Morrissey 2009.
24. Howes et al. 1988; NICHD Early Child Care Research Network 1998; Bacharach and Baumeister 2003; Loeb et al. 2004.
25. For GDP figures, see OECD 2010, 19. In 2011–2012, public expenditures for elementary and secondary education totaled $621 billion, or 3.8 percent of the U.S. GDP for 2012 (NCES 2015b). Annual per pupil expenditures of $12,401 (in 2014 dollars) were fourth-highest among thirty-two OECD countries, trailing only Switzerland, Norway, and Austria (OECD 2015). The Pew Charitable Trusts (2015b) estimate that federal, state, and local public expenditures for higher education in 2013 totaled $157.5 billion, or 0.9 percent of GDP. Per capita public expenditures for children in 2002 were $1,225, or 3.2 percent of GDP, according to estimates by Thomas Selden and Merrile Sing (2008).
26. OECD European Commission/Eurydice 2014.
27. The CCDBG was created in 1996 by combining several existing child care funding streams with additional funding as part of federal welfare reform to support parental employment. CCDBG provides block grants to states, territories, and tribes. CCDBG and the Child Care and Development Fund (CCDF) are often used interchangeably, most often with the annual allocation from CCDBG referring to the allocation from the federal budget and CCDF referring to federal and state contributions to each state's CCDF. In any case, public child care funds are provided to support the child care expenses of low-income working parents; most states do so primarily by providing eligible families with portable vouchers, which parents can use at any qualified provider of their choosing to help pay for care. CCDF is largely seen as a work support rather than as a child development intervention like Head Start.
28. Total child care spending in 2013 included $7.4 billion in state and federal child care block grant funding ($5.2 billion in federal funding and $2.2 billion in state funds). In addition, states spent $2.7 billion in federal and state TANF funds on child care assistance. Finally, states can apply some prior-year unexpended federal and state CCDBG funding; in 2013, approximately $1.2 billion of spending was from CCDBG funding from prior years (Schmit and Reeves 2015; expenditure data reported by the U.S. DHHS/ACF/OCC 2015).

    Federal CCDBG funding totaled approximately $5.2 billion (including "mandatory" and "discretionary" funding of $2.9 billion and $2.3 billion). States' share of CCDBG funding was $2.2 billion; this includes two categories of funds: states' "matching funds," which are tied to a portion of the federal mandatory funding, and "maintenance of effort" funds, which reflect the amount that the states have already been required to spend on child care prior to the incorporation of several former child care assistance funding streams within the CCDBG when it was established in 1996 (U.S. DHHS/ACF/OCC 2015).

    In addition to these CCDBG-specific funding amounts, states can also use federal funding from their TANF block grant for child care subsidies, and they may apply some portion of their required state TANF maintenance of effort funds for child care subsidies as well. In 2013, states used $1.1 billion of their federal TANF block grants and applied $1.6 billion of their state TANF maintenance of effort funding to child care subsidies (Schmit and Reeves 2015).

29. There is significant variation among the states in child care policies and rules, including:

    1. *Minimum work hours for eligibility:* Approximately half of the states require each parent to work a minimum number of hours to be eligible for child care subsidies, ranging from fifteen to thirty hours per week, while half have no requirement for a minimum number of hours worked (Minton et al. 2014, table 2).

    2. *Income eligibility thresholds:* These ranged in 2014, for a family of four, from $2,367 per month in Michigan to $5,851 per month in North Dakota. Income eligibility thresholds also ranged from 121 percent to 298 percent of FPL, with a median rate of $3,677 overall (Minton et al. 2014, table 15).

    3. *Family copayments:* Family copayments ranged in 2013, for a family of four with two children and a family income of $30,000 receiving subsidies, from $65 per month (approximately 3 percent of family income in Washington State) to $1,035 per month (43 percent of family income in Hawaii), with a median payment of $192 overall (8 percent of family income) and three states (Michigan, Missouri, and Ohio) in which a family income of $30,000 is above the income eligibility threshold in the state (Minton et al. 2014, table 34).

    4. *Maximum reimbursement levels:* These ranged in 2014, for licensed, center-based care for an infant in full-time care, from $339 per month in Mississippi to $1,430 per month in New York State, with a median rate of nearly $700 overall and an eightieth-percentile state rate of $910 in Colorado (Minton et al. 2014, table 35). For a toddler in full-time care in a licensed center, maximum reimbursement levels ranged from $326 in Mississippi to $1,148 in Virginia, with a median rate of $625 overall and an eightieth-percentile state rate of $821 in Wisconsin (Minton et al. 2014, table 35).

30. Program participation data reported by the U.S. DHHS/ACF/OCC 2015.

31. Program participation data for 2001 reported in U.S. DHHS/ACF/OCC 2001.

32. The 15 percent represents 2.11 million children, including children served through all federal and state spending on child care, including CCDBG, TANF, and Social Services Block Grants (SSBGs) (Chien 2015).

33. In addition to the 2.8 million eligible children under age three, there were 2.2 million ages three and four, 1.0 million age five, and 7.7 million ages six to thirteen. Subsidies were received by 11 percent of eligible children under age one, 23 percent of eligible children ages one and two, 28 percent of children ages three and four, and 11 percent of children ages five to twelve (Chien 2015).

34. Sixty-three percent of all families with children receiving subsidies (from federal and state CCDF funding as well as other sources) had incomes below the FPL, and 90 percent had incomes below 150 percent FPL; 14 percent of families were receiving TANF (Chien 2015).

35. Crosby, Gennetian, and Huston 2005; Forry, Daneri, and Howarth 2013. In addition to the 70 percent of infants and toddlers in center-based care in 2013, some others were in state-licensed family child care. Overall, approximately 15 percent of children whose care was subsidized were in care in home-based settings, and 63 percent of these were with a relative provider. The use of subsidies for child care not subject to

regulation varied across the states: in sixteen states it represented less than one-tenth of subsidized care arrangements, and in eleven states 25 percent or more of subsidized care arrangements were unregulated care by relative and nonrelative providers (U.S. DHHS/ACF/OCC 2015).

36. U.S. DHHS/ACF/OCC 2015.

37. See IRS website and the Tax Policy Center.

38. In 2005, families needed to earn at least $23,700 (and to pay for child care) to receive any benefit from the CDCTC, leaving out the lowest-income working families.

39. Tax Policy Center 2015.

40. Ibid.

41. Ibid.

42. Maag 2015.

43. Office of Management and Budget 2014; Tax Policy Center 2015.

44. In 2013, income eligibility for child care assistance was below the federal maximum income threshold of 85 percent of state median income in all states, and many states had waiting lists or frozen intake for child care assistance (Children's Defense Fund 2014).

45. Adams and Rohacek 2002.

46. NICHD Early Child Care Research Network 2006.

47. Initially, young children receiving care through these programs would continue to receive assistance as these programs are streamlined and simplified into a single child care program. CCDBG provides block grant funding to states for the care of children up to age thirteen (including after-school and summer care for school-age children), and approximately one-third of block grant funding is used toward care for children ages six to thirteen. In moving to the assurance model for young children under age five (for whom early care and education represents a disproportionate cost relative to family income for the primary source of out-of-home learning and care), we suggest segregating the current amount of the block grant devoted to care for children ages six to thirteen and folding that in with other existing federal funding resources for after-school and summer programs to create a single funding stream.

48. The 250 percent maximum income threshold would be at or above the current thresholds in all but one state, North Dakota, which has a threshold equivalent to 298 percent of FPL. In thirty states, the income threshold as of 2014 was below 200 percent of FPL.

49. One option for setting these levels would be to have a common national subsidy cap but to allow states to propose a higher cap based on local costs of care, with the federal share of costs remaining 80 percent up to the state-established maximum. Another option, similar to the income eligibility levels, would be for states to establish higher maximum reimbursement rates within an allowable range (for example, plus or minus 30 percent of the federally determined floor for the cap) to account for geographic variation in child care costs. In addition, states could choose—as some do now—to offer tiered-reimbursement systems based on provider quality, as measured using validated instruments. States could also decide to incentivize the provision of a particular type or area of care for which there is greater unmet need, such as modestly higher reimbursement levels for weekend, evening, or night hours.

50. Federal and state shares for CCDBG funding are currently determined according to what is called the federal medical assistance percentages (FMAPs), which reflect measures of economic strengths across the states and generally range between 50 and 75 percent. These percentages are used across a wide range of health and human services programs to determine the federal share of program costs (U.S. DHHS 2016b). Our proposal increases the federal percentage to a uniform and significantly higher percentage of the program costs across all states. Federal spending would increase significantly at the outset of the Assurance program, but state spending would probably also increase eventually in all or most states over time as program participation increased.

51. We propose a parent fee schedule that increases with income such that the fee would equal 3 percent of all income up to the FPL (or the minimum $10 per week fee, if higher); the rate on income above this level would increase with income so that for income between 100 and 150 percent of the FPL 5 percent of income would go toward the parents' fee, for income between 150 and 200 percent of the FPL 7 percent of income would go toward the parents' fee, and so forth as family income increases. For the family of three with a family income of $29,000, their fee would be calculated as 3 percent of income up to the FPL for a family of three ($20,090 in 2015) plus 5 percent of their income above that level ($8,910), which is below 150 percent of the FPL: thus, their fee is $602.70 plus $442 ($1,048.20), which they can pay weekly ($20.16) or monthly ($87.35). Figure 3.7 shows how the parent fee would increase with income for a family of four.

52. The 2014 reauthorization of the CCDBG included a minimum twelve-month period for certification and recertification of eligibility for most families receiving subsidies.

53. Sabol et al. 2013.

54. Merz et al. 2016; see also Davis et al. 2015.

55. Particularly within the initial years of developing and expanding the CCA program, the robust research and development program that 1 percent of total federal funding would provide could help ensure experimentation, more efficacious model development, and the testing of different quality improvement efforts.

56. As of 2016, twenty-two states and the District of Columbia have state CDCTC programs that in general piggyback on the federal CDCTC, with most structured so that the state credit is calculated simply as a percentage of the federal tax credit. We assume that the states would decide whether to similarly increase their own tax credits proportionately for children under age five following an increase in the federal CDCTC, to reduce the percentage of the federal credit they offer (to remain revenue-neutral), or to take some other approach. We make no specific assumption about what states might do. For more detail on states that have their own CDCTC and their features, see Corporation for Enterprise Development 2016.

57. The current limits are between 20 percent and 35 percent, with a fairly sharp phase-out rate at very low levels of family income, so the large majority of those who receive benefits receive the minimum 20 percent rate for the credit.

58. Heckman 2006; Duncan and Sojourner 2013.

59. Bainbridge, Meyers, and Waldfogel 2003; Forry and Hofferth 2011.

60. Council of Economic Advisers 2014a; Gordon 2014; Chaudry 2016.

61. Women's labor force participation increased steadily over the last quarter of the twentieth century, from 46 percent of those age sixteen and over in the labor force in 1975 to 60 percent in 2000, before declining to 57 percent in 2015 (U.S. DOL/BLS 2016).

62. For a review of the literature, see Morrissey 2016.

63. The Urban Institute has estimated expansions in the CCDF program for the Center for American Progress and the Children's Defense Fund that differ somewhat in their parameters from our proposal. Its estimates of the increase in the number of parents gaining employment range from 400,000 to 1.9 million. By contrast, our proposal would be targeted at families with younger children—thus, a smaller subset of families—but eligibility would be extended to a larger share of the subset whose employment is most severely constrained by the cost of child care. Also, our proposal includes both middle- and higher-income thresholds for eligibility and higher subsidy levels.

64. Currently relatives and informal care providers provide a significant share of all child care for infants and toddlers, owing to some families' preferences for children at that age and constraints on availability and affordability. Only 22 percent of all one- and two-year-olds were in center-based care in 2012, according to data from the NHES (see figure 3.2); however, this share has been increasing over time, particularly among families who can afford to pay for center-based care.

65. In fiscal year 2013, the states spent $2.2 billion in state funds for CCDBG and used $1.6 billion of their state TANF maintenance of effort funding for child care subsidies (U.S. DHHS/ACF/OCC 2015).

66. Connelly and Kimmel 2003; Blau and Tekin 2007; Baker, Gruber, and Milligan 2008.

Chapter 4: Universal Preschool

* The terms "pre-K," "prekindergarten," and "preschool" are commonly used to refer to publicly supported, formal, center-based programs for three- and four-year-old children. Here we use the term "preschool" as an umbrella term for such programs. When appropriate because of specific program names, we also use the term "prekindergarten" (for example, the Boston Public Schools Prekindergarten Program).

1. National Center for Children in Poverty 2015; Child Care Aware of America 2014.

2. Authors' calculations based on data from the 2013 and 2014 CPS. Among families in the top income quintile, 86 percent of four-year-old children were enrolled in preschool or other center-based care and education in October 2014, including 63 percent of three-year-olds, who had been enrolled in preschool at age three in October 2013 and remained in the CPS rotation sample the following October. For families in the top income quintile, 75 percent of all three- and four-year-olds enrolled in preschool attended private preschool. Nearly 60 percent of children in the bottom three income quintiles were enrolled in preschool or center-based care at age four, including just 34 percent of the three-year-olds who were enrolled in preschool or center-based care in the rotation sample in the prior year, suggesting that more than one-quarter were first enrolled in center-based care beginning the year before they started kindergarten, and that 40 percent had not enrolled in preschool by age four and thus

may not have received any prior center-based early learning experience before start-ing kindergarten. Among the 60 percent of families with income in the bottom three quintiles, more than 70 percent of children who were in preschool attended public preschool programs.

3. Barnett et al. 2015.

4. OECD 2015.

5. Mashburn et al. 2008.

6. Goldin and Katz 2008.

7. On the importance of stimulating early childhood experiences, see Shonkoff and Phillips 2000. On early education improving children's school readiness and promot-ing better education outcomes, see Yoshikawa et al. 2013. On the lack of such oppor-tunities for families of all incomes, see Vandell and Wolfe 2000; Blau 2001.

8. Yoshikawa et al. 2013.

9. Camilli et al. 2010; Bania et al. 2014; Li et al. 2016. These sources present large-scale meta-analyses covering evaluations between 1960 and the late 2000s.

10. Gormley et al. 2005; Weiland and Yoshikawa 2013.

11. Gormley et al. 2005; U.S. DHHS/ACF 2010; Weiland and Yoshikawa 2013; Bloom and Weiland 2015.

12. U.S. DHHS/ACF 2010; Phillips and Meloy 2012; Weiland 2016a.

13. Jones 2014.

14. Public Opinion Strategies and Hart Research 2013, 2014; Tully 2015. Each year since 2013 the participants in the poll have also been specifically asked about President Obama's proposal to allocate $10 billion per year for ten years to states to expand pre-school slots for low- to moderate-income families, as well as other efforts, and each year increasing majorities of respondents have indicated that they support the pro-posal, rising from 70 percent in 2013 to 76 percent by 2015, including 59 percent of respondents who identify as Republican and 94 percent of Democrat (Tully 2015).

15. Barnett et al. 2016.

16. Ibid.

17. Child Care Aware of America 2014.

18. Whitebook, Phillips, and Howes 2014.

19. Harris and Adams 2007.

20. Whitebook, Phillips, and Howes 2014.

21. Clarke-Stewart et al. 2002; NICHD Early Child Care Research Network 2002; Mash-burn et al. 2008.

22. NICHD Early Child Care Research Network 2002.

23. Zaslow et al. 2010; Burchinal, Kainz, and Cai 2011; Weiland et al. 2013.

24. Schumacher, Irish, and Lombardi 2003.

25. Tout et al. 2010; Washington State Department of Early Learning 2013.

26. U.S. DHHS/ACF/OHS 2014.

27. Howes et al. 2008; Mashburn et al. 2008; Burchinal, Kainz, and Cai 2011; Zaslow et al. 2016. Modest associations between observational quality ratings and children's out-comes have led to debate in the field regarding the psychometrics of these measures, particularly their validity and measurement error (see, for example, Zaslow et al.

2010; Burchinal, Kainz, and Cai 2011; Gordon et al. 2013). Despite their limitations, at present they provide the most systematic accounting of process and structural quality available nationally in care settings for children from birth to age five.

28. Burchinal, Kainz, and Cai 2011; Weiland et al. 2013.

29. Vandell et al. 2010.

30. On ELLCO, see Smith, Dickinson, and Anastasopoulos 2002. On COEMET, see Clements and Sarama 2007.

31. Gormley et al. 2005; Phillips, Gormley, and Lowenstein 2009.

32. Lipsey, Farran, and Hofer 2015a. In a representative sample, 85 percent of the classrooms in the Tennessee program were found not to meet a standard of "good" overall quality (Farran et al. 2014).

33. Hill, Gormley, and Adelstein 2015; Lipsey, Farran, and Hofer 2015a; Phillips, Gormley, and Anderson 2016.

34. Currie and Thomas 1995; Campbell et al. 2002; Schweinhart et al. 2005; Ludwig and Miller 2007; Deming 2009; Campbell et al. 2012; Yoshikawa, Weiland, and Brooks-Gunn 2016.

35. Bailey et al. 2016.

36. Zhai, Raver, and Jones 2012.

37. Jenkins et al. 2015.

38. Yoshikawa, Weiland, and Brooks-Gunn 2016.

39. Yoshikawa et al. 2013; Bailey et al. 2016; Yoshikawa, Weiland, and Brooks-Gunn 2016.

40. NICHD Early Child Care Research Network 2006; Mashburn et al. 2008; Phillips, Gormley, and Lowenstein 2009; Weiland et al. 2013.

41. On all eleven prekindergarten programs, see Mashburn et al. 2008. On the Head Start grantees, see U.S. DHHS/ACF/OPRE 2014. On Boston's prekindergarten program, see Weiland et al. 2013. On Tulsa's programs, see Phillips, Gormley, and Lowenstein 2009.

42. Mashburn et al. 2008; Moiduddin et al. 2012; U.S. DHHS, ACF, Office of Planning, Research and Evaluation 2014.

43. Mashburn et al. 2008.

44. U.S. DHHS/ACF/OPRE 2013, 2014.

45. LoCasale-Crouch et al. 2007.

46. Clements and Sarama 2007; Ginsburg, Lee, and Boyd 2008.

47. Kholoptseva 2016.

48. Beck and McKeown 2007; Neuman and Dwyer 2009; Bowne, Yoshikawa, and Snow 2016.

49. Phillips, Gormley, and Lowenstein 2009; Weiland et al. 2013; Yoshikawa et al. 2013.

50. Whitehurst et al. 1999; Starkey, Klein, and Wakeley 2004; Wasik, Bond, and Hindman 2006; Bierman et al. 2008; Clements and Sarama 2008; Klein et al. 2008; Preschool Curriculum Evaluation Research Consortium 2008; Farver, Lonigan, and Eppe 2009; Landry et al. 2009; Neuman and Cunningham 2009; Powell et al. 2010; Fantuzzo, Gadsden, and McDermott 2011; Lonigan et al. 2011.

51. Yoshikawa et al. 2013.

52. Preschool Curriculum Evaluation Research Consortium 2008.

53. Weiland 2016b.

54. Duncan et al. 2015.
55. Diamond et al. 2007; Blair and Raver 2014; Farran and Wilson 2014; Morris et al. 2014.
56. Bierman et al. 2008; Morris et al. 2014.
57. Yoshikawa et al. 2013.
58. Kohn 2016.
59. Bartik, Gormley, and Adelstein 2012.
60. Yoshikawa et al. 2013.
61. Li et al. 2016.
62. NICHD Early Child Care Research Network 2005; Loeb et al. 2007.
63. Puma et al. 2012; Li et al. 2016.
64. This approach would also counteract the moral hazards that could arise if a progressive state that advances early education sees the federal government providing disproportionate support to laggard states, or if states freeze or back-track investments while legislation and funding for a larger federal role is being debated.
65. Incentives would be established in accord with current policy structures. As of this writing, the implementation and regulations of the Every Student Succeeds Act (ESSA) are not yet clear enough on exactly how incentives for quality under this act would work for preschool education.
66. A ramp-up phase could allow programs that do not yet meet some of these requirements time to improve. For example, as access grows across mixed-delivery systems that include community providers, Head Start, and public preschool, some providers may not meet staff qualification requirements. These providers could be incentivized to satisfy these requirements within a certain number of years (for example, within three years, with scholarship support). To address compensation differentials (providers in community-based child care centers are generally paid lower salaries than Head Start teachers, who in turn are paid lower salaries than public preschool teachers), bonuses could be provided to those with much lower salaries during the transition to full parity (Whitebook, Phillips, and Howes 2014; Institute of Medicine and National Research Council 2015).
67. See the What Works Clearinghouse website at http://whatworks.ed.gov.
68. Reardon 2011.
69. Alternative teacher certification programs like the Boston Teacher Residency, New York City Teaching Fellows, and Teach for America offer models for doing so. The extra summer month could also be used to attract more promising teachers to the field. Programs that offer college students supervised opportunities to teach young children, like the national JumpStart program and the West Virginia University Extension Services/Americorps Energy Express summer program, could be expanded. To our knowledge, the effects of these programs on the choice to pursue early care and education as a profession have not been investigated.
70. For example, Georgia's universal preschool program, the first statewide program in the United States, accepted applications from only low-income communities in its initial rollout. In contrast, Boston instituted a lottery for parents interested in enrolling their child in preschool as the system expanded capacity across all families, regardless of income (Sachs and Weiland 2010).

71. In Georgia, after the initial phase focused on low-income communities, during which time no private providers applied to the program, expansion to all four-year-olds regardless of family income began in 1995; at that point, private providers began applying and became integrated into the state program. This helped to address facilities shortages in the public schools and allowed the program to expand more quickly. To facilitate the expansion of access to preschool in West Virginia, funding for universal preschool was provided directly to public schools, but half of these programs were required to collaborate with community-based preschool and Head Start programs.

72. Weiland and Yoshikawa 2014.

73. As shown by the experience of states and localities like Georgia, Oklahoma, and Washington, D.C., not everyone eligible for universal public preschool actually enrolls; some families continue to use private preschool programs, including those who might have their children privately enrolled in programs that begin at age one or two. For example, Oklahoma served approximately 56 percent of four-year-olds in public preschools in 2002, and 74 percent by 2012. Washington, D.C., served 44 percent of four-year-olds and 18 percent of three-year-olds in 2002 and now serves 92 percent of four-year-olds and 69 percent of three-year-olds. A target number at which coverage can be considered to have become "universal" may therefore be about 75 or 80 percent of four-year-olds in universal public preschool (and 70 percent of three-year-olds for those proposing to provide universal preschool starting at age three) at the end of a ten-year expansion.

74. NCES 2014.

75. Child Trends 2015b.

76. With few contexts currently offering universal preschool, scaling high-quality preschool for both three-year-olds and four-year-olds is likely to be a challenge. In states that do not offer universal preschool for three- or four-year-olds, we would expect a significant share of children to be served through the ACE subsidies and through Head Start programs.

77. Li et al. 2016.

78. Suárez-Orozco, Yoshikawa, and Tseng 2015.

79. U.S. DHHS/ACF 2015.

80. For example, number and demographic characteristics of children served; estimated number and demographic characteristics of community children not served; education, experience, and certification of teachers and paraprofessionals; average and range of class size; curriculum in place; available comprehensive services; and professional development provided, including number of coaching visits, hours of coaching per year, and topics covered in the coaching visits. Quality could be monitored through annual direct observations in random, representative samples of preschool classrooms, using a validated quality assessment tool that measures instructional quality. These data could then be reported to the state and federal governments, along with analysis of how such data guides states' quality improvement efforts.

81. Bassok, Fitzpatrick, and Loeb 2014.

Chapter 5: A New Head Start

1. Chetty and Hendren 2015.

2. Greg Duncan, Pamela Morris, and Chris Rodrigues (2011) review much of the literature and find significant negative effects of family poverty and low economic resources on the academic achievement of young children (see also Brooks-Gunn and Duncan 1997; Chaudry and Wimer 2016).

3. Maynard and Murnane 1979; Akee et al. 2010; Duncan, Morris, and Rodrigues 2011; Dahl and Lochner 2012.

4. Gassman-Pines and Yoshikawa 2006.

5. McLoyd 1998; Yoshikawa, Aber, and Beardslee 2012.

6. Cavanagh and Houston 2006, 2008.

7. Kessler et al. 2014; Herbers, Reynolds, and Chen 2013; Ziol-Guest and McKenna 2014.

8. Kalil and Ziol-Guest 2005, 2008; Johnson, Kalil, and Dunifon 2012.

9. Duncan et al. 1998; Ratcliffe and McKernan 2012; Sharkey and Elwert 2011; Wodtke, Harding, and Elwert 2011.

10. Sampson, Sharkey, and Raudenbush 2008; Sharkey and Elwert 2011.

11. Wolf, Magnuson, and Kimbro 2016; Harding 2003, 2010.

12. Sampson, Morenoff, and Gannon-Rowley 2002; Sampson 2012; Sharkey 2013.

13. Gordon and Chase-Lansdale 2001; Bassok, Fitzpatrick, and Loeb 2014; Bassok and Galdo 2016.

14. Shonkoff and Fisher 2013.

15. Heckman 2006.

16. Zigler and Muenchow 1992.

17. A multidisciplinary committee of fourteen members with expertise in health, education, and social services was formed to conceptualize Head Start and propose details of the program to the president; that committee's proposal laid the groundwork for the program's comprehensive set of services (Zigler and Muenchow 1992). The committee noted the limited reach of early education for most children at the time. Edward Zigler, a Yale psychology professor who served on the committee and is considered one of the founders of Head Start, noted that there was concern from the outset that Head Start would start too late in a child's life and was not comprehensive enough. However, there was also a sense that the program had to start with this age group because there were a few influential preschool evaluation studies with very promising results and few models of programs for children below preschool age. In 1965, public kindergarten programs did not even exist yet in thirty-two states, and the 42 percent of five-year-olds who were in kindergarten tended to be primarily from middle- and higher-income classes, with many attending private kindergarten (Vinovskis 2005). Center-based preschool for four-year-olds was still rarely used, and so earlier intervention at this age for children from poor families was seen as offering them a compensatory advantage—a "head start"—toward school readiness.

18. See Advisory Committee on Head Start Research and Evaluation 1999. This approach of combining education, health, and social supports with early education is still con-

sidered a model by leaders around the world in early childhood development and has been implemented by a few large-scale programs (Lombardi 2014).

19. Ludwig and Miller 2007. In addition, David Frisvold and Julie Lumeng (2011) find evidence that additional hours in Head Start may reduce childhood obesity.

20. These models have included home-based services (Home Start); more intensive combinations of family support and center-based services (Parent-Child Development Centers and Family Resource Centers); and transition services into early primary schooling (Follow Through).

21. Walker 2014. In 2013, 145,000 children were enrolled in Early Head Start, a figure that represents approximately 4 percent of children under age three in families with incomes below the poverty level. Though very low at 4 percent, this percentage represented a near-doubling of the number and ratio of children in poor families served through Early Head Start in 2008, when 84 million children and families were served.

22. Walker 2014.

23. Phillips and White 2004.

24. Advisory Committee on Head Start Research and Evaluation 2012.

25. McKey et al. 1985; Barnett 1995; Karoly et al. 1998. Ruth Hubbell McKey and her colleagues (1985) conducted a federally commissioned synthesis and meta-analysis that integrated findings from over 200 research studies (including 72 in the meta-analysis) from just the 1970s and early 1980s focused on Head Start outcomes; they found that Head Start had fairly sizable effects (in the 0.40 to 0.50 effect size range) across multiple developmental domains for its participants.

26. Although research consistently has shown short-term positive impacts on cognitive measures from Head Start across studies, studies have also found that these gains diminish relative to control groups when measured in the immediate subsequent years—for example, when children are tested again in first or third grade (McKey et al. 1985; Currie and Thomas 1995; Deming 2009; U.S. DHHS/ACF 2010; Puma et al. 2012). Some research indicates that the low quality of the schooling experienced by children from poor families after leaving Head Start contributes to this fade-out effect (Currie and Thomas 1995; Lee and Loeb 1995). More broadly, others have noted that fade-out is an empirical regularity in studies of educational interventions (Krueger and Whitmore 2001; Anderson 2008).

27. Currie and Thomas 1995; Garces, Thomas, and Currie 2002; Ludwig and Miller 2007; Deming 2009. Longitudinal designs involve repeated observations of the same measures over an extended period of time—in some cases many years or even decades. Quasi-experimental research designs are similar to experimental designs but lack random assignment to a treatment or control group. Thus, there may be important differences between groups at baseline that may limit the extent to which "treatment effects" can be attributed to the program or intervention being evaluated. These approaches are often more practical, however, since treatment cannot always be assigned in practice.

28. U.S. DHHS/ACF 2010; Puma et al. 2012.

29. Feller et al. 2016; Kline and Walters 2015.

30. Ludwig and Phillips 2008.

31. Studies that have looked at the variations in impact from being in Head Start have revealed several potential subgroups who may be relatively more disadvantaged (for example, dual-language learners, children whose mothers are less educated, and children whose homes offer more limited stimulation) and are more likely to show higher initial results and to sustain positive results (Bitler, Hoynes, and Domina 2014; Cooper and Lanza 2014; Miller et al. 2014; Bloom and Weiland 2015).

32. Bloom and Weiland 2015.

33. Moiduddin et al. 2012.

34. Burchinal et al. 2010; Moiduddin et al. 2012. The revised "Head Start Performance Standards of 2015" (U.S. DHHS/ACF 2015) intensified the professional development support provided to these workforces, particularly on-site mentoring.

35. These longer-term studies do not benefit from an experimental design but rely on several empirically rigorous non-experimental designs, including differential outcomes for sibling pairs in which one attended Head Start and another did not (Currie and Thomas 1995; Garces, Thomas, and Currie 2002; Deming 2009); for Head Start locations by community poverty levels (Ludwig and Miller 2005); and around the income eligibility cutoffs (Carneiro and Ginja 2014).

36. The Head Start participants were seven percentage points less likely to repeat a grade in school, six percentage points less likely to be identified as needing special education, eight percentage points more likely to graduate from high school, six percentage points more likely to attend college, seven percentage points less likely to be in poor health, and two percentage points less likely to become teen parents (Deming 2009).

37. Currie and Thomas 1995; Ludwig and Miller 2007.

38. Heckman and Raut 2016.

39. Love et al. 2005; Love et al. 2013. As with the quality measured across Head Start programs in the HSIS, the quality of both the home-visiting and classroom components of Early Head Start was found to be moderate on average, with lower quality and more variation found on measures of engaged support for learning—a finding similar to what was found for instructional quality in Head Start and state pre-K programs (Aikens et al. 2015).

40. Love et al. 2005.

41. Beginning in 1990, in addition to federal regional offices, states created Head Start offices and later state Early Learning Councils to bolster their own role in coordinating Head Start programs with primary and preventive health care, social services, and public preschool systems. See the Improving Head Start for School Readiness Act of 2007, which reauthorized Head Start.

42. Ludwig and Miller 2007.

43. The instructional quality observed in Head Start programs is broadly similar to the levels of quality observed in public pre-K classrooms—instruction in both settings varies widely in quality, but on average is not adequate for what children need. Improving process quality, particularly instructional quality, is thus a shared challenge in the field of early childhood education.

44. Duncan and Sojourner 2013; Gertler et al. 2014.

45. Chetty and Hendren 2015.

46. Some public prekindergarten programs now blend state or municipal resources with Head Start funding. We believe that this is a transitional funding approach on the pathway to universal preschool education as proposed in chapter 4.

47. Many Head Start programs remain part-day programs and also do not provide summer programming, leaving working families to scramble for temporary care arrangements during those times. Finally, Head Start programs have lagged behind some other preschool programs in the level of qualifications it requires from teachers and in the salaries and benefits offered to them. This, of course, is not a problem unique to Head Start—many community-based small preschool providers offer even lower salaries and have lower proportions of teachers with BA degrees or specialized training in early childhood education. The 2015 version of the revised "Head Start Performance Standards" tackles some of these problems (U.S. DHHS/ACF 2015). For example, the new standards call for all Head Start programs to offer full-day, full-year programming. They also provide more direction to increase the instructional quality of the program, emphasizing content-based training and professional development as well as coaching and mentoring through direct observation and feedback.

48. In 2010, 12.4 million people, or 4 percent of the U.S. population, were living in areas of highly concentrated poverty, defined as geographic areas (census tracts) in which 40 percent of the residents had incomes below the poverty level that year. Within these communities, 3.6 million residents were children under eighteen, and 600,000 were children under three.

49. Chetty and Hendren 2015; Chetty, Hendren, and Katz 2016.

50. These eligibility catchment areas would at minimum need to be large enough to include at least 180 children birth to three (or annual birth cohorts of 60 children or more) to ensure that a Head Start program with sufficient economies of scale could be located there. Areas of concentrated poverty vary in their size in the United States from isolated fairly small pockets of concentrated poverty to very large swaths that have large contiguous areas of concentrated poverty.

51. Such fluctuations have been especially powerful in recent decades: the number of children living in concentrated poverty sharply increased in the 1980s, and again since 2000, but declined in the 1990s (Jargowsky 2014).

52. Christopher Wildeman and Kristin Turney (2014) report that 670,000 cases of child maltreatment were confirmed by child protection services (CPS) in the United States in 2011; approximately 490,000 of these cases represented the first time for a CPS-confirmed case of maltreatment of a child. Children age five and younger represented half the cases of first CPS-confirmed maltreatment. In spite of the strong associations documented between child maltreatment and concentrated-poverty areas (for an extensive review of this literature, see Coulton et al. 2007), given the high number of confirmed cases of abuse and neglect, most of still occur outside of areas of concentrated poverty.

53. U.S. DHHS/ACF/OHS 2015.

54. Dodge et al. 2014.

55. For instance, there are between 300 and 400 clusters of zip codes that form areas where the poverty rate is over 33 percent and the child poverty rate is approximately 50 percent.

56. A recent review of infant and toddler early education services found four program models that have been systematically evaluated through high-quality studies and have shown evidence of positive effects on children's outcomes. The review also identified thirteen compelling models that provide or support infant and toddler early learning but have not yet been subject to rigorous evaluation, including two program models, five models for infant and toddler curricula, and six models for coaching and mentoring to improve provider quality (Monahan et al. 2015).

57. Dozier et al. 2008; Landry et al. 2008.

58. Clark, Tluczek, and Wenzel 2003; Toth et al. 2006; Suchman et al. 2011.

59. Olds et al. 2014.

60. Kitzman et al. 2010; Olds et al. 2010.

61. Dozier et al. 2009.

62. Aikens et al. 2015.

63. York and Loeb 2014; Mayer et al. 2015.

64. See, for example, Neuman and Cunningham 2009 and Landry et al. 2014.

65. Duncan and Sojourner 2013. The IHDP was a comprehensive early intervention demonstration program across eight study sites that targeted low-birthweight newborns and offered services that included frequent home visitation in the first year and full-day, high-quality early education from age one until they turned three.

66. Arbour et al. 2015.

67. See, for example, Dorn, Minton, and Huber 2014.

68. Davis et al. 2015; Merz et al. 2016.

69. This review, conducted by Mathematica Policy Research, found four program models that showed evidence of positive effects on children's outcomes—the Abecedarian Project, the IHDP, parent-child development centers, and Early Head Start (Monahan et al. 2015).

70. Advisory Committee on Head Start Research and Evaluation 2012; Shonkoff and Fisher 2013.

71. Coie et al. 1993.

72. Arbour et al. 2015. These include, for example, experiments that test aspects of scalability in early phases of causal impact evaluation and that test mechanisms, not just later outcomes, in efforts to build strong theories of change (Ludwig, Kling, and Mullainathan 2011); and mixed qualitative and quantitative research approaches that take into account diverse population experiences and preferences rather than solely quantitative evidence (Yoshikawa, Weiland, and Brooks-Gunn 2016).

73. With a good administrative data infrastructure, for example, randomization need not occur solely at the center level but could also be distributed through approaches such as birthday-based eligibility for community-level services, as utilized in the recent Durham Connects evaluation (Dodge et al. 2013, 2014). In addition, cutoff approaches based on risk status could be used in regression-discontinuity analysis (see, for example, Lipsey et al. 2015b).

74. In addition to setting targets for the portion of funded enrollment to be enrolled prenatally or in early infancy, we recommend experimenting with and testing the efficacy of model programs that limit new child enrollments at twelve or eighteen months in order to augment the dosage and continuity of interventions for the chil-

dren served. In concentrated-poverty areas, such a limit could ensure that centers focus on the earliest intervention and continuing services, while allowing them to make exceptions for hardship-based eligibility referrals from service systems—for example, children with acute and immediate needs due to homelessness or child welfare–related circumstances.

75. Early intervention services stem from what is referred to as Part C of the Individuals with Disabilities Education Act, enacted by Congress in 1975 to ensure that children with disabilities have the opportunity to receive a free appropriate public education, just like other children. Part B of the act covers services for school-age children, and Part C covers services for younger children prior to school entry.

76. The recently created Early Head Start–Child Care Partnerships were first funded in 2014 (U.S. DHHS/ACF 2016). The successful integration of these new entrants into the program could serve as a model for opening Head Start to other new entrants and for using ACE subsidies to complement Head Start funding. In addition, large investments have been made in new model programs, like Educare, that have integrated Early Head Start and Head Start resources with other funding to create comprehensive, seamless programs with long service durations and low rates of attrition (Yazejian and Bryant 2012).

77. Almond and Currie 2011a, 2011b.

Chapter 6: Conclusion: No More Tinkering at the Edges

1. Piketty and Saez 2014.
2. Atkinson and Piketty 2010.
3. Reardon 2011; Bradbury et al. 2015.
4. Deming 2009; Yoshikawa et al. 2013; McCoy et al. 2015.
5. Duncan and Magnuson 2013; Li et al. 2016.
6. Han, Ruhm, and Waldfogel 2009; Council of Economic Advisers 2014a; Winston 2014; U.S. DOL/BLS 2016.
7. Winston 2014; U.S. DOL/BLS 2015b.
8. Gormley et al. 2005; Weiland and Yoshikawa 2013.
9. Aos et al. 2004.
10. McKernan and Ratcliffe 2005.
11. Ruhm 1998; Waldfogel 2001a; Goldin and Katz 2011.
12. Ruhm 2000b; Tanaka 2005; Chatterji and Markowitz 2012; Wiese and Ritter 2012; Klevens et al. 2016. On long-term educational outcomes, see Carneiro, Løken, and Salvanes 2011.
13. NICHD Early Child Care Research Network and Duncan 2003; NICHD Early Child Care Research Network 2005; Duncan and Sojourner 2013.
14. Gormley et al. 2005; Weiland and Yoshikawa 2013.
15. Clark, Tluczek, and Wenzel 2003; Toth et al. 2006; Dozier et al. 2008; Landry et al. 2008; Suchman et al. 2012.
16. Bartik, Gormley, and Adelstein 2012; Kay and Pennucci 2014; Karoly 2016.
17. Isaacs et al. 2015.

18. Ibid. In contrast to the 2 percent of the federal budget that is spent on children, 44 percent of the entire federal budget and 9 percent of our GDP financed the nonchild expenditures for Social Security, Medicare, and Medicaid (CBO 2016).

19. Edelstein et al. 2012.

20. Anne Mitchell, Louise Stoney, and Harriet Dichter (2001) estimate that families contribute approximately 60 percent and all government funding contributes nearly 40 percent of the total funds spent on early care and education in the United States.

21. Kena et al. 2015. Total expenditures for public elementary and secondary schools in the United States amounted to $621 billion in 2011–2012, or $12,401 per public school student enrolled in the fall (in constant 2013–2014 dollars, based on the Consumer Price Index).

22. For example, the annual budgetary costs of the 2001 tax cuts, the wars in Iraq and Afghanistan between 2002 and 2012, the 2004 prescription-drug expansions (Part D) to Medicare, the 2008 Troubled Asset Relief Program (TARP), and the 2010 Affordable Care Act represented new public spending priorities in recent years that were significantly greater than what would be required to support young children and the human capital development of the future U.S. workforce.

23. Eurydice 2009. The equivalent component of our plan—universal preschool education for children starting at age three—amounts to 0.4 percent of the U.S. GDP.

24. There would be nothing to compel any state to agree to the guarantee structure. Based on the 2012 decision in *National Federation of Independent Businesses v. Sebelius,* which challenged the constitutionality of the provisions of the Affordable Care Act (ACA), the majority opinion issued by Chief Justice John Roberts indicated that the Medicaid expansions in the ACA were effectively a state option because existing Medicaid spending cannot be threatened or eliminated to compel a state to take up the expansions and incur greater costs. It is not as clear whether the same logic would apply to the CCDBG program, which may be effectively eliminated and replaced with the Assurance system, but in any case we propose that it be structured as a state option.

25. One possible approach would be to use some of the increased federal share of spending that would have been directed to the states in Assurance expenditures (based on the number of children in families with working parents and incomes below 250 percent FPL) to fund Early Head Start and Head Start, thereby generating increased supply in the most-disadvantaged areas.

26. NCES 2016.

27. U.S. DHHS/ACF/OCC 2015; Barnett et al. 2015.

28. Parental leave could be created within the Social Security Act (Senate Finance Committee and House Ways and Means Committee), the Assuring Care and Education for Young Children program through the CCDBG (Senate Health, Education, Labor, and Pensions [HELP] Committee and House Education and Workforce Committee), universal preschool through the next reauthorization of the Elementary and Secondary Education Act or a new law (Senate HELP Committee and House Education and Workforce Committee), and Head Start through the Head Start Act (Senate HELP Committee and House Education and Workforce Committee).

29. In 1971, Congress passed the Comprehensive Child Development Act on a bipartisan vote, though it was ultimately vetoed by President Nixon. The act would have provided a wide range of services, including universal child care.
30. The White House/Office of the Press Secretary 2015.
31. The White House/Office of the Press Secretary 2013a.
32. The White House/Office of the Press Secretary 2013b.
33. For example, San Antonio and Seattle voters both expanded preschool services in 2012 and 2014 voter referendums that relied on increased sales and other taxes (Kahn and Barron 2015).
34. Jones 2014.

REFERENCES

Adams, Gina, and Monica Rohacek. 2002. "More Than a Work Support? Issues Around Integrating Child Development Goals into the Child Care Subsidy System." *Early Childhood Research Quarterly* 17(4): 418–40.

Advisory Committee on Head Start Research and Evaluation. 1999. "Evaluating Head Start: A Recommended Framework for Studying the Impact of the Head Start Program" (executive summary). Washington: U.S. Department of Health and Human Services. Available at: http://www.researchconnections.org /childcare/resources/4087/pdf (accessed October 12, 2016).

———. 2012. *Advisory Committee on Head Start Research and Evaluation: Final Report.* Report submitted to the Secretary of the U.S. Department of Health and Human Services (August). Available at: http://www.acf.hhs.gov/programs/opre /resource/advisory-committee-on-head-start-research-and-evaluation-final -report (accessed August 22, 2016).

Aikens, Nikki, Yange Xue, Eileen Bandel, Pia Caronogan, Cheri A. Vogel, and Kimberly Boller. 2015. "Early Head Start Home Visits and Classrooms: Stability, Predictors, and Thresholds of Quality." Brief 2015-34. Washington: U.S. Department of Health and Human Services, Administration for Children and Families, Office of Planning, Research, and Evaluation.

Akee, Randall K. Q., William E. Copeland, Gordon Keeler, Adrian Angold, and Elizabeth J. Costello. 2010. "Parents' Incomes and Children's Outcomes: A Quasi-Experiment." *American Economic Journal: Applied Economics* 2(1): 86–115.

Albelda, Randy, and Alan Clayton-Matthews. 2016. "It's About Time: Costs and Coverage of Paid Family and Medical Leave in Massachusetts." Boston: University of Massachusetts–Boston, Center for Women in Politics and Public Policy and Center for Social Policy (May). Available at: http://scholarworks.umb.edu /cwppp_pubs/28 (accessed August 25, 2016).

Alliance for Early Childhood Finance. 2016. "Cost Modeling." Available at: http:// www.earlychildhoodfinance.org/finance/cost-modeling (accessed October 12, 2016).

Almond, Douglas, and Janet Currie. 2011a. "Human Capital Development Before Age Five." In *Handbook of Labor Economics*, vol. 4b, edited by Orley Ashenfelter and David Card (Amsterdam: Elsevier/North Holland), 1315–1486.

———. 2011b. "Killing Me Softly: The Fetal Origins Hypothesis." *Journal of Economic Perspectives* 25(3): 153–72.

Anderson, Michael L. 2008. "Multiple Inference and Gender Differences in the Effects of Early Intervention: A Reevaluation of the Abecedarian, Perry Preschool, and Early Training Projects." *Journal of the American Statistical Association* 103(484): 1481–95.

Ansari, Arya, Kelly Purtell, and Elizabeth Gershoff. 2016. "Classroom Age Composition and the School Readiness of 3- and 4-Year-Olds in the Head Start Program." *Psychological Science* 27(1, January): 53–63.

Aos, Steve, Roxanne Lieb, Jim Mayfield, Marna Miller, and Annie Pennucci. 2004. *Benefits and Costs of Prevention and Early Intervention Programs for Youth*. Olympia: Washington State Institute for Public Policy.

Appelbaum, Eileen, and Ruth Milkman. 2011. "Leaves That Pay: Employer and Worker Experiences with Paid Family Leave in California." Available at: http://www.cepr.net/documents/publications/paid-family-leave-1-2011.pdf (accessed November 8, 2016).

Arbour, Mary Catherine, Hirokazu Yoshikawa, Sidney Atwood, Francis Romina Duran, Felipe Godoy, Ernesto Trevino, and Catherine E. Snow. 2015. "Quasi-Experimental Study of a Learning Collaborative to Improve Public Preschool Quality and Children's Language Outcomes in Chile." *BMJ Quality and Safety* 24(11): 727.

Atkinson, Anthony Barnes, and Thomas Piketty, eds. 2010. *Top Incomes: A Global Perspective*. New York: Oxford University Press.

Bacharach, Verne R., and Alfred A. Baumeister. 2003. "Child Care and Severe Externalizing Behavior in Kindergarten Children." *Applied Developmental Psychology* 23(5): 527–37.

Bailey, Drew, Greg J. Duncan, Candice Odgers, and Winnie Yu. 2016. "Persistence and Fadeout in the Impacts of Child and Adolescent Interventions." Working Paper 2015-27. Indooroopilly: University of Queensland, Institute for Social Science Research, ARC Centre of Excellence for Children and Families over the Life Course (November). Available at: http://www.lifecoursecentre.org.au/wp-content/uploads/2015/11/2015-27-LCC-Working-Paper-Bailey-et-al.1.pdf (accessed November 8, 2016).

Bainbridge, Jay, Marcia K. Meyers, and Jane Waldfogel. 2003. "Child Care Policy Reform and the Employment of Single Mothers." *Social Science Quarterly* 84(4): 771–91.

Baker, Michael, Jonathan Gruber, and Kevin Milligan. 2008. "Universal Child Care, Maternal Labor Supply, and Family Well-being." *Journal of Political Economy* 116(4): 709–45.

Baker, Michael, and Kevin Milligan. 2008. "Maternal Employment, Breastfeeding, and Health: Evidence from Maternity Leave Mandates." *Journal of Health Economics* 27(4): 871–87.

Bania, Neil, Noa Kay, Steve Aos, and Annie Pennucci. 2014. "Outcome Evaluation of Washington State's Early Childhood Education and Assistance Program." Olympia: Washington State Institute for Public Policy.

Barnett, W. Steven. 1995. "Long-Term Effects of Early Childhood Programs on Cognitive and School Outcomes." *The Future of Children* 5(3): 25–50.

Barnett, W. Steven, Megan E. Carolan, James H. Squires, Kirsty Clarke Brown, and Michelle Horowitz. 2015. "The State of Preschool 2014: State Preschool Yearbook." New Brunswick, N.J.: National Institute for Early Education Research.

Barnett, W. Steven, Alison H. Friedman-Krauss, Rebecca Gomez, Michelle Horowitz, G. G. Weisenfeld, Kristy Clarke Brown, and James H. Squires. 2016. "The State of Preschool 2015: State Preschool Yearbook." New Brunswick, N.J.: National Institute for Early Education Research.

Bartel, Ann, Charles Baum, Maya Rossin-Slater, Christopher Ruhm, and Jane Waldfogel. 2014. "California's Paid Family Leave Law: Lessons from the First Decade." Report prepared for the U.S. Department of Labor, Office of the Assistant Secretary for Policy, Chief Evaluation Office (June 23). Available at: http://www.dol.gov/asp/evaluation/reports/PaidLeaveDeliverable.pdf (accessed August 22, 2016).

Bartik, Timothy J. 2011. *Investing in Kids: Early Childhood Programs and Local Economic Development*. Kalamazoo, Mich.: W. E. Upjohn Institute for Employment Research.

Bartik, Timothy J., William Gormley, and Shirley Adelstein. 2012. "Earnings Benefits of Tulsa's Pre-K Program for Different Income Groups." *Economics of Education Review* 31(6): 1143–61.

Bassok, Daphna, Maria Fitzpatrick, and Susanna Loeb. 2014. "Does State Preschool Crowd-Out Private Provision? The Impact of Universal Preschool on the Childcare Sector in Oklahoma and Georgia." *Journal of Urban Economics* 83: 18–33.

Bassok, Daphna, and Eva Galdo. 2016. "Inequality in Preschool Quality? Community-Level Disparities in Access to High-Quality Learning Environments." *Early Education and Development* 27(1): 128–44.

Bassok, Daphna, and Scott Latham. 2016. "Kids Today: Changes in School-Readiness in an Early Childhood Era." Working Paper 35. Charlottesville: University of Virginia, EdPolicyWorks. Available at: http://curry.virginia.edu/uploads/resourceLibrary/35_Kids_Today.pdf (accessed November 8, 2016).

Beck, Isabel L., and Margaret G. McKeown. 2007. "Increasing Young Low-Income Children's Oral Vocabulary Repertoires Through Rich and Focused Instruction." *Elementary School Journal* 107(3): 251–71.

Berger, Lawrence M., Jennifer Hill, and Jane Waldfogel. 2005. "Maternity Leave, Early Maternal Employment, and Child Health and Development in the U.S." *Economic Journal* 115(501): 29–47.

Berkeley School of Law and Georgetown Law. 2010. *Family Security Insurance: A New*

Foundation for Economic Security. Berkeley and Washington, D.C.: University of California/Berkeley Law/Berkeley Center on Health, Economic, and Family Security (CHEF) and Georgetown Law/Workplace Flexibility 2010 (December). Available at: http://scholarship.law.georgetown.edu/cgi/viewcontent.cgi ?article=1002&context=pub_rep (accessed August 23, 2016).

Bierman, Karen L., Celene E. Domitrovich, Robert L. Nix, Scott D. Gest, Janet A. Welsh, Mark T. Greenberg, Clancy Blair, Keith E. Nelson, and Sukhdeep Gill. 2008. "Promoting Academic and Social-Emotional School Readiness: The Head Start REDI Program." *Child Development* 79(6): 1802–17.

Bitler, Marianne P., Hilary W. Hoynes, and Thurston Domina. 2014. "Experimental Evidence on Distributional Effects of Head Start." Working Paper 20434. Cambridge, Mass.: National Bureau of Economic Research.

Blair, Clancy, and C. Cybele Raver. 2012. "Child Development in the Context of Adversity: Experiential Canalization of Brain and Behavior." *American Psychologist* 67(4): 309–18.

———. 2014. "Closing the Achievement Gap Through Modification of Neurocognitive and Neuroendocrine Function: Results from a Cluster Randomized Controlled Trial of an Innovative Approach to the Education of Children in Kindergarten." *PLoS ONE* 9(11).

Blau, David. 2001. *The Child Care Problem: An Economic Analysis.* New York: Russell Sage Foundation.

Blau, David, and Erdal Tekin. 2007. "The Determinants and Consequences of Child Care Subsidies for Single Mothers in the USA." *Journal of Population Economics* 20(4): 719–41.

Blau, Francine D., and Lawrence M. Kahn. 2013. "Female Labor Supply: Why Is the U.S. Falling Behind?" IZA Discussion Paper 7140. Bonn: Institute for the Study of Labor.

Bloom, Howard S., and Christina Weiland. 2015. "Quantifying Variation in Head Start Effects on Young Children's Cognitive and Socio-emotional Skills Using Data from the National Head Start Impact Study." Working paper. New York: MDRC March).

Boushey, Heather. 2009. "Helping Breadwinners When It Can't Wait: A Progressive Program for Family Leave Insurance." Washington, D.C.: Center for American Progress (May). Available at: https://www.americanprogress.org/wp-content /uploads/issues/2009/06/pdf/fmla.pdf.

Boushey, Heather, and Sarah Jane Glynn. 2012a. "There Are Significant Business Costs to Replacing Employees." Washington, D.C.: Center for American Progress (November 16). Available at: https://www.americanprogress.org/issues /economy/reports/2012/11/16/44464/there-are-significant-business-costs-to -replacing-employees/.

———. 2012b. "The Effects of Paid Family and Medical Leave on Employment Stability and Economic Security." Washington, D.C.: Center for American Progress (April 12). Available at: https://cdn.americanprogress.org/wp-content/uploads /issues/2012/04/pdf/BousheyEmploymentLeave1.pdf.

Boushey, Heather, and Alexandra Mitukiewicz. 2014. "Family and Medical Leave Insurance: A Basic Standard for Today's Workforce." Washington, D.C.: Center for American Progress (April). Available at: https://cdn.americanprogress.org/wp-content/uploads/2014/04/FMLA-reportv2.pdf (accessed November 29, 2016).

Boushey, Heather, Ann O'Leary, and Alexandra Mitukiewicz. 2013. "The Economic Benefits of Family and Medical Leave Insurance." Washington, D.C.: Center for American Progress (December 12). Available at: https://cdn.americanprogress.org/wp-content/uploads/2013/12/PaidFamLeave-brief.pdf (accessed November 29, 2016).

Bowne, Jocelyn Bonnes, Hirokazu Yoshikawa, and Catherine E. Snow. 2016. "Relationships of Teachers' Language and Explicit Vocabulary Instruction to Students' Vocabulary Growth in Kindergarten." *Reading Research Quarterly* (June 9): 1–23. doi:10.1002/rrq.151.

Bradbury, Bruce, Miles Corak, Jane Waldfogel, and Elizabeth Washbrook. 2015. *Too Many Children Left Behind: The U.S. Achievement Gap in Comparative Perspective.* New York: Russell Sage Foundation.

Brooks-Gunn, Jeanne, and Greg J. Duncan. 1997. "The Effects of Poverty on Children." *The Future of Children* 7(2): 55–71.

Brooks–Gunn, Jeanne, Wen–Jui Han, and Jane Waldfogel. 2002. "Maternal Employment and Child Cognitive Outcomes in the First Three Years of Life: The NICHD Study of Early Child Care." *Child Development* 73(4): 1052–72.

———. 2010. "First-Year Maternal Employment and Child Development in the First Seven Years." *Monographs of the Society for Research in Child Development* 75(2): 1–19.

Burchinal, Margaret, Kirsten Kainz, and Karen Cai. 2011. "How Well Do Our Measures of Quality Predict Child Outcomes?" In *Quality Measurement in Early Childhood Settings,* edited by Martha Zaslow, Ivelisse Martinez-Bock, Kathryn Tout, and Tamara Halle. Baltimore, Md.: Paul H. Brookes Publishing.

Burchinal, Margaret, Nathan Vandergrift, Robert Pianta, and Andrew Mashburn. 2010. "Threshold Analysis of Association Between Child Care Quality and Child Outcomes for Low-Income Children in Pre-kindergarten Programs." *Early Childhood Research Quarterly* 25(2, April): 166–76.

Burgess, Kimberly, Nina Chien, Taryn Morrissey, and Kendall Swenson. 2014. "Trends in the Use of Early Care and Education, 1995–2011: Descriptive Analysis of Child Care Arrangements from National Survey Data." Washington: U.S. Department of Health and Human Services, Office of the Assistant Secretary for Planning and Evaluation.

Camilli, Gregory, Sadako Vargas, Sharon Ryan, and W. Steven Barnett. 2010. "Meta-analysis of the Effects of Early Education Interventions on Cognitive and Social Development." *Teachers College Record* 112(3): 579–620.

Campbell, Frances A., Elizabeth P. Pungello, Margaret Burchinal, Kirsten Kainz, Yi Pan, Barbara H. Wasik, Oscar A. Barbarin, Joseph J. Sparling, and Craig T. Ramey. 2012. "Adult Outcomes as a Function of an Early Childhood Educational Program: An Abecedarian Project Follow-up." *Developmental Psychology* 48(4): 1033–43.

Campbell, Frances A., Craig T. Ramey, and Shari Miller-Johnson. 2002. "Early Childhood Education: Young Adult Outcomes from the Abecedarian Project." *Applied Developmental Science* 6(1): 42–57.

Carlson, Marcia J., and Mary E. Corcoran. 2001. "Family Structure and Children's Behavioral and Cognitive Outcomes." *Journal of Marriage and Family* 63(3): 779–92.

Carneiro, Pedro, and Rita Ginja. 2014. "Long-Term Impacts of Compensatory Preschool on Health and Behavior: Evidence from Head Start." *American Economic Journal of Economic Policy* 6(4): 135–73.

Carneiro, Pedro, Katrine V. Løken, and Kjell G. Salvanes. 2011. "A Flying Start? Maternity Leave Benefits and Long-Run Outcomes of Children." IZA Discussion Paper 5793. Bonn: Institute for the Study of Labor.

Cavanagh, Shannon E., and Aletha C. Huston. 2006. "Family Instability and Children's Early Problem Behavior." *Social Forces* 85(1): 551–81.

———. 2008. "The Timing of Family Instability and Children's Social Development." *Journal of Marriage and Family* 70(5): 1258–70.

Center on the Developing Child at Harvard University. 2007. "The Science of Early Childhood Development." Cambridge, Mass.: Center on the Developing Child. Available at: http://developingchild.harvard.edu/resources/inbrief-science-of-ecd/ (accessed August 22, 2016).

———. 2009. "Maternal Depression Can Undermine the Development of Young Children." Working Paper 8. Cambridge, Mass.: Center on the Developing Child at Harvard University. Available at: http://developingchild.harvard.edu/index.php/resources/reports_and_working_papers/working_papers/wp8/ (accessed November 8, 2016).

Chatterji, Pinka, and Sara Markowitz. 2012. "Family Leave After Childbirth and the Mental Health of New Mothers." *Journal of Mental Health Policy and Economics* 15(2): 61–76.

Chaudry, Ajay. 2004. *Putting Children First: How Working Mothers Manage Child Care.* New York: Russell Sage Foundation.

———. 2016. "The Case for Early Education in the Emerging Economy." New York: Roosevelt Institute (August).

Chaudry, Ajay, Juan Pedroza, Heather Sandstrom, Anna Danziger, Michel Grosz, Molly M. Scott, and Sarah Ting. 2011. *Child Care Choices of Low-Income Working Families.* Washington, D.C.: Urban Institute.

Chaudry, Ajay, and Christopher Wimer. 2016. "Poverty Is Not Just an Indicator: The Relationship Between Income, Poverty, and Child Well-being." *Academic Pediatrics* 16(3, supplement 1): S23–29.

Chen, Jen Hao. 2013. "Multiple Childcare Arrangements and Health Outcomes in Early Childhood." *Maternal and Child Health Journal* 17(3): 448–55.

Chetty, Raj, John N. Friedman, Nathanial Hilger, Emmanuel Saez, Diane Whitmore Schanzenbach, and Danny Yagan. 2011. "How Does Your Kindergarten Classroom Affect Your Earnings? Evidence from Project Star." *Quarterly Journal of Economics* 126(4): 1593–1660.

Chetty, Raj, and Nathaniel Hendren. 2015. "The Impacts of Neighborhoods on Inter-

generational Mobility: Childhood Exposure Effects and County-Level Estimates." Cambridge, Mass.: Harvard University and National Bureau of Economic Research (May). Available at: http://scholar.harvard.edu/files/hendren
/files/nbhds_paper.pdf (accessed November 8, 2016).

Chetty, Raj, Nathaniel Hendren, and Lawrence F. Katz. 2016. "The Effects of Exposure to Better Neighborhoods on Children: New Evidence from the Moving to
Opportunity Experiment." *American Economic Review* 106 (4, August): 90.

Chien, Nina. 2015. "Estimates of Child Care Eligibility and Receipt for Fiscal Year
2012." ASPE Issue Brief (November 24). Washington: U.S. Department of Health
and Human Services, Office of the Assistant Secretary for Planning and Evaluation (ASPE).

Child Care Aware of America. 2014. "Parents and the High Cost of Child Care."
Available at: https://www.ncsl.org/documents/cyf/2014_Parents_and_the
_High_Cost_of_Child_Care.pdf (accessed August 22, 2016).

———. 2015. "Parents and the High Cost of Child Care: 2015." Available at:
http://www.usa.childcareaware.org/advocacy-public-policy/resources/reports
-and-research/costofcare/ (accessed August 22, 2016).

Child Trends. 2015a. "Births to Unmarried Women: Indicators on Children and
Youth." Child Trends Data Bank. Available at: http://www.childtrends.org
/?indicators=births-to-unmarried-women#_edn10 (accessed August 22, 2016).

———. 2015b. "Full-Day Kindergarten: Indicators on Children and Youth." Child
Trends Data Bank. Available at: http://www.childtrends.org/?indicators=full
-day-kindergarten (accessed November 8, 2016).

Children's Defense Fund. 2014. *The State of America's Children 2014*. Washington, D.C.:
Children's Defense Fund. Available at: http://www.childrensdefense.org/library
/state-of-americas-children/2014-soac.pdf (accessed August 22, 2016).

Clark, Roseanne, Audrey Tluczek, and Amy Wenzel. 2003. "Psychotherapy for Post-
partum Depression: A Preliminary Report." *American Journal of Orthopsychiatry*
73(4): 441–54.

Clarke-Stewart, K. Alison, Deborah Lowe Vandell, Margaret Burchinal, Marion
O'Brien, and Kathleen McCartney. 2002. "Do Regulable Features of Child-Care
Homes Affect Children's Development?" *Early Childhood Research Quarterly* 17(1):
52–86.

Clements, Douglas H. 2007. "Curriculum Research: Towards a Framework for
Research-Based Curricula." *Journal of Research in Mathematics Education* 38(1): 35–
70.

Clements, Douglas H., and Julie Sarama. 2007. "Effects of a Preschool Mathematics
Curriculum: Summative Research on the Building Blocks Project." *Journal for Research in Mathematics Education* 38(2): 136–63.

———. 2008. "Experimental Evaluation of the Effects of a Research-Based Preschool
Mathematics Curriculum." *American Educational Research Journal* 45(2): 443–94.

Coie, John D., Norman F. Watt, Stephen G. West, J. David Hawkins, Joan R. Asarnow,
Howard J. Markman, Sharon L. Ramey, Myrna B. Shure, and Beverly Long. 1993.
"The Science of Prevention." *American Psychologist* 48(10): 1013–22.

Congressional Budget Office (CBO). 2016. *The 2016 Long-Term Budget Outlook.* Publication 51580. Washington: U.S. Congress, CBO (July). Available at: http://www.cbo.gov/sites/default/files/114th-congress-2015-2016/reports/51580-LTBO.pdf (accessed October 12, 2016).

Connelly, Rachel, and Jean Kimmel. 2003. "The Effect of Child Care Costs on the Employment and Welfare Recipiency of Single Mothers." *Southern Economic Journal* 69(3): 498–519.

Cooper, Brittany Rhoades, and Stephanie T. Lanza. 2014. "Who Benefits Most from Head Start? Using Latent Class Moderation to Examine Differential Treatment Effects." *Child Development* 85(6): 2317–38.

Corporation for Enterprise Development. 2016. "CFED Assets and Opportunity Scorecard: Child and Child Care Tax Credits." Available at: http://scorecard.assetsandopportunity.org/latest/measure/child-and-child-care-tax-credits (accessed October 12, 2016).

Coulton, Claudia J., David S. Crampton, Molly Irwin, James C. Spilsbury, and Jill E. Korbin. 2007. "How Neighborhoods Influence Child Maltreatment: A Review of the Literature and Alternative Pathways." *Child Abuse and Neglect* 31(11–12): 1117–42.

Council of Economic Advisers. 2014a. "The Economics of Paid and Unpaid Leave." Washington: Executive Office of the President of the United States (June). Available at: https://www.whitehouse.gov/sites/default/files/docs/leave_report_final.pdf (accessed August 25, 2016).

———. 2014b. "The Labor Force Participation Rate Since 2007: Causes and Policy Implications." Washington: Executive Office of the President of the United States (July). Available at: https://www.whitehouse.gov/sites/default/files/docs/labor_force_participation_report.pdf (accessed August 25, 2016).

Crosby, Danielle A., Lisa Gennetian, and Aletha C. Huston. 2005. "Child Care Assistance Policies Can Affect the Use of Center-Based Care for Children in Low-Income Families." *Applied Developmental Science* 9(2): 86–106.

Cunha, Flavio, and James Heckman. 2007. "The Technology of Skill Formation." *American Economic Review* 97(2): 31–47.

Currie, Janet. 2009. "Healthy, Wealthy, and Wise: Socioeconomic Status, Poor Health in Childhood, and Human Capital Development." *Journal of Economic Literature* 47(1): 87–122.

Currie, Janet, and Duncan Thomas. 1995. "Does Head Start Make a Difference?" *American Economic Review* 85(3): 341–64.

Dahl, Gordon B., and Lance Lochner. 2012. "The Impact of Family Income on Child Achievement: Evidence from the Earned Income Tax Credit." *American Economic Review* 102(5): 1927–56.

Dahl, Gordon B., Katrine V. Løken, Magne Mogstad, and Kari Vea Salvanes. 2015. "What Is the Case for Paid Maternity Leave?" Working Paper 19595. Cambridge, Mass.: National Bureau of Economic Research.

Daku, Mark, Amy Raub, and Jody Heymann. 2012. "Maternal Leave Policies and Vaccination Coverage: A Global Analysis." *Social Science and Medicine* 74(2): 120–24.

Davis, Elise, Kim-Michelle Gilson, Rahila Christian, Elizabeth Waters, Andrew Mackinnon, Helen Herrman, Margaret Sims, Linda Harrison, Kay Cook, Cathrine Mihalopoulos, Bernie Marshall, Anna Flego, and Lara Corr. 2015. "Building the Capacity of Family Day Care Educators to Promote Children's Social and Emotional Wellbeing: An Exploratory Cluster Randomised Controlled Trial." *Australasian Journal of Early Childhood* 40(2): 57–67.

Deming, David. 2009. "Early Childhood Intervention and Life-Cycle Skill Formation: Evidence from Head Start." *American Economic Journal: Applied Economics* 1(3): 111–34.

Diamond, Adele, W. Steven Barnett, Jessica Thomas, and Sarah Munro. 2007. "Preschool Program Improves Cognitive Control." *Science* 318(5855): 1387–88.

Dodge, Kenneth A., W. Benjamin Goodman, Robert A. Murphy, Karen O'Donnell, and Jeannine Sato. 2013. "Randomized Controlled Trial of Universal Postnatal Nurse Home Visiting: Impact on Emergency Care." *Pediatrics* 132(supplement): S140–46.

Dodge, Kenneth A., W. Benjamin Goodman, Robert A. Murphy, Karen O'Donnell, Jeannine Sato, and Susan Guptill. 2014. "Implementation and Randomized Controlled Trial Evaluation of Universal Postnatal Nurse Home Visiting." *American Journal of Public Health* 104(supplement 1): 136–44.

Dorn, Stan, Sarah Minton, and Erika Huber. 2014. "Examples of Promising Practices for Integrating and Coordinating Eligibility, Enrollment, and Retention: Human Services and Health Programs Under the Affordable Care Act." Washington, D.C.: Urban Institute (July 1).

Dowsett, Chantelle J., Aletha C. Huston, Amy E. Imes, and Lisa Gennetian. 2008. "Structural and Process Features in Three Types of Child Care for Children from High- and Low-Income Families." *Early Childhood Research Quarterly* 23(1): 69–93.

Dozier, Mary, Oliver Lindhiem, Erin Lewis, Johanna Bick, Kristin Bernard, and Elizabeth Peloso. 2009. "Effects of a Foster Parent Training Program on Young Children's Attachment Behaviors: Preliminary Evidence from a Randomized Clinical Trial." *Child and Adolescent Social Work Journal* 26(4): 321–32.

Dozier, Mary, Elizabeth Peloso, Erin Lewis, Jean-Philippe Laurenceau, and Seymour Levine. 2008. "Effects of an Attachment-Based Intervention on the Cortisol Production of Infants and Toddlers in Foster Care." *Development and Psychopathology* 20(3): 845–59.

Duncan, Greg J., and Jeanne Brooks-Gunn. 2000. "Family Poverty, Welfare Reform, and Child Development." *Child Development* 71(1): 188–96.

Duncan, Greg J., Chantelle J. Dowsett, Amy Claessens, Katherine Magnuson, Aletha C. Huston, Pamela Klebanov, Linda S. Pagani, Leon Feinstein, Mimi Engel, Jeanne Brooks-Gunn, Holly Sexton, Kathryn Duckworth, and Crista Japel. 2007. "School Readiness and Later Achievement." *Developmental Psychology* 43(6): 1428–46.

Duncan, Greg J., Jade M. Jenkins, Margaret Burchinal, Thurston Domina, and Marianne Bitler. 2015. "Boosting School Readiness with Preschool Curricula." Irvine, Calif.: Irvine Network on Interventions in Development (March).

Duncan, Greg J., and Katherine A. Magnuson. 2011. "The Nature and Impact of Early Achievement Skills, Attention Skills, and Behavior Problems." In *Whither Opportunity: Rising Inequality, Schools, and Children's Life Chances,* edited by Greg J. Duncan and Richard Murnane. New York: Russell Sage Foundation.

———. 2013. "Investing in Preschool Programs." *Journal of Economic Perspectives* 27(2): 109–32.

Duncan, Greg J., Pamela A. Morris, and Chris Rodrigues. 2011. "Does Money Really Matter? Estimating Impacts of Family Income on Young Children's Achievement with Data from Random-Assignment Experiments." *Developmental Psychology* 47(5): 1263–79.

Duncan, Greg J., and Aaron J. Sojourner. 2013. "Can Intensive Early Childhood Intervention Programs Eliminate Income-Based Cognitive and Achievement Gaps?" *Journal of Human Resources* 48(4): 945–68.

Duncan, Greg J., W. Jean Yeung, Jeanne Brooks-Gunn, and Judith R. Smith. 1998. "How Much Does Childhood Poverty Affect the Life Chances of Children?" *American Sociological Review* 63(3): 406–23.

Duncan, Greg J., Kathleen M. Ziol-Guest, and Ariel Kalil. 2010. "Early-Childhood Poverty and Adult Attainment, Behavior, and Health." *Child Development* 81(1): 306–25.

Edelstein, Sara, Julia Isaacs, Heather Hahn, and Katherine Toran. 2012. "How Do Public Investments in Children Vary with Age? A Kids' Share Analysis of Expenditures in 2008 and 2011 by Age Group." Washington, D.C.: Urban Institute.

Eurydice. 2009. "Tackling Social and Cultural Inequalities Through Early Childhood Education and Care in Europe." Brussels: Education, Audiovisual, and Culture Executive Agency.

Fantuzzo, John W., Vivian L. Gadsden, and Paul A. McDermott. 2011. "An Integrated Curriculum to Improve Mathematics, Language, and Literacy for Head Start Children." *American Educational Research Journal* 48(3): 763–93.

Farran, Dale C., Kerry Hofer, Mark Lipsey, and Carol Bilbrey. 2014. "Variations in the Quality of TN-VPK Classrooms" (PowerPoint slides). Presented to the meeting of the Society for Research on Educational Effectiveness. Washington, D.C. (March 8).

Farran, Dale C., and Sandra Jo Wilson. 2014. "Achievement and Self-regulation in Pre-kindergarten Classrooms: Effects of the Tools of the Mind Curriculum." Nashville, Tenn.: Vanderbilt University, Peabody Research Institute (July 27). Available at: https://my.vanderbilt.edu/toolsofthemindevaluation/files/2011/12/Tools-Submission-Child-Development-7-27-14.pdf (accessed August 22, 2016).

Farver, JoAnn M., Christopher J. Lonigan, and Stefanie Eppe. 2009. "Effective Early Literacy Skill Development for Young Spanish-Speaking English Language Learners: An Experimental Study of Two Methods." *Child Development* 80(3): 703–19.

Feller, Avi, Todd Grindal, Luke Miratrix, and Lindsay Page. 2016. "Compared to

What? Variation in the Impacts of Early Childhood Education by Alternative Care-Type Settings" (January 11). Available at SSRN: http://papers.ssrn.com /sol3/papers.cfm?abstract_id=2534811 (accessed August 22, 2016).

Fernald, Anne, Virginia A. Marchman, and Adriana Weisleder. 2013. "SES Differences in Language Processing Skill and Vocabulary Are Evident at 18 Months." *Developmental Science* 16(2): 234–48. doi:10.1111/desc.12019.

Fernández-Kranz, Daniel, and Núria Rodríguez-Planas. 2013. "Can Parents' Right to Work Part-time Hurt Childbearing-Aged Women? A Natural Experiment with Administrative Data." IZA Discussion Paper 7509. Bonn: Institute for the Study of Labor.

Forry, Nicole, Paula Daneri, and Grace Howarth. 2013. "Child Care Subsidy Literature Review." OPRE Brief 2013-60. Washington: U.S. Department of Health and Human Services, Administration for Children and Families, Office of Planning, Research and Evaluation (OPRE).

Forry, Nicole D., and Sandra L. Hofferth. 2011. "Maintaining Work: The Influence of Child Care Subsidies on Child Care–Related Work Disruptions." *Journal of Family Issues* 32(3): 346–68.

Frisvold, David E., and Julie C. Lumeng. 2011. "Expanding Exposure: Can Increasing the Daily Duration of Head Start Reduce Childhood Obesity?" *Journal of Human Resources* 46(2): 373–402.

Garces, Eliana, Duncan Thomas, and Janet Currie. 2002. "Longer-Term Effects of Head Start." *American Economic Review* 92(4): 999–1012.

Gassman-Pines, Anna, and Hirokazu Yoshikawa. 2006. "The Effects of Antipoverty Programs on Children's Cumulative Level of Poverty-Related Risk." *Developmental Psychology* 42(6): 981–99.

Gault, Barbara, Heidi Hartmann, Ariane Hegewisch, Jessica Milli, and Lindsey Reichlin. 2014. "Paid Parental Leave in the United States: What the Data Tell Us About Access, Usage, and Economic and Health Benefits." Washington, D.C.: Institute for Women's Policy Research.

Gennetian, Lisa A., Sharon Wolf, Heather D. Hill, and Pamela A. Morris. 2015. "Intra-year Household Income Dynamics and Adolescent School Behavior." *Demography* 52(2): 455–83.

Gertler, Paul, James Heckman, Rodrigo Pinto, Arianna Zanolini, Christel Vermeersch, Susan Walker, Susan M. Chang, and Sally Grantham-McGregor. 2014. "Labor Market Returns to an Early Childhood Stimulation Intervention in Jamaica." *Science* 344(6187): 998–1001.

Ginsburg, Herbert P., Joon Sun Lee, and Judi Stevenson Boyd. 2008. "Mathematics Education for Young Children: What It Is and How to Promote It." *Social Policy Report* 22. Ann Arbor, Mich.: Society for Research in Child Development.

Goldin, Claudia, and Lawrence F. Katz. 2008. *The Race Between Education and Technology.* Cambridge, Mass.: Belknap Press of Harvard University Press.

———. 2011. "The Cost of Workplace Flexibility for High-Powered Professionals." *Annals of the American Academy of Political and Social Science* 638(1): 45–67.

Gordon, Rachel A., and P. Lindsay Chase-Lansdale. 2001. "Availability of Child Care in the United States: A Description and Analysis of Data Sources." *Demography* 38(2): 299–316.

Gordon, Rachel A., Ken Fujimoto, Robert Kaestner, Sanders Korenman, and Kristin Abner. 2013. "An Assessment of the Validity of the ECERS-R with Implications for Measures of Child Care Quality and Relations to Child Development." *Developmental Psychology* 49(1): 146–60.

Gordon, Robert J. 2014. "The Demise of U.S. Economic Growth: Restatement, Rebuttal, and Reflections." Working Paper 19895. Cambridge, Mass.: National Bureau of Economic Research.

Gormley, William T., Jr., Ted Gayer, Deborah Phillips, and Brittany Dawson. 2005. "The Effects of Universal Pre-K on Cognitive Development." *Developmental Psychology* 41(6): 872–84.

Gornick, Janet C., and Marcia K. Meyers. 2003. *Families That Work: Policies for Reconciling Parenthood and Employment*. New York: Russell Sage Foundation.

Grant, Rebecca. 2015. "Silicon Valley's Best and Worst Jobs for New Moms (and Dads)." *The Atlantic,* March 2.

Grissmer, David, and Elizabeth Eiseman. 2008. "Can Gaps in the Quality of Early Environments and Non-cognitive Skills Help Explain Persisting Black-White Achievement Gaps?" In *Steady Gains and Stalled Progress: Inequality and the Black-White Test Score Gap,* edited by Katherine A. Magnuson and Jane Waldfogel. New York: Russell Sage Foundation.

Guendelman, Sylvia, Jessica Lang Kosa, Michelle Pearl, Steve Graham, Julia Goodman, and Martin Kharrazi. 2009. "Juggling Work and Breastfeeding: Effects of Maternity Leave and Occupational Characteristics." *Pediatrics* 123(1): e38–46.

Halle, Tamara, Nicole Forry, Elizabeth Hair, Kate Perper, Laura Wandner, Julia Wessel, and Jessica Vick. 2009. "Disparities in Early Learning and Development: Lessons from the Early Childhood Longitudinal Study–Birth Cohort (ECLS-B)." Washington, D.C.: Child Trends.

Hamilton, Brady E., Joyce A. Martin, Michelle J. K. Osterman, Sally C. Curtin, and T. J. Matthews. 2015. "Births: Final Data for 2014." *National Vital Statistics Reports* 64, no. 12. Washington: Centers for Disease Control and Prevention (December 23). Available at: http://www.cdc.gov/nchs/data/nvsr/nvsr64/nvsr64_12.pdf (accessed October 14, 2016).

Han, Wen-Jui. 2004. "Nonstandard Work Schedules and Child Care Decisions: Evidence from the NICHD Study of Early Child Care." *Early Childhood Research Quarterly* 19(2): 231–56.

Han, Wen-Jui, Christopher Ruhm, and Jane Waldfogel. 2009. "Parental Leave Policies and Parents' Employment and Leave-Taking." *Journal of Policy Analysis and Management* 28(1): 29–54.

Han, Wen-Jui, Christopher J. Ruhm, Jane Waldfogel, and Elizabeth Washbrook. 2008. "The Timing of Mothers' Employment After Childbirth." *Monthly Labor Review* 131(6): 15–27.

Han, Wen-Jui, and Jane Waldfogel. 2003. "Parental Leave: The Impact of Recent Legislation on Parents' Leave Taking." *Demography* 40(1): 191–200.

Harding, David J. 2003. "Counterfactual Models of Neighborhood Effects: The Effect of Neighborhood Poverty on Dropping Out and Teenage Pregnancy." *American Journal of Sociology* 109(3): 676–719.

———. 2010. *Living the Drama: Community, Conflict, and Culture Among Inner-City Boys.* Chicago: University of Chicago Press.

Hardy, Bradley L. 2014. "Childhood Income Volatility and Adult Outcomes." *Demography* 51(5): 1641–65.

Harris, Douglas N., and Scott J. Adams. 2007. "Understanding the Level and Causes of Teacher Turnover: A Comparison with Other Professions." *Economics of Education Review* 26(3): 325–37.

Heckman, James J. 2006. "Skill Formation and the Economics of Investing in Disadvantaged Children." *Science* 312(June): 1900–1902.

———. 2007. "The Economics, Technology, and Neuroscience of Human Capability Formation." *Proceedings of the National Academy of Sciences* 104(33): 13250–55.

———. 2008. "Schools, Skills, and Synapses." *Economic Inquiry* 46(3): 289–324.

Heckman, James J., and Lakshmi K. Raut. 2016. "Intergenerational Long-Term Effects of Preschool-Structural Estimates from a Discrete Dynamic Programming Model." *Journal of Econometrics* 191(1): 169–75.

Herbers, Janette E., Arthur J. Reynolds, and Chin-Chih Chen. 2013. "School Mobility and Developmental Outcomes in Young Adulthood." *Development and Psychopathology* 25(2): 501–15.

Heymann, Jody, Amy Raub, and Alison Earle. 2011. "Creating and Using New Data Sources to Analyze the Relationship Between Social Policy and Global Health: The Case of Maternal Leave." *Public Health Reports* 126(3): 127–34.

Hill, Carolyn J., William T. Gormley, and Shirley Adelstein. 2015. "Do the Short-Term Effects of a High-Quality Preschool Program Persist?" *Early Childhood Research Quarterly* 32: 60–79.

Hill, Jennifer L., Jane Waldfogel, Jeanne Brooks-Gunn, and Wen-Jui Han. 2005. "Maternal Employment and Child Development: A Fresh Look Using Newer Methods." *Developmental Psychology* 41(6): 833–50.

Hofferth, Sandra L., Kimberlee A. Shauman, Jerry West, and Robin R. Henke. 1998. *Characteristics of Children's Early Care and Education Programs: Data from the 1995 National Household Education Survey.* Washington: U.S. Department of Education, National Center for Education Statistics.

Houser, Linda, and Thomas P. Vartanian. 2012. *Pay Matters: The Positive Economic Impacts of Paid Family Leave for Families, Businesses, and the Public.* Rutgers, N.J.: Center for Women and Work.

Howes, Carollee, Margaret Burchinal, Robert Pianta, Donna Bryant, Diane Early, Richard Clifford, and Oscar Barbarin. 2008. "Ready to Learn? Children's Pre-academic Achievement in Pre-kindergarten Programs." *Early Childhood Research Quarterly* 23(1) (January): 27–50.

Howes, Carollee, Kenneth H. Rubin, Hildy S. Ross, and Doran C. French. 1988. "Peer

Interaction of Young Children." *Monographs of the Society for Research in Child Development* 53(1): i+iii+v+1–92.

Huerta, Carmen, Willem Adema, Jennifer Baxter, Jui Han, Mette Lausten, Raehyuck Lee, and Jane Waldfogel. 2013. "Fathers' Leave, Fathers' Involvement, and Child Development." OECD Social Employment and Migration Working Paper 140. Paris: OECD Publishing.

Independent Women's Forum (IWF). 2014. "Working for Women: A Modern Agenda for Improving Women's Lives." Washington, D.C.: IWF. Available at: http://pdf .iwf.org/Working_for_Women.pdf (accessed August 25, 2016).

Institute of Leadership and Management. 2014. "Shared Opportunity: Parental Leave in U.K. Business." Available at: https://www.i-l-m.com/~/media/ILM Website/Documents/research-reports/shared-leave/ilm-shared-parental-leave -report pdf.ashx (accessed August 22, 2016).

Institute of Medicine and National Research Council. 2015. *Transforming the Workforce for Children Birth Through Age 8: A Unifying Foundation.* Washington, D.C.: National Academies Press.

Isaacs, Julia B., Sara Edelstein, Heather Hahn, Ellen Steele, and C. Eugene Steuerle. 2015. *Kids' Share 2015: Report on Federal Expenditures on Children in 2014 and Future Projections.* Washington, D.C.: Urban Institute.

Jargowsky, Paul A. 2014. "Concentration of Poverty in the New Millennium: Changes in the Prevalence, Composition, and Location of High-Poverty Neighborhoods." New York: Century Foundation.

Jenkins, Jade M., Tyler W. Watts, Katherine Magnuson, Douglas Clements, Julie Sarama, Christopher B. Wolfe, and Mary Elaine Spitler. 2015. "Preventing Preschool Fadeout Through Instructional Intervention in Kindergarten and First Grade." Working paper. Graduate School of Education, University of California (February). Available at: http://inid.gse.uci.edu/files/2011/03/Jenkinsetal _Fadeout_SREE.pdf (accessed November 8, 2016).

Johnson, Katie. 2016. "Paid Leave Would Cost $159 per Worker, UMass Report Finds." *Boston Globe,* May 19, 2016. Available at: https://www.bostonglobe.com/business /2016/05/19/paid-leave-would-cost-per-worker-umass-report-finds /libpAyh03eX2d7snE3BtAM/story.html (accessed August 22, 2016).

Johnson, Rucker C., Ariel Kalil, and Rachel E. Dunifon. 2012. "Employment Patterns of Less-Skilled Workers: Links to Children's Behavior and Academic Progress." *Demography* 49(2): 747–72.

Jones, Jeffrey M. 2014. "In U.S., 70% Favor Federal Funds to Expand Pre-K Education." Gallup: Politics, September 8. Available at: http://www.gallup.com/poll /175646/favor-federal-funds-expand-pre-education.aspx (accessed November 8, 2016).

Kagan, Sharon Lynn, Evelyn Moore, and Sue Bredekamp. 1995. "Reconsidering Children's Early Development and Learning: Toward Common Views and Vocabulary." Washington, D.C.: National Educational Goals Panel.

Kahn, Matthew E., and Kyle Barron. 2015. "The Political Economy of State and Local Investment in Pre-K Programs." Discussion Paper 9337. Bonn: Institute for the Study of Labor.

Kaiser Family Foundation. 2016. "Births Financed by Medicaid Births Financed by Medicaid." Menlo Park, Calif.: Henry J. Kaiser Family Foundation. Available at: http://kff.org/medicaid/state-indicator/births-financed-by-medicaid/# (accessed August 7, 2016).

Kalil, Ariel, and Kathleen M. Ziol-Guest. 2005. "Single Mothers' Employment Dynamics and Adolescent Well-being." *Child Development* 76(1): 196–211.

———. 2008. "Parental Employment Circumstances and Children's Academic Progress." *Social Science Research* 37(2): 500–515.

Karoly, Lynn A. 2016. "The Economic Returns to Early Childhood Education." *The Future of Children* 26(2): 37–55.

Karoly, Lynn A., Peter W. Greenwood, Susan S. Everingham, Jill Houbé, M. Rebecca Kilburn, C. Peter Rydell, and James Chiesa. 1998. "Investing in Our Children: What We Know and Don't Know About the Costs and Benefits of Early Childhood Interventions." Santa Monica, Calif.: RAND.

Katz, Lawrence F., and Alan B. Krueger. 2016. "The Rise and Nature of Alternative Work Arrangements in the United States, 1995–2015." Cambridge, Mass.: National Bureau of Economic Research (March 29). Available at: http://scholar.harvard.edu/files/lkatz/files/katz_krueger_cws_v3.pdf. (accessed August 12, 2016).

Kay, Noa, and Annie Pennucci. 2014. *Early Childhood Education for Low-Income Students: A Review of the Evidence and Benefit-Cost Analysis.* Olympia: Washington State Institute for Public Policy.

Kena, Grace, William Hussar, Joel McFarland, Cristobal de Brey, Lauren Musu-Gillette, Xiaolei Wang, Jijun Zhang, Amy Rathbun, Sidney Wilkinson-Flicker, Melissa Diliberti, Amy Barmer, Farrah Bullock Mann, and Erin Dunlop Velez. 2016. *The Condition of Education 2016.* NCES 2016-144. Washington: U.S. Department of Education, National Center for Education Statistics. Available at: http://nces.ed.gov/pubs2016/2016144.pdf (accessed October 14, 2016).

Kena, Grace, Lauren Musu-Gillette, Jennifer Robinson, Xiaolei Wang, Amy Rathbun, Jijun Zhang, Sidney Wilkinson-Flicker, Amy Barmer, and Erin Dunlop Velez. 2015. *The Condition of Education 2015.* NCES 2015-144. Washington: U.S. Department of Education, National Center for Education Statistics.

Kennedy, Sheela, and Larry L. Bumpass. 2008. "Cohabitation and Children's Living Arrangements: New Estimates from the United States." *Demographic Research* 19(47): 1663–92.

Kessler, Ronald C., Greg J. Duncan, Lisa A. Gennetian, Lawrence F. Katz, and Jeffrey R. Kling. 2014. "Associations of Housing Mobility Interventions for Children in High-Poverty Neighborhoods with Subsequent Mental Disorders During Adolescence." *Journal of the American Medical Association* 311(9): 937–48.

Kholoptseva, Jenya. 2016. "Effects of Center-Based Early Childhood Education Programs on Children's Language, Literacy, and Math Skills: A Comprehensive Meta-analysis." PhD diss., Harvard University.

Khon, Alfie. 2016. "The Trouble with Calls for Universal 'High-Quality' Pre-K." Blog–Alfie Kohn. Available at: http://www.alfiekohn.org/blogs/trouble-calls-universal-high-quality-pre-k/ (accessed January 31, 2016).

Kitzman, Harriet J., David L. Olds, Robert E. Cole, Carole A. Hanks, Elizabeth A. Anson, Kimberly J. Arcoleo, Dennis W. Luckey, Michael D. Knudtson, Charles R. Henderson, and John R. Holmberg. 2010. "Enduring Effects of Prenatal and Infancy Home Visiting by Nurses on Children: Follow-up of a Randomized Trial Among Children at Age 12 Years." *Archives of Pediatrics and Adolescent Medicine* 164(5): 412–18.

Klein, Alice, Prentice Starkey, Douglas Clements, Julie Sarama, and Roopa Iyer. 2008. "Effects of a Pre-kindergarten Mathematics Intervention: A Randomized Experiment." *Journal of Research on Educational Effectiveness* 1(3): 155–78.

Klerman, Jacob A., Kelly Daly, and Alyssa Pozniak. 2013. "The Family Medical Leave Act After Two Decades." Cambridge, Mass.: Abt Associates. Available at: http://abtassociates.com/AbtAssociates/files/a5/a51185de-0104-4eff-9e9f -39eb863a7c9d.pdf (accessed August 22, 2016).

———. 2014. *Family and Medical Leave in 2012: Technical Report.* Cambridge, Mass.: Abt Associates. Available at: https://www.dol.gov/asp/evaluation/fmla/fmla-2012 -technical-report.pdf (accessed August 22, 2016).

Klevens, Joanne, Feijun Luo, Likang Xu, Cora Peterson, and Natasha E. Latzman. 2016. "Paid Family Leave's Effect on Hospital Admissions for Pediatric Abusive Head Trauma." *Injury Prevention* 22(6): 442–45.

Kline, Patrick, and Christopher Walters. 2015. "Evaluating Public Programs with Close Substitutes: The Case of Head Start." Working Paper 21658. Cambridge, Mass.: National Bureau of Economic Research.

Knudsen, Eric I., James J. Heckman, Judy L. Cameron, and Jack P. Shonkoff. 2006. "Economic, Neurobiological, and Behavioral Perspectives on Building America's Future Workforce." *World Economics* 7(3): 17–41.

Krueger, Alan B., and Diane M. Whitmore. 2001. "The Effect of Attending a Small Class in the Early Grades on College-Test Taking and Middle School Test Results: Evidence from Project STAR." *Economic Journal* 111(468): 1–28.

Lake Research Partners and Chesapeake Beach Consulting. 2013. "Work-Family Strategy Council Poll." Washington, D.C.: Lake Research Partners.

Landry, Susan H., Jason L. Anthony, Paul R. Swank, and Pauline Monseque-Bailey. 2009. "Effectiveness of Comprehensive Professional Development for Teachers of At-Risk Preschoolers." *Journal of Educational Psychology* 101(2): 448.

Landry, Susan H., Karen E. Smith, Paul R. Swank, and Cathy Guttentag. 2008. "A Responsive Parenting Intervention: The Optimal Timing Across Early Childhood for Impacting Maternal Behaviors and Child Outcomes." *Developmental Psychology* 44(5): 1335–53.

Landry, Susan H., Tricia A. Zucker, Heather B. Taylor, Paul R. Swank, Jeffrey M. Williams, Michael Assel, April Crawford, Weihua Huang, Jeanine Clancy-Menchetti, Christopher J. Lonigan, Beth M. Phillips, Nancy Eisenberg, Tracy L. Spinrad, Jill de Villiers, Peter de Villiers, Marcia Barnes, Prentice Starkey, and Alice Klein. 2014. "Enhancing Early Child Care Quality and Learning for Toddlers at Risk: The Responsive Early Childhood Program." *Developmental Psychology* 50(2): 526–41.

Laughlin, Lynda. 2011. "Maternity Leave and Employment Patterns of First-Time Mothers: 1961–2008." *Current Population Reports* P70-128. Washington: U.S. Government Printing Office.

———. 2013. "Who's Minding the Kids? Child Care Arrangements: Spring 2011." *Current Population Reports* P70-135. Washington: U.S. Census Bureau.

Lee, Valerie E., and Susanna Loeb. 1995. "Where Do Head Start Attendees End Up? One Reason Why Preschool Effects Fade Out." *Educational Evaluation and Policy Analysis* 17(1): 62–82.

Lerner, Sharon, and Eileen Appelbaum. 2014. "Business as Usual: New Jersey Employers' Experiences with Family Leave Insurance." Washington, D.C.: Center for Economic and Policy Research (June). Available at: http://cepr.net/documents/nj-fli-2014-06.pdf (accessed November 8, 2016).

Li, Weilin, Greg J. Duncan, Katherine Magnuson, Holly Schindler, Hirokazu Yoshikawa, Jimmy Leak, and Jack P. Shonkoff. 2016. "Is Timing Everything? How Early Childhood Education Program Cognitive and Achievement Impacts Vary by Starting Age, Program Duration, and Time Since the End of the Program." Manuscript under review.

Lichter, Daniel T., Deborah Roempke Graefe, and J. Brian Brown. 2003. "Is Marriage a Panacea? Union Formation Among Economically Disadvantaged Unwed Mothers." *Social Problems* 50(1): 60–86.

Lipsey, Mark, Dale Farran, and Kerry Hofer. 2015a. "A Randomized Control Trial of a Statewide Voluntary Prekindergarten Program on Children's Skills and Behaviors Through Third Grade." Nashville, Tenn.: Vanderbilt University, Peabody Research Institute.

Lipsey, Mark W., Christina Weiland, Hirokazu Yoshikawa, Sandra Jo Wilson, and Kerry G. Hofer. 2015b. "The Prekindergarten Age-Cutoff Regression-Discontinuity Design: Methodological Issues and Implications for Application." *Educational Evaluation and Policy Analysis* 37(3): 296–313.

LoCasale-Crouch, Jennifer, Tim Konold, Robert Pianta, Carollee Howes, Margaret Burchinal, Donna Bryant, Richard Clifford, Diane Early, and Oscar Barbarin. 2007. "Observed Classroom Quality Profiles in State-Funded Pre-kindergarten Programs and Associations with Teacher, Program, and Classroom Characteristics." *Early Childhood Research Quarterly* 22(1, January): 3–17.

Loeb, Susanna, Margaret Bridges, Daphna Bassok, Bruce Fuller, and Russell W. Rumberger. 2007. "How Much Is Too Much? The Influence of Preschool Centers on Children's Social and Cognitive Development." *Economics of Education Review* 26(1): 52–66.

Loeb, Susanna, Bruce Fuller, Sharon Lynn Kagan, and Bidemi Carrol. 2004. "Child Care in Poor Communities: Early Learning Effects of Type, Quality, and Stability." *Child Development* 75(1): 47–65.

Lombardi, Caitlin McPherran, and Rebekah Levine Coley. 2014. "Early Maternal Employment and Children's School Readiness in Contemporary Families." *Developmental Psychology* 50(8): 2071–84.

Lombardi, Joan. 2014. "A Great Beginning: Ensuring Early Opportunities for America's Young Children." In *Improving the Odds for America's Children: Future Directions in Policy and Practice,* edited by Kathleen McCartney, Hirokazu Yoshikawa, and Laurie Forcier. Cambridge, Mass.: Harvard Education Press.

Lonigan, Christopher J., JoAnn M. Farver, Beth M. Phillips, and Jeanine Clancy-Menchetti. 2011. "Promoting the Development of Preschool Children's Emergent Literacy Skills: A Randomized Evaluation of a Literacy-Focused Curriculum and Two Professional Development Models." *Reading and Writing* 24(3): 305–37.

Love, John M., Rachel Chazan-Cohen, Helen Raikes, and Jeanne Brooks-Gunn. 2013. "What Makes a Difference: Early Head Start Evaluation Findings in a Developmental Context." *Monographs of the Society for Research in Child Development* 78(1): vii–viii, 1–173.

Love, John M., Ellen Eliason Kisker, Christine Ross, Helen Raikes, Jill Constantine, Kimberly Boller, Jeanne Brooks-Gunn, Rachel Chazan-Cohen, Louisa Banks Tarullo, Christy Brady-Smith, Allison Sidle Fuligni, Peter Z. Schochet, Diane Paulsell, and Cheri Vogel. 2005. "The Effectiveness of Early Head Start for 3-Year-Old Children and Their Parents: Lessons for Policy and Programs." *Developmental Psychology* 41(6): 885–901.

Ludwig, Jens, Jeffrey R. Kling, and Sendhil Mullainathan. 2011. "Mechanism Experiments and Policy Evaluations." *Journal of Economic Perspectives* 25(3): 17–38.

Ludwig, Jens, and Douglas L. Miller. 2007. "Does Head Start Improve Children's Life Chances? Evidence from a Regression Discontinuity Design." *Quarterly Journal of Economics* (February): 159–208.

Ludwig, Jens, and Matthew Miller. 2005. "Interpreting the WIC Debate." *Journal of Policy Analysis and Management* 24(4): 691–701.

Ludwig, Jens, and Deborah A. Phillips. 2008. "Long-Term Effects of Head Start on Low-Income Children." *Annals of the New York Academy of Sciences* 1136: 257–68.

Lueck, Marjorie, Ann C. Orr, and Martin O'Connell. 1982. "Trends in Child Care Arrangements of Working Mothers." Current Population Reports, P-23. Washington: U.S. Government Printing Office.

Maag, Elaine. 2015. "Tax Subsidies for Childcare Expenses Target Middle-Income Families, Missing Many Poor Parents." Tax Policy Center, September 11. Available at: http://www.taxpolicycenter.org/taxvox/tax-subsidies-childcare-expenses-target-middle-income-families-missing-many-poor-parents (accessed October 12, 2016).

Maag, Elaine, James Nunns, Eric Toder, and Roberton Williams. 2014. "Analysis of Specific Tax Provisions in President Obama's FY2015 Budget." Washington, D.C.: Tax Policy Center (June 30). Available at: http://www.taxpolicycenter.org/publications/analysis-specific-tax-provisions-president-obamas-fy2015-budget/full (accessed October 14, 2016).

Magnuson, Katherine A., and Greg J. Duncan. 2006. "The Role of Family Socioeconomic Resources in the Black-White Test Score Gap Among Young Children." *Developmental Review* 26(4): 365–99.

———. 2014. "Can Early Childhood Interventions Decrease Inequality of Economic

Opportunity?" Paper prepared for the Federal Reserve Bank of Boston conference "Inequality of Economic Opportunity in the United States." Boston (October 17–18). Available at: http://www.bostonfed.org/inequality2014/papers/magnusun-duncan.pdf (accessed January 25, 2016).

Magnuson, Katherine A., Christopher J. Ruhm, and Jane Waldfogel. 2007. "The Persistence of Preschool Effects: Do Subsequent Classroom Experiences Matter?" *Early Childhood Research Quarterly* 22(1): 18–38.

Mamedova, Saida, and Jeremy Redford. 2015. "Early Childhood Program Participation, from the National Household Education Surveys Program of 2012." Washington: U.S. Department of Education, National Center for Education Statistics, Institute of Education Sciences.

Martin, Joyce A., Brady E. Hamilton, Michelle J. K. Osterman, Sally C. Curtin, and T. J. Mathews. 2015. "Births: Final Data for 2013." *National Vital Statistics Reports* (CDC) 64(1, January 15). Available at: http://www.cdc.gov/nchs/data/nvsr/nvsr64/nvsr64_01.pdf (accessed November 8, 2016).

Mashburn, Andrew J., Robert C. Pianta, Bridget K. Hamre, Jason T. Downer, Oscar A. Barbarin, Donna Bryant, Margaret Burchinal, and Diane M. Early. 2008. "Measures of Classroom Quality in Prekindergarten and Children's Development of Academic, Language, and Social Skills." *Child Development* 79(3): 732–49.

Mathur, Aparna. 2015. "A Simple Proposal to Fund Maternity Leave." *Forbes*, March 26, 2015.

Mayer, Susan E., Ariel Kalil, Philip Oreopoulos, and Sebastian Gallegos. 2015. "Using Behavioral Insights to Increase Parental Engagement: The Parents And Children Together (PACT) Intervention." Working Paper 21602. Cambridge, Mass.: National Bureau of Economic Research.

Maynard, Rebecca A., and Richard J. Murnane. 1979. "The Effects of a Negative Income Tax on School Performance: Results of an Experiment." *Journal of Human Resources* 14(4): 463–76.

McCoy, Dana C., Hirokazu Yoshikawa, Kathleen Ziol-Guest, Greg J. Duncan, Holly Schindler, Katherine Magnuson, Rui Yang, and Jack P. Shonkoff. 2015. "Long-Term Impacts of Early Childhood Education Programs on High School Graduation, Special Education, and Grade Retention: A Meta-analysis." Paper presented to the Association for Public Policy Analysis and Management conference "The Golden Age of Evidence-Based Policy." Miami (November 12–14).

McKernan, Signe-Mary, and Caroline Ratcliffe. 2005. "Events That Trigger Poverty Entries and Exits." *Social Science Quarterly* 86(special issue): 1146–69.

McKey, Ruth Hubbell, Larry Condelli, Harriet Ganson, Barbara J. Barrett, Catherine McConkey, Margaret C. Plantz, and Allen N. Smith. 1985. *The Impact of Head Start on Children, Families, and Communities: Head Start Synthesis Project.* Contract 105-81-C-026 T. Washington: U.S. Department of Health and Human Services, Administration for Children, Youth, and Families, Office of Human Development Services, Head Start Bureau (June). Available at: http://files.eric.ed.gov/fulltext/ED263984.pdf (accessed August 25, 2016).

McLoyd, Vonnie C. 1998. "Socioeconomic Disadvantage and Child Development." *The American Psychologist* 53(2): 185–204.

Merz, Emily C., Susan H. Landry, Ursula Y. Johnson, Jeffrey M. Williams, and Kwanghee Jung. 2016. "Effects of a Responsiveness-Focused Intervention in Family Child Care Homes on Children's Executive Function." *Early Childhood Research Quarterly* 34: 128–39.

Miller, Elizabeth B., George Farkas, Deborah Lowe Vandell, and Greg J. Duncan. 2014. "Do the Effects of Head Start Vary by Parental Preacademic Stimulation?" *Child Development* 85(4): 1385–1400.

Minton, Sarah, Christin Durham, Erika Huber, and Linda Giannarelli. 2014. "The CCDF Policies Database Book of Tables: Key Cross-State Variations in CCDF Policies as of October 1, 2012." OPRE Report 2014-72. Washington: U.S. Department of Health and Human Services, Administration for Children and Families, Office of Planning, Research, and Evaluation.

Mitchell, Anne, Louise Stoney, and Harriet Dichter. 2001. *Financing Child Care in the United States: An Expanded Catalog of Current Strategies.* Kansas City, Mo.: Ewing Marion Kauffman Foundation. Available at: http://sites.kauffman.org/pdf/childcare2001.pdf (accessed August 22, 2016).

Moiduddin, Emily, Louisa Tarullo, Jerry West, and Yange Xue. 2012. "Child Outcomes and Classroom Quality in FACES 2009." OPRE Report 2012-37a. Washington: U.S. Department of Health and Human Services, Administration for Children and Families, Office of Planning, Research and Evaluation.

Monahan, Shannon, Jaime Thomas, Diane Paulsell, and Lauren Murphy. 2015. "Learning About Infant and Toddler Early Education Services (LITES): A Systematic Review of the Evidence." Washington: U.S. Department of Health and Human Services, Office of the Assistant Secretary for Planning and Evaluation.

Morris, Pamela, Shira K. Mattera, Nina Castells, Michael Bangser, Karen Bierman, and Cybele Raver. 2014. "Impact Findings from the Head Start CARES Demonstration: National Evaluation of Three Approaches to Improving Preschoolers' Social and Emotional Competence" (executive summary). OPRE Report 2014-44. Washington: U.S. Department of Health and Human Services, Administration for Children and Families, Office of Planning, Research and Evaluation.

Morrissey, Taryn W. 2009. "Multiple Child Care Arrangements and Young Children's Behavioral Outcomes." *Child Development* 80(1): 59–76.

———. 2013. "Multiple Child Care Arrangements and Common Communicable Illnesses in Children Aged 3 to 54 Months." *Maternal and Child Health Journal* 17(7): 1175–84.

———. 2016. "Child Care and Parent Labor Force Participation: A Review of the Research Literature." *Review of Economics of the Household* (March). doi:10.1007/s11150-016-9331-3.

National Center for Children in Poverty. 2015. "United States Early Childhood Profile." New York: Columbia University, Mailman School of Public Health (May 13). Available at: http://www.nccp.org/profiles/pdf/profile_early_childhood_US.pdf (accessed August 22, 2016).

National Center for Education Statistics (NCES). 2014. "Types of State and District Requirements for Kindergarten Entrance and Attendance, by State: 2014" (data table). Available at: https://nces.ed.gov/programs/statereform/tab5_3.asp (accessed August 22, 2016).

———. 2015a. "Percentage of 3- and 4-Year-Olds and 5- to 14-Year-Olds Enrolled in School, by Country: 2000 Through 2013" (data table). Washington: U.S. Department of Education. Available at: https://nces.ed.gov/programs/digest/d15/tables/dt15_601.35.asp (accessed October 12, 2016).

———. 2015b. "Revenues and Expenditures for Public Elementary and Secondary Education: School Year 2011–12 (Fiscal Year 2012): First Look." NCES 2014-301. Washington: U.S. Department of Education. Available at: http://nces.ed.gov/pubs2014/2014301.pdf (accessed August 22, 2016).

———. 2016. "Public School Expenditures." In *The Condition of Education*. NCES 2016-144. Washington: NCES (May). Available at: https://nces.ed.gov/programs/coe/indicator_cmb.asp.

National Institute of Child Health and Human Development (NICHD) Early Child Care Research Network. 1998. "Relations Between Family Predictors and Child Outcomes: Are They Weaker for Children in Child Care?" *Developmental Psychology* 34(5): 1119–28.

———. 2000. "Characteristics and Quality of Child Care for Toddlers and Preschoolers." *Applied Developmental Science* 4(3): 116–35.

———. 2002. "Child-Care Structure, Process, Outcome: Direct and Indirect Effects of Child-Care Quality on Young Children's Development." *Psychological Science* 13(3): 199–206.

———, ed. 2005. *Child Care and Child Development: Results from the NICHD Study of Early Child Care and Youth Development*. New York: Guilford Press.

———. 2006. "Child-Care Effect Sizes for the NICHD Study of Early Child Care and Youth Development." *The American Psychologist* 61(2): 99–116.

NICHD Early Child Care Research Network and Greg J. Duncan. 2003. "Modeling the Impacts of Child Care Quality on Children's Preschool Cognitive Development." *Child Development* 74(5): 1454–75.

National Partnership for Women and Families. 2015a. *The Family and Medical Insurance Leave Act (The FAMILY Act)*. Washington, D.C.: National Partnership for Women and Families (March). Available at: http://www.nationalpartnership.org/research-library/work-family/paid-leave/family-act-fact-sheet.pdf (accessed August 22, 2016).

———. 2015b. "First Impressions: Comparing State Paid Family Leave Programs in Their First Years: Rhode Island's First Year of Paid Leave in Perspective." Washington, D.C.: National Partnership for Women and Families (February). Available at: http://www.nationalpartnership.org/research-library/work-family/paid-leave/first-impressions-comparing-state-paid-family-leave-programs-in-their-first-years.pdf (accessed August 22, 2016).

———. 2016. *Expecting Better: A State-by-State Analysis of Laws That Help Expecting and New Parents*. 4th ed. Washington, D.C.: National Partnership for Women and

Families (August). Available at: http://www.nationalpartnership.org/research -library/work-family/expecting-better-2016.pdf (accessed August 22, 2016).

National Scientific Council on the Developing Child. 2004. "Young Children Develop in an Environment of Relationships." Working Paper 1. Cambridge, Mass.: Center on the Developing Child at Harvard University. Available at: http://www .developingchild.net (accessed August 22, 2016).

National Survey of Early Care and Education (NSECE) Project Team. 2016. "Characteristics of Home-Based Early Care and Education Providers: Initial Findings from the National Survey of Early Care and Education." OPRE Report 2016-13. Washington: U.S. Department of Health and Human Services, Administration for Children and Families, Office of Planning, Research, and Evaluation.

Nelson, Charles A., Charles H. Zeanah, Nathan A. Fox, Peter J. Marshall, Anna T. Smyke, and Donald Guthrie. 2007. "Cognitive Recovery in Socially Deprived Young Children: The Bucharest Early Intervention Project." *Science* 318(December): 1937–40.

Nepomnyaschy, Lenna, and Jane Waldfogel. 2007. "Paternity Leave and Fathers' Involvement with Their Young Children." *Community, Work, and Family* 10(4): 427– 53.

Neuman, Susan B., and Linda Cunningham. 2009. "The Impact of Professional Development and Coaching on Early Language and Literacy Instructional Practices." *American Educational Research Journal* 46(2): 532–66.

Neuman, Susan B., and Julie Dwyer. 2009. "Missing in Action: Vocabulary Instruction in Pre-K." *The Reading Teacher* 62(5): 384–92.

Office of Management and Budget. 2014. *Fiscal Year 2015, Analytical Perspectives: Budget of the U.S. Government.* Washington: U.S. Government Printing Office. Available at: https://www.whitehouse.gov/sites/default/files/omb/budget/fy2015 /assets/spec.pdf (accessed August 25, 2016).

———. 2016. *Fiscal Year 2017, Analytical Perspectives: Budget of the U.S. Government.* Washington: U.S. Government Printing Office. Available at: https://www .whitehouse.gov/sites/default/files/omb/budget/fy2017/assets/spec.pdf (accessed November 29, 2016).

Olds, David L., Harriet J. Kitzman, Robert E. Cole, Carole A. Hanks, Kimberly J. Arcoleo, Elizabeth A. Anson, Dennis W. Luckey, Michael D. Knudtson, Charles R. Henderson, Jessica Bondy, Amanda J. Stevenson et al. 2010. "Enduring Effects of Prenatal and Infancy Home Visiting by Nurses on Maternal Life Course and Government Spending: Follow-up of a Randomized Trial Among Children at Age 12 Years." *Archives of Pediatrics and Adolescent Medicine* 164(5): 419–24.

Olds, David L., Harriet Kitzman, Michael D. Knudtson, Elizabeth Anson, Joyce A. Smith, and Robert Cole. 2014. "Effect of Home Visiting by Nurses on Maternal and Child Mortality: Results of a 2-Decade Follow-up of a Randomized Clinical Trial." *Journal of the American Medical Association: Pediatrics* 168(9): 800–806.

Organization for Economic Cooperation and Development (OECD). 2010. "Gender Brief." Paris: OECD Social Policy Division (March). Available at: http://www .oecd.org/social/family/44720649.pdf (accessed August 25, 2016).

———. 2014. *Public Spending on Childcare and Early Education*. Paris: OECD, Social Policy Division, Directorate of Employment, Labour, and Social Affairs. Available at: http://www.oecd.org/els/soc/PF3_1_Public_spending_on_childcare_and_early_education.pdf (accessed August 25, 2016).

———. 2015. *Education at a Glance 2015: OECD Indicators*. Paris: OECD Publishing. Available at: download.ei-ie.org/Docs/WebDepot/EaG2015_EN.pdf (accessed October 14, 2016).

OECD European Commission/Eurydice. 2014. "Proposal for Key Principles of a Quality Framework for Early Childhood Education and Care." Paris: OECD (October). Available at: http://ec.europa.eu/education/policy/strategic-framework /archive/documents/ecec-quality-framework_en.pdf (accessed August 25, 2016).

Parker, Kim, and Wendy Wang. 2013. *Modern Parenthood: Roles of Moms and Dads Converge as They Balance Work and Family*. Washington, D.C.: Pew Research Center.

Patnaik, Ankita. 2015. "'Daddy's Home!' Increasing Men's Use of Paternity Leave." Briefing paper prepared for the Council on Contemporary Families (April 2). Available at: https://contemporaryfamilies.org/ccf-briefing-report-daddys -home/ (accessed November 29, 2016).

Pew Charitable Trusts. 2015a. "Raising Kids and Running a Household: How Working Parents Share the Load." Washington, D.C.: Pew Charitable Trusts (November 4). Available at: http://www.pewsocialtrends.org/2015/11/04/raising-kids -and-running-a-household-how-working-parents-share-the-load/ (accessed January 18, 2016).

———. 2015b. "Federal and State Funding of Higher Education: A Changing Landscape" (issue brief). Washington, D.C.: Pew Charitable Trusts (June 11). Available at: http://www.pewtrusts.org/en/research-and-analysis/issue-briefs/2015/06 /federal-and-state-funding-of-higher-education (accessed November 8, 2016).

Pew Research Center. 2009. "Trends in Political Values and Core Attitudes: 1987– 2009: Independents Take Center Stage in Obama Era" (press release). Washington, D.C.: Pew Research Center, May 21. Available at: http://www.people-press .org/2009/05/21/independents-take-center-stage-in-obama-era/ (accessed August 15, 2016).

Phillips, Deborah, William Gormley, and Sara Anderson. 2016. "The Effects of Tulsa's CAP Head Start Program on Middle-School Academic Outcomes and Progress." *Developmental Psychology* 52(8): 1247–61.

Phillips, Deborah A., William T. Gormley, and Amy E. Lowenstein. 2009. "Inside the Pre-kindergarten Door: Classroom Climate and Instructional Time Allocation in Tulsa's Pre-K Programs." *Early Childhood Research Quarterly* 24(3): 213–28.

Phillips, Deborah A., and Mary E. Meloy. 2012. "High-Quality School-Based Pre-K Can Boost Early Learning for Children with Special Needs." *Council for Exceptional Children* 78(4): 471–90.

Phillips, Deborah A., Miriam Voran, Ellen Kisker, Carollee Howes, and Marcy Whitebook. 1994. "Child Care for Children in Poverty: Opportunity or Inequity?" *Child Development* 65(2): 472–92.

Phillips, Deborah, and Sheldon H. White. 2004. "New Possibilities for Research on Head Start." In *The Head Start Debates,* edited by Edward F. Zigler and Sally J. Styfco. Baltimore, Md.: Brookes Publishing.

Piketty, Thomas, and Emmanuel Saez. 2014. "Income Inequality in Europe and the United States." *Science* 344(6186): 838–43.

Powell, Douglas R., Karen E. Diamond, Margaret R. Burchinal, and Matthew J. Koehler. 2010. "Effects of an Early Literacy Professional Development Intervention on Head Start Teachers and Children." *Journal of Educational Psychology* 102(2): 299–312.

Preschool Curriculum Evaluation Research Consortium. 2008. "Effects of Preschool Curriculum Programs on School Readiness." Washington: U.S. Department of Education, Institute of Education Sciences, National Center for Education Research.

Public Opinion Strategies and Hart Research. 2013. "Key Findings from a National Survey of 800 Registered Voters Conducted July 8–11, 2013." Available at: https://assets.documentcloud.org/documents/743383/poll-findings-report.pdf (accessed January 25, 2016).

———. 2014. "Key Findings from a National Survey of 800 Registered Voters Conducted May 28–June 1, 2014." Available at: http://growamericastronger.org/wp-content/uploads/2014/06/FINAL_FFYF-National-Results_071414.pdf?a63b61 (accessed January 20, 2016).

Puma, Michael, Stephen Bell, Ronna Cook, Camilla Heid, Pam Broene, Frank Jenkins, Andrew Mashburn, and Jason Downer. 2012. "Third Grade Follow-up to the Head Start Impact Study Final Report." OPRE Report 2012-45. Washington: U.S. Department of Health and Human Services, Administration for Children and Families, Office of Planning, Research and Evaluation.

Ramirez, Miriam. 2012. "The Impact of Paid Family Leave on New Jersey Businesses." New Brunswick, N.J.: Bloustein School of Planning and Public Policy (Fall). Available at: http://bloustein.rutgers.edu/wp-content/uploads/2012/03/Ramirez.pdf (accessed August 22, 2016).

Ratcliffe, Caroline, and Signe-Mary McKernan. 2012. "Child Poverty and Its Lasting Consequence." Washington, D.C.: Urban Institute. Available at: http://www.urban.org/research/publication/child-poverty-and-its-lasting-consequence/view/full_report (accessed August 22, 2016).

Reardon, Sean F. 2011. "The Widening Academic Achievement Gap Between the Rich and the Poor: New Evidence and Possible Explanations." In *Whither Opportunity? Rising Inequality, Schools, and Children's Life Chances,* edited by Greg J. Duncan and Richard J. Murnane. New York: Russell Sage Foundation.

Reardon, Sean F., and Ximena A. Portilla. 2016. "Recent Trends in Income, Racial, and Ethnic School Readiness Gaps at Kindergarten Entry." *AERA Open* 2(3): 1–18.

Rigby, Elizabeth, Rebecca M. Ryan, and Jeanne Brooks-Gunn. 2007. "Child Care Quality in Different State Policy Contexts." *Journal of Policy Analysis and Management* 26(4): 887–907.

Ros Pilarz, Alejandra, and Heather D. Hill. 2014. "Unstable and Multiple Child Care

Arrangements and Young Children's Behavior." *Early Childhood Research Quarterly* 29(4): 471–83.

Rossin, Maya. 2011. "The Effects of Maternity Leave on Children's Birth and Infant Health Outcomes in the United States." *Journal of Health Economics* 30(2): 221–39.

Ruhm, Christopher J. 1998. "The Economic Consequences of Parental Leave Mandates: Lessons from Europe." *Quarterly Journal of Economics* 113(1): 285–317.

———. 2000a. "Are Recessions Good for Your Health?" *Quarterly Journal of Economics* 115(2): 617–50.

———. 2000b. "Parental Leave and Child Health." *Journal of Health Economics* 19(6): 931–60.

Ruzek, Erik, Margaret Burchinal, George Farkas, and Greg J. Duncan. 2014. "The Quality of Toddler Child Care and Cognitive Skills at 24 Months: Propensity Score Analysis Results from the ECLS-B." *Early Childhood Research Quarterly* 29(1): 12–21.

Sabol, Terri J., Sandra Soliday Hong, Robert C. Pianta, and Margaret R. Burchinal. 2013. "Can Rating Pre-K Programs Predict Children's Learning?" *Science* 341(6,148): 845–46.

Sachs, Jason, and Christina Weiland. 2010. "Boston's Rapid Expansion of Public School-Based Preschool: Promoting Quality, Lessons Learned." *Young Children* (September): 74–77.

Sampson, Robert J. 2012. *Great American City: Chicago and the Enduring Neighborhood Effect*. Chicago: University of Chicago Press.

Sampson, Robert J., Jeffrey D. Morenoff, and Thomas Gannon-Rowley. 2002. "Assessing 'Neighborhood Effects': Social Processes and New Directions in Research." *Annual Review of Sociology* 28: 443–78.

Sampson, Robert J., Patrick Sharkey, and Stephen W. Raudenbush. 2008. "Durable Effects of Concentrated Disadvantage on Verbal Ability Among African-American Children." *Proceedings of the National Academy of Sciences* 105(3): 845–52.

Schmit, Stephanie, and Rhiannon Reeves. 2015. "Child Care Assistance in 2013." Washington, D.C.: CLASP (March). Available at: http://www.clasp.org/resources -and-publications/publication-1/Spending-and-Participation-Final.pdf (accessed August 22, 2016).

Schumacher, Rachel, Kate Irish, and Joan Lombardi. 2003. "Meeting Great Expectations: Integrating Early Education Program Standards in Child Care." Brief 3. Washington, D.C.: CLASP (August). Available at: http://www.clasp.org /resources-and-publications/files/0146.pdf (accessed August 22, 2016).

Schweinhart, Lawrence J., Jeanne Montie, Zongping Xiang, W. Steven Barnett, Clive R. Belfield, and Milagros Nores. 2005. *Lifetime Effects: The High/Scope Perry Preschool Study Through Age 40*. Ypsilanti, Mich.: High/Scope Educational Research Foundation.

Selden, Thomas M., and Merrile Sing. 2008. "Aligning the Medical Expenditure Panel Survey to Aggregate U.S. Benchmarks." Working Paper 8006. Rockville, Md.: Agency for Healthcare Research and Quality.

Seward, Rudy Ray, Dale E. Yeatts, and Lisa K. Zottarelli. 2012. "Parental Leave and

Father Involvement in Child Care: Sweden and the United States." *Journal of Comparative Family Studies* 33(3): 387–99.

Sharkey, Patrick. 2013. *Stuck in Place: Urban Neighborhoods and the End of Progress Toward Racial Equality.* Chicago: University of Chicago Press.

Sharkey, Patrick, and Felix Elwert. 2011. "The Legacy of Disadvantage: Multigenerational Neighborhood Effects on Cognitive Ability." *American Journal of Sociology* 116(6): 1934–81.

Shonkoff, Jack P., W. Thomas Boyce, and Bruce S. McEwen. 2009. "Neuroscience, Molecular Biology, and the Childhood Roots of Health Disparities." *Journal of the American Medical Association* 301(21): 2252–59.

Shonkoff, Jack P., and Philip A. Fisher. 2013. "Rethinking Evidence-Based Practice and Two-Generation Programs to Create the Future of Early Childhood Policy." *Development and Psychopathology* 25(4pt2): 1635–53.

Shonkoff, Jack P., Andrew S. Garner, and the Committee on Psychosocial Aspects of Child and Family Health, Committee on Early Childhood, Adoption, and Dependent Care, and Section on Developmental and Behavioral Pediatrics. 2012. "The Lifelong Effects of Early Childhood Adversity and Toxic Stress." *Pediatrics* 129(1): e232–46.

Shonkoff, Jack P., and Deborah A. Phillips, eds. 2000. *From Neurons to Neighborhoods: The Science of Early Childhood Development.* Washington, D.C.: National Academy Press.

Smith, Miriam W., David K. Dickinson, and Louisa Anastasopoulos. 2002. *User's Guide to the Early Language and Literacy Classroom Observation Toolkit: Research Edition.* Baltimore, Md.: Brookes Publishing.

Starkey, Prentice, Alice Klein, and Ann Wakeley. 2004. "Enhancing Young Children's Mathematical Knowledge Through a Pre-kindergarten Mathematics Intervention." *Early Childhood Research Quarterly* 19(1): 99–120.

State of California, Department of Workforce Development Agency. 2014. "Paid Family Leave: Ten Years of Assisting Californians in Need." Available at: http://www.edd.ca.gov/disability/pdf/Paid_Family_Leave_10_Year _Anniversary_Report.pdf (accessed August 22, 2016).

Stiglitz, Joseph E. 2012. *The Price of Inequality: How Today's Divided Society Endangers Our Future.* New York: W. W. Norton & Co.

Suárez-Orozco, Carola, Hirokazu Yoshikawa, and Vivian Tseng. 2015. "Intersecting Inequalities: Research to Reduce Inequality for Immigrant-Origin Children and Youth." New York: William T. Grant Foundation (February). Available at: http:// wtgrantfoundation.org/library/uploads/2015/09/Intersecting-Inequalities -Research-to-Reduce-Inequality-for-Immigrant-Origin-Children-and-Youth.pdf (accessed August 22, 2016).

Suchman, Nancy E., Cindy DeCoste, Thomas J. McMahon, Bruce Rounsaville, and Linda Mayes. 2011. "Effects of Parental Supportiveness on Toddlers' Emotion Regulation over the First Three Years of Life in a Low-Income African American Sample." *Infant Mental Health Journal* 27(1): 5–25.

Suchman, Nancy E., Cindy DeCoste, Patricia Rosenberger, and Thomas J. McMahon.

2012. "Attachment-Based Intervention for Substance-Using Mothers: A Preliminary Test of the Proposed Mechanisms of Change." *Infant Mental Health Journal* 33(4): 360–71.

Tanaka, Sakiko. 2005. "Parental Leave and Child Health Across OECD Countries." *Economic Journal* 115(501): F7–28.

Tax Policy Center. 2015. "How Does the Tax System Subsidize Child Care Expenses?" In *Key Elements of the U.S. Tax System.* Washington, D.C.: Urban Institute and Brookings Institute. Available at: http://www.taxpolicycenter.org/briefing -book/how-does-tax-system-subsidize-child-care-expenses (accessed August 25, 2016).

Thomas, Adam, and Isabel V. Sawhill. 2005. "For Love and Money? The Impact of Family Structure on Family Income." *The Future of Children* 15(2): 57–74.

Thomas, Mallika. 2015. "The Impact of Mandated Maternity Benefits on the Gender Differential in Promotions: Examining the Role of Adverse Selection." January 22. Available at: http://www.economics.cornell.edu/sites/default/files/files /events/Thomas paper.pdf (accessed August 22, 2016).

Toth, Sheree L., Fred A. Rogosch, Jody Todd Manly, and Dante Cicchetti. 2006. "The Efficacy of Toddler-Parent Psychotherapy to Reorganize Attachment in the Young Offspring of Mothers with Major Depressive Disorder: A Randomized Preventive Trial." *Journal of Consulting and Clinical Psychology* 74(6): 1006–16.

Tout, Kathryn, Rebecca Starr, Margaret Soli, Shannon Moodie, Gretchen Kirby, and Kimberly Boller. 2010. "Compendium of Quality Rating Systems and Evaluations." Report prepared for the U.S. Department of Health and Human Services, Administration for Children and Families, Office of Planning, Research, and Evaluation (April 15). Available at: http://www.acf.hhs.gov/opre/resource /compendium-of-quality-rating-systems-and-evaluations (accessed August 22, 2016).

Tully, Sarah. 2015. "Poll: Voters Increasingly Support Early Education Investments." EdSource, October 20. Available at: https://edsource.org/2015/poll-voters -increasingly-support-early-education-investments/89281 (accessed October 12, 2016).

U.S. Census Bureau. 1982. "Trends in Child Care Arrangements of Working Mothers." *Current Population Reports* P23-117. Washington: U.S. Census Bureau.

———. 1987. "Who's Minding the Kids? Child Care Arrangements: Winter 1984–85." *Current Population Reports* P70-9. Washington: U.S. Census Bureau.

———. 2002. "Who's Minding the Kids? Child Care Arrangements: Spring 1997." *Current Population Reports* P70-86. Washington: U.S. Census Bureau.

———. 2014. "Single Grade of Enrollment and High School Graduation Status for People 3 Years Old and Over, by Sex, Age (Single Years for 3 to 24 Years), Race, and Hispanic Origin" (data table). Washington: U.S. Census Bureau. Available at: https://www.census.gov/hhes/school/data/cps/2014/tables.html (accessed 21, 2016).

U.S. Department of Health and Human Services (DHHS). 2016a. "U.S. Federal Poverty Guidelines Used to Determine Financial Eligibility for Certain Federal Programs." Washington: U.S. Department of Health and Human Services, Office of the Assistant Secretary for Planning and Evaluation. Available at: https://aspe .hhs.gov/poverty-guidelines (accessed August 15, 2016).

———. 2016b. "Federal Medical Assistance Percentages FY2016." Washington: U.S. Department of Health and Human Services, Office of the Assistant Secretary for Planning and Evaluation. Available at: https://aspe.hhs.gov/basic-report /fy2016-federal-medical-assistance-percentages (accessed October 12, 2016).

U.S. Department of Health and Human Services (DHHS), Administration for Children and Families (ACF). 2010. "Head Start Impact Study: Final Report." Washington: U.S. Department of Health and Human Services.

———. 2015. "Head Start Performance Standards." Available at: https://www .federalregister.gov/articles/2015/06/19/2015-14379/head-start-performance -standards (accessed January 20, 2016).

———. 2016. "Early Head Start–Child Care Partnerships." Available at: http://www .acf.hhs.gov/programs/ecd/early-learning/ehs-cc-partnerships (accessed August 25, 2016).

U.S. Department of Health and Human Services (DHHS), Administration for Children and Families (ACF), Office of Child Care (OCC). 2001. "FY 2001 CCDF Data Tables and Charts (TABLE 1-CCDF Average Monthly Adjusted Number of Families and Children Served (FY 2001))." Available at: http://www.acf.hhs.gov/occ /resource/ccdf-data-01acf800-0 (accessed November 6, 2016).

———. 2015. "Characteristics of Families Served by Child Care and Development Fund (CCDF) Based on Preliminary FY 2014 Data." Washington: U.S. Department of Health and Human Services (October 22). Available at: http://www.acf .hhs.gov/programs/occ/resource/characteristics-of-families-served-by-child -care-and-development-fund-ccdf (accessed January 31, 2016).

U.S. Department of Health and Human Services (DHHS), Administration for Children and Families (ACF), Office of Head Start (OHS). 2014. "A National Overview of Grantees Class Scores in 2014." Available at: https://eclkc.ohs.acf.hhs .gov/hslc/data/class-reports/docs/national-class-2014-data.pdf (accessed November 6, 2016).

———. 2015. "Office of Head Start—Services Snapshot: National All Programs (2014–2015)." Available at: http://eclkc.ohs.acf.hhs.gov/hslc/data/psr/2015 /services-snapshot-all-programs-2014-2015.pdf (accessed August 22, 2016).

U.S. Department of Health and Human Services (DHHS), Administration for Children and Families (ACF), Office of Planning, Research, and Evaluation (OPRE). 2013. "2013 Head Start Grantee-Level Data from the Classroom Assessment National Statistics by Dimension National Statistics by Domain." Available at: http://eclkc.ohs.acf.hhs.gov/hslc/data/class-reports/docs/national-class-2013 -data.pdf (accessed January 31, 2016).

———. 2014. "2014 Head Start Grantee-Level Data from the Classroom Assessment Scoring System (CLASS®)." Available at: http://eclkc.ohs.acf.hhs.gov/hslc/data /class-reports/docs/national-class-2014-data.pdf (accessed January 31, 2016).

U.S. Department of Labor (DOL), Bureau of Labor Statistics (BLS). 2014. "Leave

Benefits: Access: Table 32: Leave Benefits: Access, Civilian Workers, National Compensation Survey, March 2014." Available at: http://www.bls.gov/ncs /ebs/benefits/2014/ownership/civilian/table32a.htm (accessed January 18, 2016).

———. 2015a. "The Cost of Doing Nothing: The Price We All Pay Without Paid Leave Policies to Support America's 21st Century Working Families." Washington: U.S. Government Printing Office.

———. 2015b. "Number of Jobs Held, Labor Market Activity, and Earnings Growth Among the Youngest Baby Boomers: Results from a Longitudinal Survey" (press release). Washington, D.C.: U.S. Department of Labor (March 31). Available at: http://www.bls.gov/news.release/nlsoy.nr0.htm (accessed February 1, 2016).

———. 2016. "Employment Characteristics of Families Summary" (press release). April 22. Available at: http://data.bls.gov/cgi-bin/print.pl/news.release/famee .nr0.htm (accessed August 7, 2016).

U.S. Social Security Administration (SSA), Office of Research, Evaluation, and Statistics. 1997. "Temporary Disability Insurance." In *Social Security Programs in the United States*. Publication 13-11758. Washington: SSA (July). Available at: https://www.ssa.gov/policy/docs/progdesc/sspus/tempdib.pdf (accessed August 21, 2016).

Vandell, Deborah Lowe, Jay Belsky, Margaret Burchinal, Laurence Steinberg, Nathan Vandergrift, and the NICHD Early Child Care Research Network. 2010. "Do Effects of Early Child Care Extend to Age 15 Years? Results from the NICHD Study of Early Child Care and Youth Development." *Child Development* 81(3): 737–56.

Vandell, Deborah Lowe, and Barbara Wolfe. 2000. "Child Care Quality: Does It Matter and Does It Need to Be Improved?" Special Report 78. Madison, Wisc.: Institute for Research on Poverty (November).

Vinovskis, Maris A. 2005. *The Birth of Head Start: Preschool Education Policies in the Kennedy and Johnson Administrations*. Chicago: University of Chicago Press.

Waldfogel, Jane. 1998. "Understanding the 'Family Gap' in Pay for Women with Children." *Journal of Economic Perspectives* 12(1): 137–56.

———. 1999. "The Impact of the Family and Medical Leave Act." *Journal of Policy Analysis and Management* 18(2): 281–302.

———. 2001a. "International Policies Toward Parental Leave and Child Care." *The Future of Children* 11(1): 99–111.

———. 2001b. "Family and Medical Leave: Evidence from the 2000 Surveys." *Monthly Labor Review* (September): 17–23.

Waldfogel, Jane, Wen-Jui Han, and Jeanne Brooks-Gunn. 2002. "The Effects of Early Maternal Employment on Child Cognitive Development." *Demography* 39(2): 369–92.

Waldfogel, Jane, Yoshio Higuchi, and Masahiro Abe. 1999. "Family Leave Policies and Women's Retention After Childbirth: Evidence from the United States, Britain, and Japan." *Journal of Population Economics* 12(4): 523–45.

Walker, Christina. 2014. "Early Head Start Participants, Programs, Families and Staff in 2013." Washington, D.C.: CLASP (August). Available at: http://www.clasp.org /resources-and-publications/publication-1/EHSpreschool-PIR-2013-Fact-Sheet .pdf (accessed October 12, 2016).

Washbrook, Elizabeth, Christopher J. Ruhm, Jane Waldfogel, and Wen-Jui Han. 2011. "Public Policies, Women's Employment After Childbearing, and Child Well-being." *BE Journal of Economic Analysis and Policy* 11(1): 1–48.

Washington State Department of Early Learning. 2013. "Early Achievers, Washington's Quality Rating and Improvement System Standards: A Framework to Support Positive Child Outcomes." Olympia: Washington State Department of Early Learning.

Wasik, Barbara A., Mary Alice Bond, and Annemarie Hindman. 2006. "The Effects of a Language and Literacy Intervention on Head Start Children and Teachers." *Journal of Educational Psychology* 98(1): 63–74.

Weiland, Christina. 2016a. "Impacts of the Boston Prekindergarten Program on the School Readiness of Young Children with Special Needs." *Developmental Psychology* 52(11): 1763–76.

———. 2016b. "Launching Preschool 2.0: High Quality Public Programs at Scale." *Behavior Science and Policy* 2(1): 37–46.

Weiland, Christina, Kchersti Ulvestad, Jason Sachs, and Hirokazu Yoshikawa. 2013. "Associations Between Classroom Quality and Children's Vocabulary and Executive Function Skills in an Urban Public Prekindergarten Program." *Early Childhood Research Quarterly* 28(2): 199–209.

Weiland, Christina, and Hirokazu Yoshikawa. 2013. "Impacts of a Prekindergarten Program on Children's Mathematics, Language, Literacy, Executive Function, and Emotional Skills." *Child Development* 84(6): 2112–30.

———. 2014. "Does Higher Peer Socio-economic Status Predict Children's Language and Executive Function Skills Gains in Prekindergarten?" *Journal of Applied Developmental Psychology* 35(5): 422–32.

Whitebook, Marcy, Deborah Phillips, and Carollee Howes. 2014. *Worthy Work, Still Unlivable Wages: The Early Childhood Workforce 25 Years After the National Child Care Staffing Study.* Berkeley: University of California, Center for the Study of Child Care Employment.

Whitehurst, Grover J., Andrea A. Zevenbergen, Deane A. Crone, Margaret D. Schultz, and Olivia N. Velting. 1999. "Outcomes of an Emergent Literacy Intervention from Head Start Through Second Grade." *Journal of Educational Psychology* 91(2): 261–72.

The White House, Office of the Press Secretary. 2013a. "Fact Sheet: President Obama's Plan for Early Education for All Americans" (press release). Washington: The White House, February 13). Available at: https://www.whitehouse.gov /the-press-office/2013/02/13/fact-sheet-president-obama-s-plan-early -education-all-americans (accessed April 26, 2016).

———. 2013b. "Remarks by the President on Economic Mobility" (press release). Washington: The White House, December 4). Available at: https://www

.whitehouse.gov/the-press-office/2013/12/04/remarks-president-economic
-mobility (accessed April 23, 2016).

———. 2015. "Fact Sheet: Helping All Working Families with Young Children Afford
Child Care" (press release). Washington: The White House, January 21). Available at: https://www.whitehouse.gov/the-press-office/2015/01/21/fact-sheet
-helping-all-working-families-young-children-afford-child-care (accessed April
26, 2016).

Wiese, Bettina S., and Johannes O. Ritter. 2012. "Timing Matters: Length of Leave
and Working Mothers' Daily Reentry Regrets." *Developmental Psychology* 48(6):
1797–1807.

Wildeman, Christopher, and Kristin Turney. 2014. "Positive, Negative, or Null? The
Effects of Maternal Incarceration on Children's Behavioral Problems." *Demography* 51(3): 1041–68.

Williams, Roberton, and Howard Gleckman. 2009. "An Updated Analysis of the
2008 Presidential Candidates' Tax Plans." Washington, D.C.: Tax Policy Center.
Available at: http://tpcprod.urban.org/UploadedPDF/411742_updated
_candidates_summary.pdf (accessed October 14, 2016).

Winston, Pamela. 2014. "Work-Family Supports for Low-Income Families: Key Research Findings and Policy Trends." Washington: U.S. Department of Health
and Human Services, Office of the Assistant Secretary for Planning and Evaluation (March 1). Available at: http://aspe.hhs.gov/hsp/14/WorkFamily/rpt
_workfamily.cfm (accessed August 23, 2016).

Wodtke, Geoffrey T., David J. Harding, and Felix Elwert. 2011. "Neighborhood Effects
in Temporal Perspective: The Impact of Long-Term Exposure in Concentrated
Disadvantage on High School Graduation." *American Sociological Review* 76(5):
713–36.

Wolf, Sharon, Katherine Magnuson, and Rachel Tolbert Kimbro. 2016. "Family Poverty and Neighborhood Poverty: Link with Children's School Readiness Before
and After the Great Recession." Unpublished manuscript.

Wolf, Sharon, and Taryn Morrissey. 2015. "Examining the Intersections of Economic
Instability, Food Insecurity, and Child Health During and After the Great Recession." Working paper, University of Pennsylvania and American University.

Yazejian, Noreen, and Donna M. Bryant. 2012. "Educare Implementation Study
Findings—August 2012." Chapel Hill: University of North Carolina, Frank Porter
Graham Child Development Institute.

York, Benjamin N., and Susanna Loeb. 2014. "One Step at a Time for Parents of Preschoolers." Working Paper 20659. Cambridge, Mass.: National Bureau of Economic Research.

Yoshikawa, Hirokazu, J. Lawrence Aber, and William R. Beardslee. 2012. "The Effects
of Poverty on the Mental, Emotional, and Behavioral Health of Children and
Youth: Implications for Prevention." *The American Psychologist* 67(4): 272–84.

Yoshikawa, Hirokazu, Christina Weiland, and Jeanne Brooks-Gunn. 2016. "When
Does Preschool Matter?" *The Future of Children* 26(2): 21–36.

Yoshikawa, Hirokazu, Christina Weiland, Jeanne Brooks-Gunn, Margaret R. Burchinal, Linda M. Espinosa, William T. Gormley, Jens Ludwig, Katherine A. Magnuson, Deborah Phillips, and Martha J. Zaslow. 2013. "Investing in Our Future: The Evidence Base on Preschool Education." Ann Arbor, Mich., and New York: Society for Research in Child Development and Foundation for Child Development (October).

Yoshikawa, Hirokazu, Thomas S. Weisner, and Edward Lowe, ed. 2006. *Making It Work: Low-Wage Employment, Family Life, and Child Development*. New York: Russell Sage Foundation.

Zaslow, Martha, Rachel Anderson, Zakia Redd, Julia Wessel, Louisa Tarullo, and Margaret Burchinal. 2010. "Quality Dosage, Thresholds, and Features in Early Childhood Settings: A Review of the Literature." OPRE 2011-5a. Washington: U.S. Department of Health and Human Services, Administration for Children and Families, Office of Planning, Research and Evaluation (August).

Zaslow, Martha, Margaret Burchinal, Louisa Tarullo, and Ivelisse Martinez-Beck. 2016. "Quality Thresholds, Features, and Dosage in Early Care and Education: Discussion and Conclusions." *Monographs of the Society for Research in Child Development* 81(2): 75–87.

Zhai, Fuhua, C. Cybele Raver, and Stephanie M. Jones. 2012. "Academic Performance of Subsequent Schools and Impacts of Early Interventions: Evidence from a Randomized Controlled Trial in Head Start Settings." *Children and Youth Services Review* 34(5): 946–54.

Zielewski, Erica H., and Shelley Waters Boots. 2010. "Exploring Policy Models for Extended Time Off." Washington, D.C.: Urban Institute. Available at: http://scholarship.law.georgetown.edu/cgi/viewcontent.cgi?article=1025&context=legal (accessed August 23, 2016).

Zigler, Edward F., and Susan Muenchow, eds. 1992. *Head Start: The Inside Story of America's Most Successful Educational Experiment*. New York: Basic Books.

Zigler, Edward F., Susan Muenchow, and Christopher J. Ruhm. 2012. *Time Off with Baby: The Case for Paid Care Leave*. Washington, D.C.: Zero to Three.

Ziol-Guest, Kathleen M., and Claire C. McKenna. 2014. "Early Childhood Housing Instability and School Readiness." *Child Development* 85(1): 103–13.

INDEX